Science Fiction Film

*For my parents, Gerda and Henry*

# Science Fiction Film

Predicting the Impossible in the
Age of Neoliberalism

Eli Park Sorensen

EDINBURGH
University Press

Edinburgh University Press is one of the leading university presses in the UK. We publish academic books and journals in our selected subject areas across the humanities and social sciences, combining cutting-edge scholarship with high editorial and production values to produce academic works of lasting importance. For more information visit our website: edinburghuniversitypress.com

© Eli Park Sorensen, 2021, 2023

Edinburgh University Press Ltd
The Tun—Holyrood Road
12 (2f) Jackson's Entry
Edinburgh EH8 8PJ

First published in hardback by Edinburgh University Press 2021

Typeset in 11/13 Monotype Ehrhardt by
Manila Typesetting Company

A CIP record for this book is available from the British Library

ISBN 978 1 4744 8184 7 (hardback)
ISBN 978 1 4744 8185 4 (paperback)
ISBN 978 1 4744 8186 1 (webready PDF)
ISBN 978 1 4744 8187 8 (epub)

The right of Eli Park Sorensen to be identified as author of this work has been asserted in accordance with the Copyright, Designs and Patents Act 1988 and the Copyright and Related Rights Regulations 2003 (SI No. 2498).

# Contents

*Acknowledgements*     vi

   Introduction: Science Fiction Film in the Age of Neoliberalism     1
1  Between Friends and Enemies: Ridley Scott's *Alien*     32
2  Monopolizing the Future: Steven Spielberg's *Minority Report* and Schmitt's Exception     53
3  The Anomalous World: *Elysium* and the Invention of the Med-Bay Machine     72
4  *Blade Runner* and the Right to Life     91
5  Terminating the State of Exception: *Oblivion* and the Problem of Exceptional Being     105
6  Escaping the Production of Bare Life: *Blade Runner 2049* and the Miracle of Birth     126
   Conclusion     145

*Works Cited*     148
*Index*     157

# Acknowledgements

This book owes a great debt of thanks to many people. I have had many important conversations and discussions with friends, colleagues, and students, hugely benefitting the thoughts and ideas that went into this book. I am very grateful to the editorial team at Edinburgh University Press, especially Gillian Leslie, Wendy Lee, Eddie Clark, Caitlin Murphy, and Richard Strachan, and to the anonymous readers for their invaluable comments. Thanks to all my colleagues and students at CUHK, especially David Huddart, Jette Hansen Edwards, Grant Hamilton, Michael O'Sullivan, Eddie Tay, Li Ou, Julian Lamb, Simon Haines, Jason Gleckman, and Evelyn Chan. Thanks also to Marvin Lee, Anjuli Gunaratne, Tammy Lai-Ming Ho, Suk-koo Rhee, Peter Paik, Kim Su Rasmussen, Mariko Watanabe, Raphaël Lambert, Sarah Winters, and Pavlina Radia for creating opportunities to present and discuss my research.

Parts of Chapter 1 and Chapter 4 were published in *Trans-Humanities: Ewha Institute for the Humanities* (2015 and 2016). I am grateful to the editors for permission to republish the aforementioned parts. I am also extremely grateful to the Faculty of Arts at CUHK for providing a Direct Grant (2019) and a Publication Subvention Grant (2020).

This book is dedicated to my parents, Gerda and Henry, for all the support they have given me over the years. Lastly, thanks to Hee-sook, Saerom, and Bori for your patience, love, and support.

INTRODUCTION

# Science Fiction Film in the Age of Neoliberalism

## Fear of the Future

An anxious moment occurs in Francis Fukuyama's otherwise confident book *The End of History* (1992), when the author of the grand narrative about liberalism's final and permanent global triumph at one point briefly imagines the future as the dystopian world evoked in George Miller's sci-fi film *Mad Max II: The Road Warrior* (1981). It is a scenario in which all the stable and well-known institutions, states, borders, and civilizations have broken down—a time when the jungle has yet again recaptured the surface of the Earth. Fukuyama uneasily observes that the "possibility of the cataclysmic destruction of our modern, technological civilization and its sudden return to barbarism has been a constant subject of science fiction" (82).[1] It is a rather odd passage in the book, and Fukuyama quickly dismisses the fear and replaces it with the more familiar thesis of a buoyant, peaceful Western-style liberal democracy as history's absolute, normative endpoint.

But the anxiety Fukuyama briefly identifies via the *Mad Max* franchise gradually intensifies in his later works, especially after 9/11, during which he himself on several occasions rejects the controversial thesis of the end of history, while at the same time indicating a growing concern about the vulnerability and survivability of liberal democracy.[2] Fukuyama shares this sentiment with a number of other political commentators, including Samuel Huntington, Lawrence Harrison, Robert Kagan, John Mearsheimer, Robert Merry, and David Runciman, who likewise have recently expressed their fearful conjectures about the future of liberal democracy in the twenty-first century in increasingly high-pitched formulations.[3]

To contextualize this current return of the fear of the future, it is worth taking a brief look at the past. In her book *The Future of the World* (2018), Jenny Andersson outlines the history of how the concept of the future in the years after World War II and the beginning of the Cold War emerged as a distinct field of knowledge production in Western societies. Given the possibility of all-out nuclear war, future research (a field including historians, scientists, philosophers, and other intellectuals) reflected a growing obsession with the notion of the future as radically unpredictable—a *shock*, as the futurist Alvin Toffler popularly labelled it[4]—and which, through various logical, rational, or intellectual procedures, might become *predictable* and hence *controllable*. However, after the end of the Cold War, Andersson observes, the acute interest in future predictability was gradually replaced by a focus on more retrospective and introspective concepts like loss, trauma, nostalgia, and melancholia.[5]

Today's chrono-phobic tendencies in many ways mark a return to a preoccupation with the concept of an unpredictable, open future that, for decades, had seemed almost absent from the political landscape. This return perhaps also explains why an increasing number of scholars have turned towards Carl Schmitt's thoughts again, which in itself is thought-provoking since he has, for a long time, been a *persona non grata* among the liberal elite.[6] There is no doubt that Carl Schmitt is a controversial figure, primarily due to his membership and active involvement in the NSDAP (Nazi Party) from 1933 to 1936, as well as the anti-Semitic tendencies in some of his writings.[7] This involvement has obviously influenced the postwar reception of Schmitt's authorship. While the interest in and controversy surrounding Schmitt's works have existed ever since they were first published, for many years their reception was limited to more conservative circles. Over the last few decades, however, Schmitt's works have gradually moved closer to mainstream thought, and, moreover, have been recognized to some extent as a significant contribution to contemporary political thought among left-wing and center–liberal thinkers and collectives such as Agamben, Derrida, and the people around the journal *Telos*.[8] More specifically, one reason why many people have returned to Schmitt is that he critically focuses on liberalism's tendency to *depoliticize* social life and, by implication, its elimination of the specifically political. To Schmitt, liberalism undermines the political unity of the state and its existential premise—the always-present possibility of war—through its ideology of pluralism and individuality, conventions, legal norms, and unwavering belief in rationality. Schmitt's concerns furthermore involve the concrete *consequences* derived from such a process of depoliticization: on the one hand, an increasingly frustrated population feeling ignored and marginalized, and on the other hand, an insufficient ability to deal with crisis situations.[9]

While it would, no doubt, be too hasty to claim that this process of depoliticization constitutes a stage that we have passed today, in the last couple of decades we have witnessed the emergence of a new political situation that has distinctly moved away from the global vision of the post-political 1990s: that is, the post-Cold War epoch creating the basis for cosmopolitan and postmodern visions such as Tony Blair's Third Way and Bill Clinton's progressive economic policies, which seemed to confirm empirically Fukuyama's vision of the end of history.[10] This seemed true especially after 9/11, the War on Terror, the wars in the Middle East, in particular, the controversial invasion of Saddam Hussein's regime on the basis of spurious intelligence claims; and, later, the devastating financial crisis, the US and European governments' exceptional measures to save the banking industry,[11] the intensification of ecological destruction, Donald Trump's divisive presidential campaign and presidency, the hateful and deceptive Brexit campaign, the gradual rise of right-wing–oriented national–democratic parties across Europe such as AFD in Germany, Viktor Orbán's party in Hungary, Le Pen's party in France, UKIP in the UK, Danish People's Party in Denmark, Swedish Democrats in Sweden, the Finns Party in Finland, violent protests and clashes from Chile to Hong Kong, and, more recently, a pandemic paralyzing large parts of the world, in response to which we have witnessed the (possibly permanent) implementation of a series of authoritarian measures and surveillance technologies. All of this could, no doubt, make one feel somewhat skeptical regarding the idea of a dominant, liberal global world order.[12] Quite simply, the post-political vision of the 1990s seems rather distant today. It was a vision that coincided with a series of political, economic, and technological developments that promised so much and constituted the culmination of the vision that a peace-seeking postwar generation, through great efforts, had created in the aftermath of World War II, and which, at least during one generation, had everyone believe that this was the norm of an everlasting peace, and that the world would only become a better, more wealthy, conflict-free, rational, and safe place—the future as the perpetual present, only more peaceful, secure, fulfilling, meaningful, and intense.[13]

## Science Fiction and Realism

This was the dream of an everlasting peace, *pax romana* in the late twentieth century, not dystopian prospects like those that, according to Fukuyama, we typically find in sci-fi films. But what does sci-fi actually mean? Part of its irresistible charm is that sci-fi is unafraid to ask big and often naive questions. It is a genre that occupies a central cultural position in modern society because it focuses on the temporal idea of radical change and difference—in other words, the concept of the future. Although Fredric

Jameson and others may be right in arguing that the genre, first and foremost, is about our own time,[14] it is, at the same time, important to stress the fact that sci-fi acutely—probably more than any other genre—focuses explicitly on the very imagination of the future: what we understand collectively, and thereby in a political sense, by the concept of the future.[15] By "collective," I am not referring to a notion of universality, but rather to the historical formation of a political subject, one that transcends the sphere of oikos, the private-individual realm.

It is against this background that I make the argument that a considerable part of contemporary research on the sci-fi film genre to some extent, explicitly or implicitly, is still caught up in Fukuyama's end-of-history thesis. In other words, much of the academic research on sci-fi works is formulated within a post-political discourse (that is, the explicit or implicit assumption that discussions of the specifically political belong to a bygone stage, or that it simply means a utopian alternative to Fukuyama's thesis). Even though sci-fi film criticism has often focused on political topics or topics with a clear political dimension such as artificial intelligence, cloning, alien invasion, and so on, I would argue that many of these often fail to address the *specifically political*: that is, what it takes to create and ensure the survival of an autonomous political unity within which the normative situation of the present becomes a sustainable possibility. Here it is important to distinguish my argument from the considerable amount of critical work on the concept of utopia and sci-fi films. For many sci-fi critics, the political simply means something along the lines of a utopian impulse.[16] And often, one could add, an explicitly *international* utopian impulse: the imagination of a future world above and beyond parochial nationalism.[17] At the end of history, as Jameson and others have argued, the desire for the utopian has never been stronger, precisely because all other alternatives seem to have vanished—a form of desperate critical negativity intent on breaking out of the iron cage of the global capitalist system.[18] This book is an attempt to move beyond the current sentiment of an everlasting present, or the future-as-the-present, albeit without simultaneously constructing an argument about science fiction in terms of a utopian horizon.

Overall, my argument here is that an important dimension of the late twentieth-century/early twenty-first-century science fiction film genre consists of an aesthetic imagination of what the present, our present, may look like *politically* in the future—how we will organize ourselves, think, act, and do collectively, in the future. To Schmitt, the future as *future* is precisely defined by its radical *unpredictability* and its potential to transform the present radically in a political sense: who we are, our associations or dissociations, principles, and values. The Schmittian concept of the future is one that arrives in the form of an event so radical that it fundamentally changes the political coordinates of the present. That is to say, the future constitutes the point at which we realize that we no longer inhabit the same political system, and, with this realization, that the collective "we" of the body politic has likewise radically changed. The implication here is that if a future event does not radically change the present in a specifically political sense, it would not really constitute the future proper, but rather what one could call "the-present-plus-new-gadgets"—that is, the same, only extended, expanded, and deepened.[19] Thus, the future is not simply anything happening tomorrow; it is only the future to the extent that it involves an existential transformation of the present. It is in this sense, I would argue, that sci-fi as a genre pre-eminently preoccupied with the concept of the future in a very direct way is tied to the thinking of the specifically political.

The sci-fi genre has a particularly complicated relationship to history—or, as Csicsery-Ronay formulates it, "SF lacks the gravity of history, because it lacks the gravity of lived experience. It is *weightless*. Its represented futures incur no obligations" (*Seven Beauties* 83). Here, it is important to acknowledge that the sci-fi film genre has its own unique history within the modern cultural landscape, one that often developed independently of any explicitly political concerns.[20] Many critical works on sci-fi have often established too-straightforward allegorical links between a given socio-historical background and aesthetic plot dynamics. Thus, as Johnston argues, it is common to see many of the 1950s alien invasion films as Cold War allegories, although this is also problematic because it "reduces the narrative and thematic complexity of an entire decade of science fiction films to one perspective; it then assumes that those films . . . simply 'reflected' the whole of American society" (73). Importantly, as Johnston points out with reference to sci-fi film, "Genres are not fixed, set categories; they are flexible, changing concepts that can be better understood by appreciation of the discursive network surrounding them" (11)—that is, a discursive network that may include specific historical contexts, but also other genres (like the detective genre or war film). Here, I want to acknowledge the importance of this scholarly work on the internal history of sci-fi film, but at the same time stress that it will not be the focus of this book.[21] Nor do I intend to explore further what almost seems like a ritualistic opening of most academic sci-fi books: namely, the acknowledgment of how difficult it is to define and delineate the genealogy of the history of this genre—a sentiment with which I can only agree.[22] Since plenty of excellent books have already engaged this question thoroughly, I largely put aside problems regarding an overall common definition of the sci-fi genre. Instead, I am interested in what Paik has more narrowly described as science fiction's ability to achieve "profound and probing insights into the *principal dilemmas* of political life" (1; italics mine). This book looks at a certain intensified version of sci-fi articulated within the horizon of what constitutes the present as the end of history—a version that strives to address one of the main concerns of the genre: the imagination of the future, and hence, by implication, the future as a political problem.

As several critics have observed, a change seems to occur broadly in the sci-fi film genre around the late 1970s, the period roughly corresponding to the emergence of a new political paradigm of neoliberal world dominance. Fredric Jameson traces the beginning of this stage of neoliberalism to the recession of the 1970s, the time around the end of the Bretton Woods agreement, at which point we seem to have "become incapable of dealing with time and history" ("Postmodernism" 10). Or, as he puts it in an even more strikingly apocalyptic formulation, "we seem condemned to seek the historical past through our own pop images and stereotypes about the past, which itself remains forever out of reach" (10). To Jameson, this reality has evaporated into a series of surfaces, postcards, and hotel lobbies, while the dimension of time has dissolved into a perpetual flow of present moments—a cancelled future, or endless capitalism. Sobchack views the late 1970s as a kind of renaissance for the sci-fi film, when the genre seems to take a decidedly darker and more paranoid turn, one that "became particularly dominant in the late 1990s and has continued into the present years of the twenty-first century" ("American" 272).[23] While earlier sci-fi visions often demonstrated a curious, if not enthusiastic, attitude towards new technology, the latter was increasingly seen as something ominous and dangerous by the late twentieth century. In his essay "Visions of the Future," Franklin looks at the 1970s and early 1980s as "a period of unending and deepening social and economic crisis, and visions of the future projected in Anglo-American SF films during this period have been overwhelmingly pessimistic" (20). Out of the fifty-two films Franklin looks at, not one of them "shows a functioning democracy in the future. Many display future societies ruled by some form of conspiracy, monopoly, or totalitarian apparatus" (22). As Franklin quips, the "only future that seems unimaginable in Hollywood is a better one" (31). It is a period, as Glass has observed, that seems to herald a "new bad future" (2).

Or, what one could call the future as a political problem. In the following chapters, I will pursue a particularly narrow aspect of a certain type of sci-fi works: namely, what one oxymoronically could call the realist sci-fi film. This is a particular and late chapter in the sci-fi film genre's history, which coincides with the fin-de-siècle atmosphere of the late twentieth century and the beginning of the twenty-first century. The works I discuss in this book all address a collective—and, as I will explain a bit later, *realist*—vision of the future; this future is connected to the present in the form of a permanent state of exception, precisely because the future arrives in the form of an event that radically changes the coordinates of the present and thus *demands* a political answer (that is, a state of exception that becomes permanent).

The notion of realist sci-fi designates a temporally dislocated fictional discourse that articulates a stage of future technology that is nonetheless realistically imaginable, precisely because this future technology is envisioned as realistically validated within its own diegesis (that is to say, realistically explained within the internal logic of its own fictional universe)—and which thus, from the perspective of the present, would not seem impossible at some point in the future.[24] In fact, oftentimes the *development* of this cognitively defamiliarizing future technology from our present becomes the starting point of a given sci-fi story, which thus further underlines its adherence to a realist impulse.

This description of realist sci-fi in particular draws on Darko Suvin's now classic concept of the novum.[25] To Suvin,

> SF should not be seen . . . in terms of science, the future, or any other element of its potentially unlimited thematic field. Rather, it should be defined as a fictional tale determined by the hegemonic literary device of a *locus* and/or *dramatis personae* that (1) are *radically or at least significantly different from the empirical times, places, and characters* of "mimetic" or "naturalist" fiction, but (2) are nonetheless—to the extent that SF differs from other "fantastic" genres, that is, ensembles of fictional tales without empirical validation—simultaneously perceived as *not impossible* within the cognitive (cosmological and anthropological) norms of the author's epoch. (viii)

In other words, what Suvin stresses here is the significance of something that does not seem impossible at some point within the horizon of the present, and, more specifically, the *normative* present. Thus, Suvin's concept of the novum involves the idea that the imagination of the future constitutes an innovation that does not simply undermine the realist discourse of the present, but one that evolves, so to speak, "organically" out of this discourse: for example, a form of anachronistic technology that necessarily alters or modifies our concept of realism—that is, the known world's physical laws—albeit in a way that would still not seem unrealistically imaginable from the perspective of the present. This is the novum; it signals, by way of what Suvin describes as a process of "cognitive estrangement," that we find ourselves in a different world that is *causally* or even *organically* connected to the normative present. In other words, we (the people of the present) are still the protagonists—it is still, despite the temporal dislocation, the cognitive estrangement, *our world*.[26]

As several critics have observed, there is a slight limitation to Suvin's elegant but rather formulaic theory.[27] What I am especially interested in here is Suvin's *realist–formalist* definition of the sci-fi genre, which essentially and formally articulates a collective–realist imagination of what the future might look like. It is precisely this realist–formalist definition that ties the sci-fi works I discuss in this book most explicitly to the specifically political.

Suvin's notion of the novum usefully demarcates the sci-fi genre from that of *fantasy*. The sci-fi genre crucially contains fantastical or distinctly non-realist elements, which I will address later in this chapter; at the same time, however, it is a genre that should be distinguished from the fantasy genre.[28] The realistic dimension in sci-fi works generally emerges in connection with the political imagination of the future or what the future realistically will look like—that is, seen from the collective imagination of the present. From a narrow political perspective, fantasy is mainly centered around the individual, the introverted fantasy of the individual, and, more specifically, the individual's range of imaginative freedom within a politically conceived space.[29]

More specifically, I am interested in exploring the political dimension of Suvin's concept of the novum as a form of future realism—that is, imagining the future as it might emerge from the collective imagination of the present. Sci-fi criticism often acknowledges the genre's close ties to realism. Thus, Marc Angenot follows Suvin's distinction between sci-fi and fantasy by arguing that the former aspires to a realist aesthetic, albeit situated in the future (which thereby makes it somewhat "unrealistic" at the same time). Angenot explains: "The 'realism' of SF resides in a paradigmatic delusion: codes, series, coordinates, systems, are simultaneously absent yet indispensable for the coherence of the syntagm" (10). Christine Brooks-Rose's systematic discussion of what she views as "the close link between science fiction and realistic fiction" (82) likewise offers a series of observations along these lines,[30] while Tom Shippey has drawn attention to the necessary abundance of specific and concrete details in sci-fi works—a "high-information" genre, as he calls it—which, among other things, means that the plot narrative becomes less dynamic.[31] The latter is also a point that Brooks-Rose develops: that sci-fi is often incredibly inventive when it comes to technical ideas and descriptions, but not particularly original when it comes to narrative structure.

Here it is important to clarify what we mean by the concept of realism. Those sci-fi critics who have explicitly connected the genre to realism often see the latter as a largely epistemological endeavor, reflecting a tendency within literary criticism and film studies.[32] There is no doubt that realism, as an aesthetic form in a historical perspective, has been closely connected to the epistemological desire of expressing and representing the world truthfully and accurately. At the same time, I want to stress another important aspect of realist discourse: namely, its *political* dimension. This latter dimension has often been overlooked in those endless debates regarding realism's mimesis, where the main issue is to argue either for or against the effects of realism's epistemological powers.[33] My argument here is that we fail to grasp the political potential of the sci-fi genre properly unless we take into account realism's political dimension. By "political" in realist aesthetics, I am primarily referring to the notion of realism as a stylistic or aesthetic articulation of the concept of reality understood or defined in terms of the premise of a collective unity, the formation, protection, and normalization of an autonomous political community. J. P. Stern has described realism's implicit "premise of a single, undivided reality" (63), while Ayelet Ben-Yishai defines realism as embodying a notion of "what is commonly accepted as real" (15). The notion of realism that I am interested in exploring here follows recent critical studies that seek to expand realism's potential: a potential that, in addition to its epistemological value, also contains important aesthetic work on dynamics related to consensus, commonality, common identity, collectivities, and communities—in short, the political.[34] This approach also implies that sci-fi, at least as long as we connect it to the idea of realism, is committed to the imagination of a *collective* future.[35] When Suvin talks about the future growing out of the present—that is, the sci-fi work's novum—what this notion implies at the same time, I would argue, is that it is *collectively* imagined: the present collectively imagining the future in a different time in different circumstances.[36] A unique, private–subjective, individual fantasy of the future would precisely undermine the genre's realism, and instead bring it too close to the genre of fantasy. The genre of film, I would argue, is, to some extent, an even stauncher adherent of this particular realist doctrine than literature, the latter being primarily a subjective–individual endeavor, while film production tends to be a collective endeavor.

In this sense, the sci-fi film genre is closely connected to the political. The latter is likewise a dimension that implicitly insists on a collective imagination. The apolitical, to the contrary, is something that constitutes the frames for the individual fantasy. Here, one could think of a recent attempt to revitalize Suvin's concept of the novum: namely,

Seo-Young Chu's ambitious book *Do Metaphors Dream of Literal Sleep?* from 2010. Chu is particularly interested in the idea of cognitive estrangement or cognitively estranging objects, which, according to Chu, are made "available for representation" (34) through science fiction. These objects constitute objects of wonder, phantasmagoria, and "high-intensity" forms of mimesis that would otherwise have been unrepresentable—with examples such as trauma, cyberspace, globalization, Korean "han," surrealism, lyric poetry, and so on. However, this rethinking of Suvin's novum runs into the problem of subjectivism, which, I believe, Chu's theoretical framework never fully addresses. In this sense, Chu's otherwise innovative and highly original argument risks dissolving the imagination of the collective future into a private fantasy; the consequence of this is, I would argue, a *depoliticization* of the genre. More generally, I believe that much of the critical scholarship on sci-fi works often ends up with arguments along these lines—that is, critical positions that tend to depoliticize the genre.

## The Dream of the Eternal Present

It is against this horizon that I would like to turn to Carl Schmitt's concept of the political.[37] Schmitt was and still is a controversial figure, as I mentioned earlier, in the sense that not only was he a member of the Nazi Party in the 1930s, but he also actively participated in the formulation of the regime's criminal activities; some of his writings reveal a persistent anti-Semitic dimension; and finally, like Heidegger, Schmitt never fully acknowledged the extent of his involvement with the Nazi regime after the war.[38] Furthermore, his writings possibly inspired later development of fascist ideology on a few occasions.[39] It is meaningless to defend Schmitt's wartime activities, although I would maintain that one can and should, to a certain extent, distinguish between Schmitt's practical engagement and his theoretical work.[40] Thus, I would argue that it is a misreading of his theoretical works to conclude that they necessarily constitute the foundation for fascist ideology.[41]

To Schmitt, the political essentially comes down to the ability to distinguish friends from enemies. Thus, Schmitt writes:

> The specific political distinctions to which political actions and motives can be reduced is that between friend and enemy... The distinction of friend and enemy denotes the utmost degree of a union or separation, of an association or dissociation. (*Concept* 26)

Brutal in its simplicity, Schmitt's definition essentially comes down to one crucial assumption: that the specifically political designates the possibility that some social conflicts within or around the body politic are fundamentally *irresolvable* via peaceful negotiation or parameters of reason alone.[42] Schmitt employs the Latin distinction between *hostis* (a collective or public enemy, stemming from the etymological root of "hostile"), and *inimicus* (an individual and private enemy, from the etymological root of "inimical"). Private enemies are not public enemies—in fact, they are not really enemies in the political sense. The ability to make distinctions implies that the enemy cannot be determined or identified as an *essence* or *substance*; the enemy can be identified only in a concrete or strategically specific situation. Thus, Schmitt argues that

> The political enemy need not be morally evil or aesthetically ugly . . . *But he is, nevertheless, the other, the stranger; and it is sufficient for his nature that he is, in a specially intense way, existentially something different and alien, so that in the extreme case conflicts with him are possible.* These can neither be decided by a previously determined general norm nor by the judgment of a disinterested and therefore neutral third party. (*Concept* 27)

It is because of the enemy's perpetual unpredictability and *indefinability* that the sovereign must—at all times, according to Schmitt—possess the right to declare a state of exception. This sovereign's right to declare the state of exception should not be understood as an essence, but rather as the sovereign's condition of possibility. Only in moments of existential crisis, when the very survival of the state is at stake, does the sovereign emerge; at other times, the sovereign remains dormant, indecisive.[43] The state of exception constitutes a gap in the normative law, the constitution, one that is precisely defined negatively—that is, as ultimately empty, not bound by anything (for example, a legal set of norms)—in order to anticipate that which, in principle, can never be predicted: namely, the perpetual unpredictability of the future.[44] In *The Concept of the Political*, Schmitt argues that liberalism (which Schmitt understands as the rational–technological conceptualization of politics) potentially leads to disaster because it reduces and ultimately eliminates the political—that is, liberalism transforms the state into a blind, bureaucratic, and technocratic institution, utterly incapable of confronting the real political challenges of the state.[45] In Schmitt's view, liberalism is unable to deal with the future as radically unpredictable.[46]

The culmination of liberalism presents itself as a post-political society in which the political entity—that is, the technologized, bureaucratized, and industrialized society—runs by itself, like a machine, with minimal state intervention. Thus, Schmitt observes that "Technology ... appeared to be a domain of peace, understanding, and reconciliation" (*Concept* 91), but "precisely because [technology] serves all, it is not neutral. No single decision can be derived from the immanence of technology, least of all for neutrality" (91). This is why "technology can do nothing more than intensify peace or war; it is equally available to both" (95). Since technology merely constitutes an instrument, it simply intensifies irresolvable conflicts. The political authority in the liberal state thus, as Schmitt writes in his Hobbes book, turns into a "gigantic mechanism" (35), a "technical state-administrative (*staatsverwaltungstechnischer*) rationalization" (44), which runs according to a harmonic set of fixed, mechanical procedures, like a clock.[47]

The liberal norm is based on the conviction that a juridically binding act becomes meaningful to the extent that it is *normative*, that it is causally connected to a set of prescriptive rules equal to all, and valid in all situations.[48] As Schmitt observes, "Every general rule demands a regular, everyday frame of life to which it can be factually applied and which is submitted to its regulations" (*Theology* 16). This is a society safely couched in its belief in an unchangeable legal norm, the constitution—and thus a society that no longer dreams about the future: a futureless society. In such a society, the political has largely been reduced, if not eliminated, or transformed and relegated to the market, civil society, or the private sphere. These are depoliticized spheres, devoid of political conflicts or decisions. This is the liberal vision of a depoliticized society, the highest purpose of which is to realize values—or, at least, to create the optimal conditions for their possible realization—such as freedom, equality, welfare, dignity, rights, fairness, and security. The point here is that liberalism is a society intensely devoted to the *present*, a society that no longer wants to think about the future as radically unpredictable; it can envision the future only as essentially the same as the present, albeit perhaps with more gadgets—that is, the same in extended form. Or, to put it differently, it is a society that has normatively reached the collective consensus that its political situation can no longer be improved in any fundamental sense (that is, Fukuyama's thesis of the end of history)—even if many aspects of liberal society still generate dissatisfaction, or even if many countries in the world are not (as yet) encompassed by the liberal vision. Finally, one could argue that the liberal vision, in its fullest and purest sense, has yet to manifest itself empirically anywhere on Earth.[49] In spite of all this, it is nonetheless striking that, apart from depoliticized, utopian fantasies, our present has yet to come up with a political vision that, in any significant sense, seems capable of improving the liberal vision.[50] To such a present, there is nothing to gain from the future, only something to be lost or deprived of. It is in this sense, as Butler observes, that the future "becomes a lawless future, not anarchical, but given over to the discretionary decisions of a set of designated sovereigns" (65).

## The State of Exception

According to Schmitt, what makes the liberal–technocratic state fatally weak is that it is at all times tied to a set of predetermined, general norms—that is, the constitution.[51] However, Schmitt argues that the state, as the ultimate legislator and executor of the law, cannot protect itself adequately, to the extent that it must operate solely on the basis of a general, preformulated set of laws, applicable to all possible and thinkable scenarios. There is, according to Schmitt, no absolute norm applicable to all possible and thinkable situations—for example, the future as the radically unpredictable event. Therefore, a political executor, constitutionally bound by a norm-based set of laws, will be unable to act meaningfully in the exceptional situation—that is, that which breaks with all possible norms—because he or she necessarily will attempt to act in accordance with the procedures of the normative situation.[52] Thus, Schmitt writes:

> There are rarely today any parliamentary majorities that still seriously believe that their statutory decisions will be valid 'in perpetuity'. The situation is so incalculable and so abnormal that the statutory norm is losing its former character and becoming a mere measure. (*Legality* 82–3)[53]

The future, to Schmitt, constitutes the radically unpredictable event, and it is precisely for that very reason that he defines the sovereign as *the one who has the right to declare the state of exception*.[54] In the state of exception, the sovereign elevates him or herself—whose power is based on the assumption that the future is radically unpredictable, which means that the one possessing power, and thereby the responsibility to protect the state, must be prepared for that which *cannot* be prepared for—above the general constitutional law; the sovereign is no longer bound or limited by ordinary, legal norms. This is essential to Schmitt: as the representative of the state, the sovereign must, at all times, be prepared for the extreme situation, the return of the state of nature, at which point all rules and norms become meaningless and invalidated. This aspect is usually hidden in normal situations, says Schmitt, but emerges in times of existential crisis, when the very survival of the state is at stake.[55] In fact, it is the figure of the exceptional sovereign that guarantees the very possibility of a normal situation—and hence the possibility of a legal realm—in the first place. Thus, Schmitt writes that the "exception reveals most clearly the essence of the state's authority ... authority proves that to produce law it need not be based on law" (*Theology* 13).[56] The state of exception is, according to Schmitt, a limit concept, *Grenzbegriff*, which is tied to the law but at the same time not subsumed by it.[57] In his reading of Schmitt, Agamben puts it this way; "The state of exception is not a special kind of law (like the law of war); rather, insofar as it is a suspension of the juridical order itself, it defines law's threshold or limit concept" (*State* 4). When Schmitt defines the state of exception as a limit concept, he underlines at the same time that this condition is basically unthinkable, unimaginable; it can never be concretized in advance, concretely anticipated, never be given concrete content—until it happens. One simply does not know what is around the corner. Thus, Schmitt writes:

> The precise details of an emergency cannot be anticipated, nor can one spell out what may take place in such a case, especially when it is truly a matter of an extreme emergency and of how it is to be eliminated. (*Theology* 6–7)

What Schmitt stresses here is that the state of exception, as we understand it in the present, is a future event that can never fully be described in advance; the only description, and what ultimately justifies its identification and declaration, is an extreme, existential danger—that is, something that threatens the very survival of the state in its present form.[58] Facing this dangerous event, the state is always in an acutely vulnerable situation. The future event constitutes a possibility that never entirely disappears, however far we move away from the prehistoric state of nature. In other words, this is the event that heralds the future proper. To Schmitt, the future is quite simply an event that possesses the potential force and ability to radically change the political coordinates of the society of the present—and hence, ultimately, change who we are. In the future proper, the "we" becomes another people immersed in another political reality.

It is important here to keep in mind that Schmitt's exception is not simply a defense of the right to suspend the constitution in a general sense. Rather, it is limited to those unpredictable and indefinable situations which potentially could emerge in the future—or, more precisely, that which defines what the future actually is.[59] This is worth keeping in mind, given that Schmitt has often been characterized as a thinker promoting totalitarianism and dictatorship, that, with his insistence on the right to declare the state of exception, Schmitt believes that the sovereign holds the right to implement the lawless situation at any time in a concrete sense, and thus that sovereignty is within its right to entirely ignore any concerns about individual rights and so forth. This would constitute a misreading of Schmitt's argument. What Schmitt essentially addresses is a *gap* between the general (system of norms) and the particularity of the body politic, between which Schmitt inserts the sovereign's decision.[60] As Sava puts it, it is this gap

> that explains why the state cannot identify with its norm, with its constitution. This argument contends, therefore, that there is a place of the decision and of the exception, which is born in the gap between the general norm and the particular reality. (26)

Precisely because the future is radically unpredictable, no one, no legal complex can contain it within a normative frame of law. When Schmitt defines the sovereign's power as the right to declare the state of exception, he is, at the same time, saying that the sovereign is the one who has the right to define *when* the future arrives (and to reject events that do not announce the arrival of the future)—that is, the right to identify what constitutes a threat as sufficiently dangerous to threaten the existence of the state.[61] In this right lies, at the same time, a regressive obligation; the sovereign suspends the order of law with the purpose of defending and preserving it, and finally of bringing it back when the right moment arrives—in other words, to bring back the present, to save it from the event of the future, which threatens to change everything. The state of exception is, in other words, a kind of temporal suspension that, like a protective shell around the temporarily suspended constitution, carries out the dirty (or rather unconstitutional) work in order to leave the constitution pure, innocent, intact, albeit without force so that the latter can be reinserted in explicit form, uncontaminated and uncorrupted as before.[62] This is precisely the distinction that Schmitt makes in the work *Dictatorship* between commissarial dictatorship and sovereign dictatorship: commissarial dictatorship attempts, in contrast to the latter, to re-establish order on the exceptional situation when the right time arrives.[63]

It is in this connection that one should understand Schmitt's comment in *Political Theology*: "All significant concepts of the modern theory of the state are secularized theological concepts" (36). A little later in the same paragraph, Schmitt adds: "The exception in jurisprudence is analogous to the miracle in theology" (36). What makes a miracle a miracle is essentially a *political* decision in the modern, secular society. This point is furthermore repeated in the 1938 work *The Leviathan in the State Theory of Thomas Hobbes*, in which Schmitt argues even more explicitly that "Nothing here is true: everything is command. A miracle is what the sovereign state authority commands its subjects to believe is a miracle . . . Miracles cease when the state forbids them" (55). Thus, political acts cannot simply be justified or explained mechanically, rationally, or logically; like God, the sovereign is the one who has been given the task of making political decisions based on something that cannot fundamentally be predicted, anticipated, or prepared for. This is why the sovereign's political decisions cannot be limited or bound by scientific rationality or legal norms. The sovereign rules in exceptional times as if guided by miracles.[64]

In the above passages, I have attempted to outline what I see as a Schmittian concept of the future.[65] The sovereign is the one whose duty it is to protect us against the event that holds the potential to change everything. This is the future: it arrives in the form of an event that radically changes the way we currently live. When Schmitt talks about the friend/enemy distinction, and states that the political really comes down to a question about the ability to distinguish these figures, he is at the same time saying that the political really is a matter of identifying the future—that is, the unthinkable, unpredictable event: is it good or bad for us, in the present? Confronted with this question, we are faced with a choice: to change or to resist the event. The sovereign is the one who resists the future, to the extent that it threatens to radically change the way we live in the present.

## Science Fiction and the Exception

Whereas Schmitt's state of exception serves the purpose of suspending or arresting time in order to bring back the law from the lawlessness of the future, something interesting happens when this dynamic is deferred to a genre discourse premised on thinking and imagining the future. This book attempts to identify a recurring structure, which we find especially in connection with the type of sci-fi works that, in the last decades of the twentieth century and into the twenty-first century, have implemented, either directly or indirectly, the vision of the end of history, and more precisely, the liberal–democratic vision of the last imaginable stage of what the perfect society looks like. It is this horizon that creates an interesting but also challenging chapter of the sci-fi film genre: namely, the point at which the genre not only generates utopian or dystopian visions, but perhaps more disconcertingly, also faces the ideological conundrum of a present society that, in a political sense, has reached the *culmination* of political thought—a society that has reached its maximum potential, one that, in principle, can no longer generate more individual freedom, justice, peace, and affluence.

What thus emerges is a recurrent structure in each of the films I will be discussing, which may be divided into several key stages. We typically begin with a scenario characterized by what Suvin has described as the novum, a future society that is cognitively estranging but, at the same time, not impossible to imagine from the perspective of the present as the collective future, one that organically develops from our own time.

However, in the realist sci-fi work, the specifically political is, I would argue, precisely *not* embodied in the novum as such, but rather centered around a radical element, often in the form of a transgressive, almost magical, fantastical, but definitely unthinkable and thereby unrealistic technological invention, which precisely undermines or departs from the general or hegemonic idea of the novum, the realistic future (seen from our present), and which potentially propels the genre towards fantasy.[66] Obviously, it would be possible to imagine this radical element in its concrete manifestation (for example, a time machine, and so on); the challenge, however, consists in understanding this radical element as deterministic in terms of its political implications—that is, the notion of a political society based on this new premise.

On the other hand, what prevents the genre from descending into pure fantasy is precisely the novum, the genre's future realism. It is, in other words, still committed to the collectively imagined future. The novum, the genre's adherence to the aesthetic doctrine of realism, albeit deferred into the future, is centered around the radical element precisely in an attempt to *normalize the exceptional situation.*

The works I discuss in this book envision imagined future societies built around an exceptional event that has fundamentally changed the political coordinates of the present. This event could, for example, consist of a technological invention—which, from the perspective of our time, might appear so unrealistic that it no longer seems to grow organically out of the collective notion of the present. It constitutes, in other words, a radical departure from the present. Precisely here, the limit or the unthinkable, the unpredictable, manifests itself and thus offers a glimpse of the future proper. It is, in reality, this radical event that propels the political into the future (that is, the reason why society has changed); it changes the basic coordinates, the normative rules, and it is in relation to this situation that the political enters the state of exception. The state of exception is an attempt to grasp the future from the location of the present, to hold on to ourselves, who we are at present, in the future.

It is in this sense, one could argue via Schmitt, that the political can only think the unthinkable concretely in the form of a concrete–literal state of exception. It is precisely the unthinkable, undefinable event that propels us into the future, and which political power confronts in the form of the state of exception. Thus, the sci-fi scenarios discussed in this book typically envision a future society that, in some way or other, is connected to the state of exception. What often happens is that this situation—which, seen from the perspective of the present, constitutes a state of exception—becomes *elevated to the norm*: what is normal, that is, a situation conditioned by normality within this future society's present. In reality, it involves a suspension of time. This is, of course, where we encounter the *permanent state of exception*.[67] To some extent, all states of exception are detemporalized and hence at least potentially permanent, but the permanent exception is the one according to which the nature of the exception has been elevated to that of a normative situation. As sci-fi, however, the genre is caught between an inaccessible past (due to the radical nature of the future event) and an absent future (in the sense that it *is* the future).

The tension we find in these sci-fi films is generated through the problematic relations between power and the people, the individuals; it is a political tension that precisely testifies to a situation in which the state of exception has been elevated to a normative, and thereby most often undemocratic or totalitarian, political situation. It follows that the crisis and the culmination in these films often arrive in the form of a breakdown of the unstable political situation: that is, the regime is overturned, or the people in power are replaced. Quite literally, what we see is a breakdown of technology. When this happens, it is striking to notice how often we witness the re-emergence of sovereignty: that is, the sovereign holding the right to declare the state of exception in order to eliminate the existential threat at any cost. The aim of these sci-fi works is thus to destroy the false facade of normality—that is, the permanent state of exception—and to rediscover the true face of power: the sovereign who explicitly claims the right that, in the first place, made the exceptional situation possible, and further, made it normative or permanent—the one who has the right to declare the state of exception.

However, the initial task of the future sovereign is to stabilize the exception-turned-into-the norm, not to bring us back to the present. The latter is typically the task of the people, often represented through the protagonist. In the sci-fi films discussed in this book, we thus find—after the direct confrontation between the explicit sovereign and the individuals—the reintroduction of a potential future, again: that is, a return to the present. What does it mean to return to the present? It is a political gesture that restores the deferred balance between norm and exception, which thus again creates the space for a proper state of exception—that is, as an always-present potential in the normative society, and whose ultimate purpose is self-preservation, to bring back order. As such, the genre recreates the potential for the political again: the utmost danger, which thus again is identified as the radically unpredictable future itself.[68]

## Overview

*Science Fiction Film: Predicting the Impossible in the Age of Neoliberalism* discusses six films: *Alien* (1979), *Minority Report* (2002), *Elysium* (2013), *Blade Runner* (1982), *Oblivion* (2013), *and Blade Runner 2049* (2017). Each film discussion addresses specific aspects of the political dimension in the post-political age, such as the end of liberalism (and ideology), politics-as-administration, security, the state of emergency, totalitarianism, and biopolitics, that, insofar as one can talk about a demarcated genre paradigm, situate these films apart from their predecessors. These films, in different ways, reactivate political potentials through plots that involve envisioning a radically unpredictable future at a time when we, perhaps more intensely than ever before, have become aware of the limits of our imagination, of our ability to think beyond ourselves. Examining the sci-fi film genre emerging during the neoliberal epoch within the context of consolidated, stable, and individualized Western societies leads to the following argument: if the collective imagination of the present can no longer think beyond the notion of a post-political society, the sense of the political, albeit in deferred form, may be resuscitated precisely through a genre that intensely explores political images of our future and thus allows us to rediscover the possibility of moving beyond the current post-political malaise. What this late version of the sci-fi film genre ultimately attempts to articulate is the impossible: to predict the political implications of a future that remains radically unpredictable in the present.

The first chapter presents a reading of Ridley Scott's sci-fi classic *Alien* (1979), with a specific focus on the film's latent political conflict.[69] In a political sense, what happens to our understanding of the political if we no longer need it? *Alien* has often been read through feminist and psychoanalytic approaches, but such approaches essentially draw attention away from the literalness of the film's political dimension, which comes close to the problem Schmitt used to explain his concept of the state of exception. During the state of exception, the sovereign may legally suspend the constitution in order to protect, defend, and preserve it.

However, in the absence of danger, the state becomes increasingly depoliticized and irrelevant. Thus, the state must establish a relation to the anomaly (the enemy, Behemoth, or the state of nature) in order to reassert itself. *Alien* tells the story of Ripley, a loyal citizen fighting against power's sinister attempt to restore fear and terror. She simultaneously comes to personify both the absolute unlimited sovereign and the alien; Ripley is both the outlawed, banned life and the hero of the state, both friend and enemy at the same time. Read against Schmitt's thoughts, the film traces and explores the tensions between sovereignty and the citizen in a post-political age.

Chapter 2 looks at some of the political implications emerging in Steven Spielberg's sci-fi film *Minority Report* (2002). What happens politically if we can predict the future? Drawing on Schmitt's notions of the political and the state of exception, I argue that *Minority Report* envisions a stage at which it has become possible to predict a violent future. The film implies that if the state could eliminate that future via advanced technology, a new situation would emerge in which there would no longer be any need for a sovereign. To Schmitt, state sovereignty must preserve the right to identify a future event that poses an existential threat. In *Minority Report*, technology has reached such an advanced stage and spread that the political no longer plays any significant role. Once the possibility of Schmitt's radically unpredictable future has been eliminated, the need for the political and hence the sovereign disappears. I argue that, in Spielberg's film, the sovereign returns when the technological precog system is most vulnerable—that is, the moment the system cannot protect itself. The film thus ends with the collapse of technology and a return to the present—in other words, a return to the political. Overall, the film suggests that in the encounter with the disruptive future event, the political ultimately will reassert itself in the form of a state of exception to preserve the present.

In Chapter 3, I further explore Schmitt's notion of the exceptional and its relation to a normative situation. In a political sense, what happens if we invent a machine that can cure almost everything? I argue that Neill Blomkamp's *Elysium* (2013) presents a scenario that constitutes the future because the emergence of a radical new technological invention has disturbed the political coordinates of the present; with the invention of the so-called Med-Bay machine, it is now possible to cure almost everything—illness, aging, even death. In such a society, the political (that is, power's ability to provide control and security) collapses, but it restores itself by devising a premodern political construction: the city gate in the form of Elysium's architecture as a floating space paradise, physically distanced from Earth. This distance prevents access to the

Med-Bay machines, transforming Earth (where no one has access to the Med-Bays) into a gigantic concentration camp, an anomaly that turns into the norm. Elysium has become the exception, even if its politicians stubbornly (perhaps hypocritically) adhere to a liberal–humanistic norm that, in peaceful times, allows them to keep believing that they still represent civilization. That this civilized world can exist only by elevating itself to an exception—which thereby turns Earth's miserable and lost population into the norm—constitutes a political conundrum that the film never fully manages to resolve.

Chapter 4 investigates the notions of "human" and "rights" in connection with a discussion of the first volume of Michel Foucault's *History of Sexuality* and Ridley Scott's *Blade Runner* (1982). What happens, politically, if humans can reproduce a life form that is almost indistinguishable from human life? Foucault's concept of sovereignty in many ways extends Schmitt's notion of the sovereign's right to declare the exception. In an essay on the politics of life, Foucault develops a series of arguments as to what he describes as "The 'right' to life, to one's body, to health, to happiness, to the satisfactions of needs, and beyond all the oppressions or 'alienations,' the 'right' to rediscover what one is and all that one can be" (*History of Sexuality* 145). This right to life is one of the main themes in *Blade Runner*, which tells the story of a group of replicants (human-like robots) returning to Earth in search of more life. On Earth, however, they are outlawed, and most of the film's plot consists of Deckard, the main character, hunting down and killing the replicants. I argue that *Blade Runner* explores what one could call the culmination of biopower, the imagination of a life whose absolute perfection is simultaneously the expression of absolute monstrosity, a threat to life that legitimizes the death penalty. Questioning and exploring the notions of "human" and "rights" in a sci-fi context, *Blade Runner* develops some of the implications of what sovereignty means when the border between natural life and artificial life erodes.

In Chapter 5, I discuss Joseph Kosinski's *Oblivion*, a 2013-sci-fi film about the aftermath of an alien attack. The film, I argue, asks the following question: in a political sense, what happens when we try to return from the state of exception to a normal situation? *Oblivion* follows Jack Harper, who believes that humans survived an alien attack by using nuclear weapons, which made Earth uninhabitable. However, what he does not know is that the hostile aliens won the war, and that he himself is a human clone. I argue that the film addresses the challenges of the state of exception, in which everything is potentially turned upside down to the extent that it is no longer possible to fully comprehend the scale, implications, or consequences of this upheaval. This is the great danger of being in the state of exception after the sovereign's decision on the exception has been made. In *Oblivion*, the war continues—we just do not know it; we no longer understand which side we are on or, in the end, who we ourselves are. The film thus articulates a paradoxical self-consciousness that is born and shaped within the exceptional situation. To Schmitt, the sovereign identifies the exceptional situation and decides what to do about it. However, once we are in the state of exception, Kosinski's film suggests, it is difficult, if not impossible, to recognize it, much less terminate it and return to normality. The film thus highlights the dangers of declaring the state of exception, especially when it comes to defending the present against a transformative future event.

The book's last chapter discusses Denis Villeneuve's *Blade Runner 2049* (2017) in connection with its precursor, Ridley Scott's 1982 film *Blade Runner*. What happens politically when artificially produced life can reproduce on its own, beyond human control? If Scott's *Blade Runner* was mainly occupied with the emergence of the traditional sovereign and the right to kill in those situations when the boundary between humans and non-humans break down, Villeneuve's sequel *Blade Runner 2049* shifts the focus to questions about the right to produce life. In the sequel, set some thirty years after the first film, it is revealed that Deckard and Rachael had a child together—an event that has huge political implications, not only because replicant birth is supposed to be a physical impossibility, but also because it raises the question of who holds the right to produce life. In the 1982 film, the replicant represents the absolute culmination of the biopolitical production of bare life, and thereby the ultimate expression of sovereign power. Using Agamben and Arendt's developments of Schmitt's political ideas, I argue that *Blade Runner 2049* attempts to articulate something that escapes this sphere of sovereign power: the miracle of birth. Birth is the most radical questioning of sovereign power precisely because it once again brings together life and its form in a way that prevents the production of bare life. Overall, the film envisions a future scenario in which the individual life may articulate itself beyond or even in defiance of sovereign power.

## Notes

1. In a similarly alarming tone, the American political scientist Robert Kagan has argued that the American-led liberal world order today is on the wane, and that *The Jungle Grows Back*—as his book from 2018 is called.
2. See Menand (2018).

3. Huntington (2005); Harrison and Huntington (2000); Kagan (2008); Mearsheimer (2014); Merry (2005); and Runciman (2018).
4. See Toffler (1970).
5. See Andersson 16. Fred Polak reaches a similar conclusion in *The Image of the Future*, which traces the vision of a utopian future from antiquity to the present, at which point the concept is weakened and replaced by an increasingly detemporalized notion of a permanent present.
6. For a discussion of this issue, and in particular Habermas's critique of Schmitt, see Specter 426–54.
7. On this issue, see in particular Gross (2016) and Bendersky (1983).
8. See, for example, Derrida (2005); Benoist (2002); Agamben (2005); and Mouffe (2005).
9. As Mouffe writes—with reference to Schmitt—"The mistake of liberal rationalism is to ignore the affective dimension mobilized by collective identifications and to imagine that those supposedly archaic 'passions' are bound to disappear with the advance of individualism and the progress of rationality" (6).
10. Fukuyama's thesis was, and perhaps still is, badly misunderstood—that is, as if he argued that historical events would no longer occur, or that all the world's problems had now been solved. What Fukuyama, via Hegel-Kojève, suggested was that liberal democracy paired with market capitalism constituted the culmination of modern political thought—at the end of which liberal democracy, in a normative sense, offered the individual the greatest amount of dignity, freedom, and rights.
11. Thus, in his televised speech to the American people, President George W. Bush used an emergency rhetoric to successfully convince Congress to take over vast sums of debt to save the banks. For a full transcript of Bush's speech, see: http://www.nytimes.com/2008/09/24/business/economy/24text-bush.html (last accessed October 2020).
12. For a critical discussion of this skepticism, see Brown 1–22.
13. As Robert Kagan observes, in *The Return of History*, "The world has become normal again. The years immediately following the end of the Cold War offered a tantalizing glimpse of a new kind of international order, with nation-states growing together or disappearing, ideological conflicts melting away, cultures intermingling . . . But that was a mirage" (3). It was a mirage, which the time following 9/11 in particular made clear, and which, in recent years, has escalated into a serious questioning of the liberal paradigm within Western societies.
14. See Jameson, *Archaeologies* 288–9. Similarly, to Delany, "SF is not about the future; it uses the future as a narrative convention to present distortions of the present" (*Starboard* 48).
15. Although the sci-fi genre, given its preoccupation with the concept of the future, has often been connected with predictive powers, I agree with Suvin's comment that "SF is material for futurology (if at all) only in the

very restricted sense of reflecting on the author's own historical period and the possibilities inherent in it" (76). For further discussions of this issue, see Westfahl, Wong and Chan (2011) and Roberts (2006): 24–8. See also Alkon's important study of the emergence of narratives set in the future—*Origins of Futuristic Fiction*—which focuses on the integral role of science fiction in the historical development of the concept of the future as something more and different than simply the continuation of the present.

16. For example, see Telotte 124; MacLeod 230; Jameson, *Archaeologies* 281–95; and Wegner 27–61. For a critical approach to the concept of utopia within the context of science fiction, see Paik 1–22.
17. See Csicsery-Ronay's essay "Dis-Imagined Communities" 217–37.
18. Or, as Canavan argues, contemporary society is characterized by "a time in which our own capacity to imagine alternative futures to capitalism has become deeply impoverished" (xxix). For further arguments along those lines, see Mark Fisher's *Capitalist Realism* 1–11.
19. The future, as Slavoj Žižek observes, is not simply that which inevitably happens, but rather that which arrives in the form of a radical departure: "There are in French two words for 'future' which cannot be adequately rendered in English: *futur* and *avenir*. *Futur* stands for 'future' as the continuation of the present, as the full actualization of tendencies already in existence; while *avenir* points more towards a radical break, a discontinuity with the present—*avenir* is what is to come (*à venir*), not just what will be" (*The Year* 134). Likewise, to Derrida, the "future can only be anticipated in the form of an absolute danger . . . a sort of monstrosity" (*Grammatology* 5).
20. As I will clarify a little later, I am primarily looking at the late twentieth-/early twenty-first-century science fiction film—rather than the entire (and predominantly literary) genre of science fiction. There is an important discussion about films versus literary texts within sci-fi studies: for instance, whether we are talking about different genres or simply different forms of expression within the same genre paradigm (see, for example, Sobchack (1988) *Screening Space* and Landon (1992)), but also the extent to which sci-fi film studies could even be seen as a serious genre (a notion sometimes met with disdain from literary practitioners within the sci-fi field)—that is, a process of critical legitimation that sci-fi literature itself went through at an earlier stage. It is true, as Blackford observes, that "many SF movies are formulaic" (17), that many are the products of a commercial Hollywood discourse, and that many perhaps lack the philosophical and cognitive intricacies that one finds in much sci-fi literature. At the same time, I agree with Cornea's point that it is also possible to overstate "the differences between science fiction literature and film at the expense of their affiliations" (5). That being said, I do see an advantage in looking at film precisely because this medium—typically being grounded in a pronounced collective effort (such as directing, filming, script writing, sound editing, and so on, all in unison, in an effort to create a product typically intended for mass consumption, the

semi-hypnotic collective experience of sitting in the darkness of the cinema, experiencing the same, simultaneously)—underlines my overall argument about sci-fi realism and the specifically political in a more explicit and direct way than literary expression would have done.

21. For critical overviews of the sci-fi film genre, see especially Cornea (2007), Johnston (2011), Sobchack (1988), and Telotte (2001).
22. Thus, John Rieder indicatively writes that "SF has no essence, no single unifying characteristic, and no point of origin" (193). To Cornea, "There are almost as many definitions of science fiction as there are critics who have attempted to define it as a genre" (2). Likewise, Roberts opens his *Science Fiction* with the line, "The term 'science fiction' resists easy definition" (1), which echoes Seed's opener in *Science Fiction: A Very Short Introduction*: "Science fiction has proven notoriously difficult to define" (1).
23. Other critics who comment on this change in the late 1970s include Luckhurst 167–219; Redmond 134–43; Bould and Vint 146–64; Johnston 91–103; and Sobchack (1988) 223–41.
24. The important thing here is, to a lesser extent, whether the future technology (such as 'speed-of-light' space travel or the ability to dematerialize in one place and rematerialize in another place) is realistic in a strictly scientific sense, but rather if this future technology—and the characters' use of and engagement with this technology—is envisioned in realistic terms: that is, a way of imagining how the future world would operate realistically, and not magically, fantastically, or psychically.
25. Suvin borrows this concept from Ernst Bloch's *The Principle of Hope* (1959/1995); see Suvin 64. As Csicsery-Ronay points out, "Suvin's novum differs from Bloch's in important ways . . . Suvin downplays Bloch's messianic framework . . . [the novum is] a figural device that so 'dominates' (Suvin's term) its fiction, that every significant aspect of the narrative's meaning can be derived from it: the estranged conditions caused by a radically new thing, the thematic unity of the work, and even changes in its readers' attitudes toward their own world, after reading" (*Seven Beauties* 49). Whereas Bloch's Novum (capitalized in English translations) constitutes a messianic potential of newness that awakens the present from its slumber, Suvin's concept is a futurist discourse that rationally and scientifically follows the inherent possibilities of the present.
26. The novum exercises a form of *hegemony* in the sense that it conditions the building blocks of the plot's world, and furthermore links this world to the concerns and interests of the present. See Suvin 63.
27. For example, Renault 113–41; and Telotte 4. Both critics find the sharp border between sci-fi and fantasy too absolute. Furthermore, Csicsery-Ronay observes that the concept of the novum seems most "useful for reading narratively simple fictions, such as short stories and novels with relatively simple narrative arcs" (*Seven Beauties* 62)—and, one might add, the genre of film (which, like the short story, tends to present relatively simple plots).

28. There is a longstanding and important debate about the relationship between science fiction and fantasy in the history of sci-fi criticism. See, for example, Baker 440; Brooks-Rose 73; Cornea 3–4; Suvin 66; and Telotte 11.
29. Thus, I largely agree with Freedman's argument that science fiction is a genre strongly adhering to some kind of historical concreteness precisely because it insists on what he calls "a cognitive continuum with the actual," which sharply distinguishes it from "irrationalist estrangements of such essentially ahistorical modes as fantasy or the Gothic, which may secretly work to ratify the mundane status quo by presenting no alternative to the latter other than inexplicable discontinuities" (43). At the same time, it is important to stress that sci-fi—obviously—is a fantastic genre in the sense that it imagines something non-existent. What connects the genre to realism is the adherence to a collective imagination—even if this imagination trespasses into the realm of the fantastic.
30. See also Russ (116), Delany ("About 5750 Words" 8), Roberts (15), and Johnston (15) for similar observations.
31. See Shippey 16. Realism here should not be confused with the notion of "hard sci-fi," even if it also involves a stronger commitment to the "exactness" of real science. The point here is, rather, that realistic sci-fi is sharply distinguished from fantasy, comedy, and other distinctly anti-realist aesthetic modes.
32. An important exception here would be Paik's reading of science fiction through realism, where the latter is understood in terms of political philosophy, meaning "a discourse which analyzes in an impartial and dispassionate manner the workings of power" (19).
33. For a discussion of this, see Shaw 3–36.
34. See, in particular: Ben-Yishai (2013); Duncan (2007); Ermarth (1998); Gallagher (1994); Greiner (2012); Petrey (1988); and Shaw (1999).
35. One could also refer here to the distinction that Ursula Le Guin makes between fantasy as originally inwards-oriented, while science fiction—as an intellectual–scientific genre—constitutes an external fantasy (see Le Guin 114).
36. Realism as a notion involving the idea of collectivity is related to Suvin's definition of the novum: that is, as a figure of the future rationally or scientifically evolving from the present. Science is, by definition, not an individual–subjective endeavor; it involves a degree of consensus and objectivity, if only within a given community of knowledge. By contrast, as Csicsery-Ronay points out, "*Invalidated novums* are those that cannot be unambiguously validated by (fictive) science. Their ontology is unclear, and readers cannot determine whether the imaginary universe they occur in is rational and material, oneiric, or hallucinatory" (*Seven Beauties* 53).
37. Apart from a few references in Jameson's *Archaeologies of the Future*, Peter Paik's *From Utopia to Apocalypse* is one of the few academic books that engages with Schmitt's thoughts in connection with the sci-fi genre.

38. In 1933, Schmitt became a member of NSDAP, which came as a surprise for many around him, since he had fought actively against the Nazis before they came to power. From 1933 to 1936, Schmitt wrote a series of highly problematic texts defending Hitler and the Nazis; he served on several committees for the Nazi regime; and on several occasions explicitly contributed to the demonization of Jewish people and their culture. In 1936, after critique from the Gestapo, Schmitt was marginalized but continued to teach until the end of the war. After the war, Schmitt was imprisoned by the Allies on two occasions, and spent around a year in a prison camp. He was sent to the Nuremberg trials, but never given a sentence. Throughout the rest of his life, Schmitt was barred from teaching or practicing law. He returned to his place of birth, Plettenberg, where he lived a quiet life until his death in 1985—never once admitting to any wrong-doing during the war years. On the contrary, Schmitt compared himself, rather unconvincingly, to Melville's protagonist Benito Cereno, the captain of a ship that has been taken over by mutineers, who force him to act as if everything is normal (see Linder 157).

39. Here see Tanaka 5 and Kalyvas 1527.

40. For a thorough discussion of Schmitt's anti-Semitism, see Raphael Gross's "The 'True' Enemy," which concludes with the damning verdict: "Against this backdrop, I find it difficult, as a historian, to imagine how contemporary political theory could profit from Schmitt's work" (111). However, I agree with Joseph Bendersky's opinion that Schmitt's "attitudes do not constitute an ideological antisemitism" ("Schmitt's Diaries" 124), even if it would be difficult to argue that Schmitt's involvement in the Nazi Party may be reduced to a matter of opportunism. For a discussion of Schmitt's Nazi affiliations, see Bendersky's *Carl Schmitt: Theorist for the Reich* (esp. 195–218).

41. Here see, for example, Kalyvas's important work on Schmitt's relevance to contemporary democratic theory (1529).

42. Schmitt's notion of the political draws on a tradition of *Realpolitik* within political history that focuses on the inherent conflictual dimension of politics. Here, the obvious precursor is Machiavelli and, more specifically, his—in some people's view, cynical—attempt to separate political thinking from ethical concerns (that is, what is necessary to maintain power versus what is the right thing to do) in *The Prince* (1513). Machiavelli's reflections on dictatorship are central to Schmitt's argument in the early work *Dictatorship* (see 1–33). Historically, Schmitt's career also, to some extent, resembles Machiavelli's. Between 1498 and 1512, Machiavelli worked as a diplomat and political advisor for the Republican rule of Florence. When the Medici family reclaimed power in 1512, Machiavelli was dismissed and, soon after, imprisoned and accused of conspiracy against the Medicis. As some historians have claimed, this is one of the reasons why Machiavelli writes *The Prince*: as a desperate attempt to win the new rulers' sympathies, and possibly even make a career within the new regime (see Lucchese 65–84).

43. On this issue, see Kalyvas 1538–9, fn57. See also Cristi 117.
44. As Schmitt observes, "Looked at normatively, the decision emanates from nothingness" (*Political Theology* 31–2)—precisely because of the unpredictability of the future, the ever-present possibility of a concrete situation involving the necessity of warfare.
45. As Kalyvas, writes, "According to Schmitt, liberalism emerged as a theory aimed at the limitation and fragmentation of political power, and it has pursued this aim by seeking to neutralize or eliminate the constituent power of the people" (1546).
46. To Schmitt, this is a general characteristic of *modern* society: "Today," as he writes in *Political Theology*, "nothing is more modern than the onslaught against the political. American financiers, industrial technicians, Marxist socialists, and anarchic–syndicalist revolutionaries unite in demanding that the biased rule of politics over unbiased economic management be done away with. There must no longer be political problems, only organizational–technical and economic–sociological tasks. The kind of economic–technical thinking that prevails today is no longer capable of perceiving a political idea" (65).
47. See in particular, Chapter III (31–40) of *The Leviathan in the State Theory of Thomas Hobbes*.
48. As Sava writes, "A juridical act or fact acquires its juridical meaning precisely through the same mechanism, using a concept analogous to that of causality, i.e. a legal causal link, provided by the norm . . . The norm can therefore be defined as a juridical causality" (22). As Sava goes on to point out, with reference to Schmitt, "There will always be a remainder between the particular and the general," which precisely opens up the space for the decision, "an element that exceeds the direct causality, since there is a gap between the general nature of the law and the particular nature of reality" (26).
49. See Derrida for an elaboration of the point that democracy arrives in the form of a "structure of a promise—and thus the memory of that which carries the future, the to-come, here and now" (*The Other Heading* 78). Derrida's concept of democracy builds, among other things, on an attempt to move beyond Schmitt's dichotomic friend/enemy distinction, and hence an attempt to formulate a new (anti-)concept of the political.
50. Or, as Slavoj Žižek puts it: "It is easy to make fun of Fukuyama's notion of the End of History, but the dominant ethos today *is* 'Fukuyamian': liberal–democratic capitalism is accepted as the finally found formula of the best possible society, all that one can do is render it more just, tolerant, and so forth" (*Defense* 421).
51. Schmitt's great opponent here is the Austrian jurist Hans Kelsen, who, in the words of Tracy B. Strong, envisioned "a theory of law that would be universally valid for all times and all situations" (Foreword to *Political Theology* xvii). In Kelsen's view, the sovereign decision and the state of exception are dangerous elements that put the constitution—or what he calls the "basic norm"—at risk. On this issue, see also Sava 17; and Kalyvas 1536, fn43.

52. On this issue, see in particular Chapter 5 ("The Extraordinary Lawgiver *Ratione Necessitatis*") in Schmitt's *Legality and Legitimacy* 67–83.
53. This argument should be understood in terms of Schmitt's wider critique of constitutional legalism, which—in Schmitt's view—eventually erodes the essence of law. On this issue, see Berkmanas 112–16.
54. This is the opening sentence of *Political Theology*: "Sovereign is he who decides on the exception" (5). As Schmitt explains, "It is precisely the exception that makes relevant the subject of sovereignty ... [the sovereign] decides whether there is an extreme emergency as well as what must be done to eliminate it. Although he stands outside the normally valid legal system, he nevertheless belongs to it, for it is he who must decide whether the constitution needs to be suspended in its entirety. All tendencies of modern constitutional development point toward eliminating the sovereign in this sense" (6–7).
55. See Schmitt, *Political Theology* 30. As Georg Schwab memorably puts it, Schmitt's "sovereign is, so to speak, slumbering, and he is suddenly awakened at a crucial moment: namely, at the borderline between normalcy and the state of exception" (50).
56. The point here is that, to Schmitt, no basic set of rules can anticipate all possible situations to come; hence, what defines sovereignty is his or her ability to *decide* what constitutes an exceptional situation. But this decision, as Tracy B. Strong points out, is never simply a decision, "if by that one means simply that choice is necessary and any choice is better than none" (Foreword to *Political Theology* xiv–xv). The "genuine decision," as Schmitt puts it, is one that ultimately stems from his understanding of the political—which is not identical with the state or the constitution; the political stems from the idea of a specific community of people, defined in opposition to other communities (hence, Schmitt's friend/enemy distinction). The reality of this community is what Schmitt at times refers to as human life, and which cannot be governed by a set of abstract laws, valid at all times and in all situations.
57. See Schmitt, *Political Theology* 5.
58. See Schmitt, *Political Theology* 6.
59. A concept close to this notion of the future would be Taleb's "black swan theory" about extreme events unpredictably disrupting the normative order (see Taleb (2010)).
60. Also, it is important to remember here that, in German, all nouns are assigned a gender, which, in the English language, creates a more personalized impression than what was probably intended by Schmitt: for example, the sovereign or enemy as "he."
61. As Tracy B. Strong has pointed out, Schmitt's opening sentence in *Politisches Theologie*, "Souverän ist, wer über den Ausnahmezustand entscheidet," is ambiguous in the sense that it may be translated as both "*what* is the exceptional situation" and "*what to do* about the exceptional situation." "Schmitt," Strong writes, "is saying that it is the essence of sovereignty *both* to decide what is an exception *and* to make the decisions appropriate to that exception,

indeed that one without the other makes no sense at all" (Foreword to *Political Theology* xii).

62. As Barbour observes, the exception "inserts a sudden, abrupt, miraculous wedge into the normal, mechanical repetitive application of rules . . . the sovereign, the sovereign exception or sovereign decision does not repeat an established rule, nor can it be repeated by, or subjected to, a future rule. It is, in short, a pure event, without past or future" (149).

63. See Schmitt, *Dictatorship* 1–33. As Schwab writes in reference to Schmitt's *Dictatorship*: "A sovereign dictatorship utilizes a crisis to abrogate the existing constitution in order to bring about a 'condition whereby a constitution [that the sovereign dictator] considers to be a true constitution will become possible,' whereas a commissarial dictatorship endeavors to restore order so that the existing constitution can be revived and allowed to function normally" (Foreword to *Political Theology* xlv).

64. In *The Leviathan in the State Theory of Thomas Hobbes*, Schmitt writes: "Sovereign power . . . is God's highest representatives on earth" (55). In Schmitt's political theology—according to which all important political concepts are secularized theological concepts—the sovereign is a kind of secularized god or a monster, a superman.

65. I should stress here that this is my own interpretation; Schmitt never talked extensively about the future in this theoretical sense, and never wrote about the sci-fi genre. He did, however, write an early short story about a post-human future, *Die Buribunken* (1918), a speculative piece of fiction about a future society, published in the journal *Summa*. See, in particular, Balke (2016) for a discussion of this early work.

66. Suvin himself seems to indicate the possibility of such a radical element when he writes: "Though I would be hard put to cite an SF tale the novelty in which is not in fact continuous with or at least analogous to existing scientific cognitions, I would be disposed to accept theoretically a faint possibility of a fictional novum that would at least seem to be based on quite new, imaginary cognitions, beyond all real possibilities known or dreamt of in the author's empirical reality" (66). Suvin stresses that, in so-called "hard" sci-fi, this possibility would be close to zero, since it is committed to the notion of a "real possibility." Some scholars might argue that the novum simply constitutes the new, hence also a radically transgressive element, although, in that case, the distinction between sci-fi and fantasy collapses.

67. As Walter Benjamin writes, clearly in reference to Schmitt, "The tradition of the oppressed teaches us that the 'state of emergency' in which we live is not the exception but the rule" ("History" 392). I will discuss this notion further in the coming chapters.

68. Within this perspective, one could further argue that the genre's fascination with the topos of time travel—especially those films involving some kind of dystopian dimension from the 1980s and onwards (such as the *Terminator* franchise, see Penley, "Time Travel" 126–35)—reveals precisely this desire

to return to the normative present: that is, the time before the future event changed the political coordinates of the present. As Csicsery-Ronay observes, time travel SF and what-if fiction "gravitate toward primal scenes, the world-transforming events most commonly held to have been decisive for the fate of the nation or the species" (*Seven Beauties* 104). An example here would be *Terminator 2: Judgment Day*, in which the character Dyson develops a microprocessor that eventually will become Skynet, and which thus must be destroyed before it happens.

69. It should be mentioned here that the works discussed in this book are not organized according to a chronological principle, mainly because the overall argument is not centered around a genealogical–historical approach, but rather organized according to conceptual trajectories of certain political themes.

CHAPTER 1

# Between Friends and Enemies: Ridley Scott's *Alien*

## Introduction

In an academic context, Ridley Scott's sci-fi classic *Alien* (1979) has most commonly been understood and discussed through feminist and psychoanalytic vocabularies, often with a specific focus on the relationship between the main character, Ripley, and the monster. That the film lends itself to these perspectives is underscored, above all, by the spaceship's peculiar architecture (for example, narrow, dark ventilation shafts), which, at times, looks like a materialization of the unconscious. To Bell-Mettreau, the film thus explores issues regarding "maternal attachment" ("Woman" 217), while Kavanaugh focuses on the film's generally "strong feminist message" (99). This message is further elaborated by Rushing, who reads *Alien* as "an archetypical view of the evolution of feminine consciousness" (2), whereas Jeffords critically argues that the feminist ideology of the film is "victorious only because it accepts the view of a corporate masculism at the expense of relations between women" (73). To Torry, however, the film's ultimate purpose is "finally an exposure of the distressing aspects of the phallic ideal represented in the triumphant Ripley, an ideal initially embodied in the alien creature itself, the Imaginary Other whose position she ultimately assumes" (344). Other readings focus more narrowly on the birth motif. Cobbs argues accordingly that "sexual symbolism and iconography of a singular kind are pervasive throughout the film and may actually be its *leitmotif*. What *Alien* is about is gestation and birth" (198). From a more historical perspective, albeit still with a strong emphasis on the feminist/psychoanalytic view, Hoffman has argued more recently that *Alien* (and *Rosemary's Baby*) constitute "social documents of the growing horror of pregnancy experienced by both women and sympathetic men from the 1960s up to the 1980s, as reproductive technology and legal actions colluded to empower the fetus at the expense of the previously sacrosanct pregnant woman" (241). Although differing as to the assessment of the film's critical potential, the discussions seem to agree on reading *Alien* as, in Vaughn's words, "a template for tracing the cultural contest over the meaning of the feminine, especially in relation to gendered social practices such as motherhood" (424).[1]

In this chapter, however, I want to pursue an argument suggesting that such theoretical frameworks, however powerful and compelling, at the same time deflect attention from the *literalness* of what is perhaps the film's most fundamental, albeit at the same time most latent conflict, namely, one that touches upon the question that sets in motion the entire plot of the film: why is it so crucial for the Company to bring back a specimen of this strange and dangerous life form to Earth?

Initially, the film seems to suggest that the reason why this life form is so valuable to the Company—much more valuable than 20,000,000 tons of mineral ore, not to speak of the lives of the crew—relates to business matters: a perfect biological weapon that would yield an enormous advantage in warfare. This premise remains, however, *literally* unspoken, even if it is hinted at by Science Officer Ash, who expresses uninhibited admiration for the creature. Ash's semi-erotic admiration of this strange being, as well as MUTHR's brutal rejection of the crew's ever more desperate requests for help to pacify it, seems to indicate that the real issue at stake here is rather different than simply business matters; even if one accepts the premise that the alien life form is valuable in a commercial sense (for example, as a valuable new weapon), it is an ironic value because it is so destructive that it threatens to destroy everything, including the realm of the commercial. But what is this value that exceeds commercial interests? To answer this question, I want to argue that it is necessary to pursue the *literal* traces in the film: that is, not the film as a psychological allegory, but as a concrete articulation of a political problem. At the beginning of the film, as the crew wakes up from a long slumber, a remarkably radiant atmosphere of tranquility and Edenic peace surrounds the place, as if we were momentarily witnessing the dawn of the first people on Earth.[2] This slow-motion opening scenario transitions into a breakfast scene during which the mood is jovial, cozy, and cantankerous at times. The camera moves slowly around the breakfast table, where people still in bathrobes, others casually dressed (with the exception of Ash, who is wearing a uniform), exchange jokes, high fives, plates, and jars while the cat sits comfortably on the table in front of Ripley. Stylistically, the literalness of the film's opening is pivotal to creating a contrast to what is about to happen (that is, alien carnage). Thematically, however, it also plays a crucial role in that it plants the seeds for the remaining plotline; this is, in other words, an overture that literally reveals *why* it is so important to establish a relation to the alien life form.

Jovial, cozy, and cantankerous at times: the crew members evidently feel safe and secure, even cheerful, as they expect to be back on Earth soon. Some people grumble about banalities like feeling cold and salary issues. The conflicts (such as that between Captain Dallas and Engineer Parker) are everyday and trivial. In other words, the crew members find themselves in the midst of MUTHR's safe bosom. Parker and Brett want higher bonuses, which apparently everyone else receives, but Dallas firmly reminds them what they initially signed up for: "You get what is agreed in your contract." When Dallas informs the crew that a strange transmission has been intercepted, Science Officer Ash reminds everyone that they have a duty to investigate it—again, by referring to their contractual obligations.[3] The scene ends with Parker sullenly observing that the only good thing on board is the coffee. Banal, mundane, and seemingly irrelevant in terms of what follows, the breakfast scene is nevertheless absolutely central because it *literally* portrays a conflict between individual desire (Parker and Brett's wish for a higher bonus) on the one hand and collective duties (the contract) on the other. This conflict, I want to argue in the following, constitutes the entire raison d'être of what subsequently unfolds; what we witness here, in embryonic form, is nothing less than the subversion of social life or the weakening of the state through citizens dissatisfied with the social contract because of their individual desires.[4]

Carl Schmitt feared the weak state above anything else;[5] far more dangerous than any alien monsters, in his view, is the *discontent citizen* like Engineers Parker and Brett, who simply want more for themselves, while deliberately disregarding, if not undermining, the community.[6] Captain Dallas insists on the contract's legal validity; the contract is legal, bureaucratic, and commercial, or, one could say that it is *depoliticized*, containing no *political* value. Schmitt wanted to restore the concept of the political—which, I argue in this chapter, is precisely what the secret mission of the *Nostromo* spaceship is essentially about: to restore the political within the realm of a weakened political discourse, a weakened state in which individuals increasingly have become obsessed with narrow egotistical and commercial interests, as well as individual rights.[7]

Thus, I want to present a reading of *Alien* that seeks to illuminate the film's latent political conflict, which, in many ways, approximates Schmitt's concept of the political, especially his reinterpretation of Thomas Hobbes's *Leviathan*. The chapter will particularly focus on Schmitt's notion of the state of exception, the sovereign, and the connections between these concepts and the specifically political, the friend–enemy distinction. In other words, this chapter will attempt to illuminate the political dynamic played out in *Alien*, a dynamic that has constituted one of the most acute (and as yet unresolved) socio-political problems regarding the organization of collective life.

## Leviathan and Behemoth

According to Carl Schmitt, a depoliticized or weak state leads to discord, and eventually civil war and chaos, and the most fundamental task of the state is to prevent this scenario. Hence, the state's ideological task, which at the same time becomes the film's ideological task, is to shift the focus from the real danger (the discontented citizen) to an external, perhaps imagined or random danger like the alien. One of the crucial foundations of Schmitt's concept of the political is his interpretation of Thomas Hobbes's political theory, or more specifically Leviathan's struggle against Behemoth. At the core of this theory, we find an anecdotal narrative of a distant past, during which individuals coexisted in a society ruled by no one—the so-called "state of nature."[8] In this state of nature, nothing of real value exists; there are no communal values, no justice, no prosperity or creativity. Even though each individual, in principle, possesses absolute rights, these rights are worthless insofar as there is no entity except the individual to enforce the validity of these rights. Thus, no one can be satisfied with a situation in which everyone may be radically free but at the same time must fear everyone else (who would equally be entitled to do whatever he or she likes—for example, rob your house). Life in the state of nature is, as Hobbes formulates it in a famous quotation from *Leviathan*, "solitary, poor, nasty, brutish, and short" (78). The disorganized, bewildered, and hostile individuals of the state of nature eventually realize the benefits of abandoning their claim to absolute individual freedom in order to attain peace, security, and prosperity.[9] Precisely this rational impulse becomes the foundation of the state, the Leviathan, the state that miraculously transforms individuals into citizens.[10]

Hobbes's theory of the foundation of the modern political state has been interpreted in widely different ways. According to the liberal tradition, the rational impulse of the individual, or that which eventually leads to the forfeiture of absolute individual rights, eventually triumphs in the creation of the state.[11] The state creates a legal framework devoted solely to the promotion of individual prosperity and development.[12] The relation between state and citizens thus essentially becomes a question about contractual justification—that is, the extent to which there is a legitimate *correspondence* between the actions of the state and the interests of the individuals; if this is not the case, the state, according to the liberalists, becomes illegitimate and unlawful.[13]

Schmitt fiercely rejects this liberal interpretation of Hobbes because such a reading ignores the presence of Behemoth, the creator of chaos and destruction.[14] In his political theory, Schmitt argues, Hobbes essentially describes a strong government that requires the presence of a powerful sovereign authority. In Schmitt's version of Hobbes, the struggle between Leviathan and Behemoth is a permanent one; the horror of the state of nature remains a latent possibility, even within the legal state. Indeed, this latent horror is the very foundation of the legal state. As McCormick writes, "Schmitt's implicit reading of Hobbes, therefore, suggests that a return to the state of nature is an ever-present possibility for any society" ("Teaching in Vain" 278). The state of nature is not merely a historical or geographical place, a place to be avoided once and for all. Rather, the state of nature is a part of our psyche; as humans, we are, at one and the same time, driven by an intense, if destructive and irrational, egotistical lust for power, *and* a capacity for rational thinking, or reason.[15]

The lawlessness of the state of nature entitles the individual to absolute rights (for example, to plunder and enrich him- or herself through force or violence), but at the same time one's neighbor possesses the exact same rights, which makes life constantly insecure.[16] This is a situation that undermines the possibility of progress insofar as one must constantly be cautious of the other's actions and doings, instead of expending one's energy on more productive activities.[17]

To Schmitt, the relationship between nature and culture is thus never permanently resolved, and hence the Leviathan's role is most definitely not simply that of a *historical* nature, but very much one that is needed in the present. If there were no sovereign, chaos would reign—that is, the state of nature. The implication here is that the sovereign should not be understood simply as the *expression* or *representative* of individuals' wills (even if it is *produced* by them, their rationality); rather, Leviathan to some extent stands in *opposition* to these individual wills. Thus, in *Political Theology*, Schmitt observes, "the necessity by which the people always will what is right is not identical with the rightness that emanated from the commands of the personal sovereign . . . The unity that a people represents does not possess this decisionist character" (48–9). Leviathan is the embodiment of this decisionist character, and is hence a figure ultimately more powerful—more ruthless, more hungry for power—than the individuals, in order to control them.[18]

## Friend or Enemy

It is Ash as a representative figure of the Company (representing Schmitt's Leviathan) who insists on letting in Executive Officer Kane when the latter has been infected by, or rather *with*, a mystical alien life form. This may seem a bit ironic because Ash actually looks as if he is doing something humane, in contrast to Ripley, who refuses to open the gate per standard quarantine procedures.[19] Soon after, however, Ash shows his real intentions: what he really cares about is not Kane's survival, but rather the alien life form that has colonized his body. What is interesting here is that whereas Ripley insists on standard procedures—that is, fixed laws, rules, and regulations (even if this means putting Kane's life at risk), Ash insists on the right to make an *exception*. But what is the nature of this exception, which initially looks like something derived from humane motivation? Here we need to look more closely at Schmitt's definition of the specifically political—that is, *the ability to distinguish between friends and enemies*. This ability implies that the enemy cannot be determined as an *essence* or *substance*, but can be identified only in a concrete situation.[20] Ash, one could argue, suspends the law (makes an exception) in order to establish a relation to the ambiguous, or a potential enemy.

In *The Concept of the Political*, Schmitt argues that liberalism (the rational–technological conception of politics) potentially leads to disaster because it reduces and eventually eliminates the political. Liberalism transforms the state into a blind, bureaucratic, and technocratic institution, utterly incapable of confronting the real political challenges of government.[21] Thus, the state, as the ultimate legislator and enforcer of the law, can never protect itself adequately, insofar as it must act on the basis of a general, prelegislated set of laws in relation to any possible situation. The future is profoundly unpredictable, and this is why Schmitt defines the sovereign as the one who can declare a state of exception.

In the concrete situation, when the critically ill Kane stands helplessly outside the spaceship's gate, desperately in need of medical help, this person constitutes an ambiguous being—half friend, half enemy, still recognizable as "Kane" but carrying an alien life form that has covered his face. Ash as a representative figure of the state desperately wants to *investigate* it, *study* the ambiguity of a life form never observed before, even if he must suspend the rules in order to do so;[22] or, one could argue, *determine* whether it is a friend or enemy, by which, in the same gesture, he restores the *specifically political*.[23] Ripley refuses to open the gate for Kane, while Ash disobeys her order; here, the film provides a neat exemplification of the difference between the geospatial concept of the state of nature and Schmitt's concept of the state of exception. In the geospatial notion, the state of nature is essentially that which is *outside* the city gate, the wilderness; to Schmitt, this wilderness has now moved *within* the city walls as the state of exception.[24] In the state of exception, the sovereign, whose rule is premised on the assumption that the future is radically unpredictable, is raised above the general constitutional law; the sovereign is no longer limited or bound by ordinary legal norms. To Schmitt, this is essential; as the embodiment of the state, the powerful sovereign must, at all times, be prepared for the extreme situation, its possibility—the state of nature where rules become invalid, meaningless. Schmitt thus defines the specifically political as something that constitutes its own right, in need of no further justification or explanation, a *causa sui*. It is in this context that one should understand Schmitt's comment in *Political Theology*: "All significant concepts of the modern theory of the state are secularized theological concepts" (36). In the secular world, the miraculous essentially comes down to the maxim, *auctoritas non veritas facit legem*—"it is authority, not truth, which makes the law." The sovereign is a god-like figure who miraculously transforms wolves into obedient, peaceful citizens of the state.

In *The Leviathan in the State Theory of Thomas Hobbes*, Schmitt argues that Hobbes's figure of the Leviathan has been misinterpreted, to the extent that it has come to signify a "huge machine" (19); this is the liberal interpretation, according to which the state is reduced to a mechanical, rational, and entirely depersonalized operator, ruling according to a fixed set of procedures. In *Alien*, this mechanical conception is initially reflected in the crew's relation to the ship's control center, "MUTHR," an entity that, in the beginning, seems neutral, functional, and machine-like, but later in the film develops into a sovereign in the Schmittian sense, acting independently of the individuals' wills (or, more specifically, *against* the wills of the individuals). Likewise, the job contract (referred to at the beginning of the film when Brett and Parker express dissatisfaction with their salary) and the standard quarantine procedures (referred to when Ripley refuses to open the hatch for Kane) stem from this discourse of a bureaucratic, mechanistic version of Leviathan, or the state. Schmitt, as we have seen, wants to move away from this bureaucratic, mechanical, and predictable concept of the state; Leviathan is not only a machine, or merely a representative person, but above all a mythical force: "In its mixture of huge animal and huge machine, the image of the leviathan attains the highest level of mythical force. It strikes at the foundation that is indestructible in the relations between great powers" (49). In order to carry out its highest task, the state, according to Schmitt, must possess a mythical force, an ability to instill fear, for it is by instilling fear in people that the political order is most efficiently created.[25]

Consequently, when citizens once again are confronted with the terrible consequences of their selfishness and greed, they will seek strong authority, or the state as a mythical force, and thus (re-)sign the covenant with the Leviathan. The Leviathan is the one, according to Schmitt, who will make the necessary political decision to distinguish friends from enemies in a borderland of ambiguity, torn between peace and war, culture and nature. The clarity that the sovereign creates in this borderland of ambiguity, Schmitt believed, would definitively reduce the risk of civil war and state disintegration.[26]

## Transgression and Power

The need to seek out the ambiguous in order to distinguish friends from enemies is most actively pursued by Science Officer Ash. More generally, however, this movement is reflected in the film's overall structure, which can be divided into four sequences. The first sequence covers the beginning and ends when the alien is brought on board; at this point, a limit is transgressed by Ash, who ignores Ripley's order to keep Kane in quarantine. The second part begins with Kane's body being investigated and lasts until the emergence of the alien, during which Kane dies. The third sequence—by far the longest—stretches from the lunch table scene to the point when everyone except Ripley is dead. Finally, the last sequence deals with the escape, the detonation of the ship, and Ripley's ultimate battle against the alien, after which she sends a message to Earth and goes into hibernation along with Jones, the cat. The first sequence could be called insemination (whereby Kane's body becomes a kind of host). The second sequence would thus aptly be called the "birth scene," during which the alien crawls out of Kane's stomach. The third sequence is essentially the battle (at this point, everyone knows that the alien is indeed an enemy—the Behemoth—not a friend), and the final sequence covers the victory over the Behemoth.

What initiates this development from a peaceful, scientific, or even humanitarian engagement with a mysterious, ambiguous life form to full-scale war, and eventually life-and-death struggle, is the Company's insistence upon bringing back a specimen to Earth—that is, the secret mission, of which, initially, only MUTHR and Ash are fully aware.[27] As mentioned, the Company apparently wants the alien specimen for military purposes, despite the fact that MUTHR is a commercial ship, and that no one among the crew seems particularly trained in military techniques, let alone equipped for a full-scale war or life-or-death struggle. Here a question emerges: why would a company send a commercial ship on a hostile mission that involves terrible risks and actually ends up destroying the entire cargo and the spaceship, and killing all the crew members except Ripley? And, conversely: why would the Company not simply send a specially trained military unit to capture the alien life form? Above all, why does all this have to be so *secret*?[28] One is tempted here to suggest that the alien form *in itself* seems less important; what *is* important is, perhaps, rather the *transgression*, the one that relates to the inner/outer distinction, or the state of nature versus the legal state.

As we observed previously, the film begins with a peaceful scene of tranquility and banality, all of which is replaced by an atmosphere of ambiguity as soon as the alien is on board, and which quickly escalates into a climate of pure terror as the alien becomes extremely hostile. From this point, the entire spaceship becomes a zone of exception. In *Alien*, the safe space is radically sabotaged as the borderline separating the outside (the state of nature) and the inside (inside the gate) is eliminated when the alien is brought on board. But what is this strange alien life form? The alien not only is a physical other, but literally emerges from the self: that is, from the body of the crew.[29] It is, furthermore, at times an *immaterial* being, an intangible, formless threat, one that constantly changes shape (for example, it grows from an embryo to a huge monster in a very short time), adapts to its surroundings, becomes invisible, untraceable, and disappears in the darkness. At one point the alien almost looks human-like, walking on two legs; at other times, it resembles a fantasy creature from the world of Hieronymus Bosch. The monster seems to possess neither any particular motive nor personality, no intention, no drive except to destroy and kill. As Ash observes at one point, it is a "survivor without conscience, without guilt or delusion of morality." The alien does not seem to have its own home, its own planet; it seems capable of existing only by literally taking someone else's place, a form of life that exists only by invading our home, our territory (Schmitt's definition of the enemy). In a political reading, the film uses the image of the spaceship as a microcosm of civilized, collective life, drifting and floating around in an endless cosmic state of nature outside the gate, which is transformed into a state of exception, or the breakdown of the inner/outer distinction. In that sense, the film is, to a lesser extent, about Ripley's ultimately successful attempt to eliminate the creature (thus restoring the safe zone), but rather about the fact that they both eventually, in this vast zone of exception, are reduced to *homines sacri*.[30] Here, one is never entirely clear about what is inside or outside, or who is friend or enemy. The place turns into a zone of indistinction,[31] where everything is confusing, since there are no longer any clear boundaries; nothing is safe or stable in this zone—it is the ultimately dangerous place, a location of absolute fear. It is here, in this tormenting space of absolute fear and terror, that power as a mythical force once again finds its legitimacy. This is where we, yet again, yearn for Leviathan, the secular god powerful enough to take up the fight against the Behemoth, the monster that reduces collective life to terror and fear, ready to reaffirm our allegiance, to (re-)sign the covenant that rescues us from the state of nature.

## The Reaffirmation of the Original Social Contract

From a political perspective, *Alien* basically articulates an attempt to restore fear in society in order to revive the specifically political and to restore the state as a mythical force rather than bureaucracy or machine (which, according to Schmitt, eventually produces discontented, irrational, selfish, and disobedient individuals). By refusing to open the gate for the dying Kane because of her allegiance to standard quarantine procedures—and, in a further sense, constitutional laws—Ripley thus refuses to participate in this restoration of fear. The state (or, in the film, euphemized as "the Company") wants to re-establish a relation between individuals and the fearful state of nature precisely because this would create the possibility of the political (or, the possibility of the state as a mythical force, the sovereign who has the right to declare a state of exception). Thus, *Alien* basically tells the story of the state and citizens mutually reaffirming their allegiance to the original social contract; it is the fear of the monster, whatever it may be, that persuades the individuals to lay down their weapons, to abandon their demands for absolute rights, and to sign the contract with the sovereign Leviathan, who, in return, promises security and protection. To Schmitt, as we observed earlier, this fight against the Behemoth never ends; it is a continuing and potentially infinite struggle, and because this struggle never really ends, we must continue to seek the sovereign. Moreover, this is why Schmitt believes that we must continue to *support* the sovereign, even though our fight might not seem ethical, for the good as such, or that we ultimately have the right on our side (and, conversely, that the monster or whatever is out there constitutes absolute evil, which at all times must be destroyed), regardless of how arbitrary or bizarre the sovereign's decisions may seem.[32] In liberal society, Schmitt believes, individuals eventually forget why they initially agreed to the social contract; after an extended period of security and prosperity, citizens begin to believe that the barbarism of the past is, finally and definitively, a thing of the past.[33] To Schmitt, this is a moment of the utmost danger for the state and for individuals. *Alien* is essentially a film that plays through this—some would perhaps call it paranoid, fictitious, or deluded—original scenario at the heart of Hobbes's political theory, or the reason why we have a social contract in the first place and why power acts in the way it does, its raison d'être.[34]

But in *Alien* the danger is not fictitious or imaginary; it is very real. The monster is ruthless, lethal, and unreasonable in the extreme. Evidently motivated by reasons beyond the rational or comprehensible, the alien is the ultimate killer. At the same time, the film asks the question of whether this danger is not, in fact, actually a danger we ourselves are creating. *Alien* seems to indicate that, in the biopolitical epoch, the state needs to renegotiate the original social contract because its subjects have become indifferent, self-satisfied, and complacent like Nietzsche's last man.[35] In other words, the state needs to restore the state of nature in order to relocate and redefine itself as the sovereign, the one with absolute power, offering peace and protection in return for allegiance and support. The power to send citizens into their deaths, for example, if the state feels threatened: this was the original agreement.[36] Here, it is rather the state sending its citizens to their deaths so that they might remember why they would need the absolute sovereign in the first place.

## Power's Desire for Power

The alien is the ultimate other-as-enemy, impossible in every way, a life that cannot live, a death that cannot die. It is a figure of indifference (unreasonable, motivated by nothing, tempted only by the prospect of killing indiscriminately), a continual transition between human and animal, nature and culture. The alien is a perfect organism, as Ash observes, perhaps life in its purest form, yet at the same time a pure monstrosity, a life that is outlawed, but which also threatens the law that outlaws it.[37] The state is aware that such a dangerous life form cannot simply be kept outside the city gates; it must be controlled in a different way. Ripley is, in a sense, the old-fashioned soldier who attempts to keep out the state of nature and protect the city gate in order to maintain a clear distinction between outer and inner. Thus, she attempts to defend and preserve the realm of blissful, communal ignorance where people may peacefully interact and do business with each other (which is precisely the state's problem; this activity makes the state's absolute sovereignty superfluous).[38] The latent project in the film is thus a reorganization of power, one that is capable of dealing with the ambiguities of a new geospatial reality, an *exceptional* power. This also explains why the film operates with a covert plot; the secret mission of the *Nostromo* spaceship, unbeknownst to the crew, is the concrete expression of power's desire for the state of exception, the suspension of the rules.[39] The spaceship's control center, MUTHR, constitutes the voice of the state, anonymous yet omnipresent. It is MUTHR, as well as Ash, the physical embodiment of MUTHR, who covertly wants to bring the alien life form back to Earth. The state has one set of interests, while the citizens have another. The citizens are interested in commercial, material aspects: the salary, the bonus, the room temperature, the food, and coffee. To Schmitt, all of this leads to a weakening of the state (that is, the state as pure machine), gradually being undermined by discontented, selfish individuals. Only when the alien turns out to be a pure enemy will these individuals begin to understand the importance of collaboration, collectivity, sacrifice, and thus the raison d'être of the state, instead of blindly pursuing their individual material concerns.

The film's actual theme is thus less related to the battle against the alien, even if most of the film consists of that battle; that is to say, *when* the battle begins, very little actually happens in terms of plot development. At this point, the subjects yet again find themselves in the state of nature, yet again positioned in direct relation to a monstrous scenario that legitimizes power's right to declare a state of exception. The more monstrously the anomaly acts, the more the state is justified in acting monstrously. *Alien* illustrates how the sovereign—first and foremost represented through MUTHR and Ash, but subsequently through the citizens, the crew, and finally Ripley the individual—and the state of nature (embodied by the alien) are united in an indissoluble alliance that forms the basis of the social contract. The alien is that which challenges the law, and the guardian of the law, the sovereign, thus necessitating that the law suspends itself in order to remain intact, that is, lawful. The law must operate in a vacuum, an empty space (or, literally, outer space), in order to defend itself.[40] It is thus to a lesser extent important whether the alien may eventually be defeated (and similarly, to Schmitt, it is less important whether the state of nature is a real, prehistoric stage or simply a necessary fiction). What *is* important is that it may always potentially be activated, and if the state of nature is potentially always present, the sovereign's right to declare a state of exception must also be possible at all times. Conversely, if the anomaly or the state of nature is no longer potentially present, one would no longer need the sovereign, whose real manifestation of power is always, in the end, the right to declare the exception, and suspend the constitution, in which case the social contract would be void, and the state would become superfluous.

In *Alien* and its subsequent sequels, power constantly attempts to bring back the monster.[41] Power is the unarticulated position in the film, operating indirectly through intermediaries, proxies, representatives, and agents. In its immediate representation, it constitutes a kind of malign capitalism ("the Company"), which cares little for human lives[42] or 20,000,000 tons of mineral ore in its brutal pursuit of profit. But underneath this immediate representation, one finds a more purified version of power whose interests go far beyond the commercial; it is power's desire for power, pure and simple, absolute and sovereign. Power needs to re-establish itself, even in the remotest corners of the universe (again, literally, in outer space), which comes about through the figure of the alien.[43] This is the reason why power cannot stop itself from bringing back the alien, making contact, baiting and provoking it into action because, without this monstrous anomaly, power would have no legitimacy or substance. In a liberal interpretation of Hobbes's *Leviathan*, the unwitting and unfortunate resurrection of the alien would constitute a horror scenario: a warning of what power's ruthless desire for power may turn into when things go wrong.[44] From the Schmittian perspective, however, the point is rather that if one forgets the state's power, things will escalate into terror leading to the victory of pure monstrosity and, consequently, the defeat of civilization as such.

## Ripley, Citizen: Enemy of the State

The heroism of Ripley is underlined throughout the film; at every turn she opposes the sovereign's project. As the Warrant Officer on board the spaceship, Ripley is the first to realize that the distress signal is, in fact, a warning signal, and she therefore rightly refuses to open the hatch for Kane and has no interest in investigating the alien (again, Ash is her direct opponent here), and she finally destroys the monster, thus preventing it from being brought back to Earth (which, of course, was the main objective of the secret mission). If the Company's ethos mostly follows the Schmittian interpretation of Hobbes's *Leviathan*, Ripley represents the liberal perspective. Ripley is the one who insists on the *literalness* or the *fixity* of the social contract, the foundation of the idea of the state as a machine. Ash attempts to kill her, rather than the alien, precisely because she constitutes a greater threat to power. For Schmitt, as we have seen, this liberal interpretation weakens and ultimately undermines the state and its absolute power. The crew on board the spaceship *Nostromo* is devoted to commercial mine harvesting, but unwittingly becomes part of a war mission that is essentially about establishing a relation to the state of nature, whose possibility everyone seems to have forgotten in the beginning of the film. This is also the reason why no one carries any weapons; they believe that there is no longer anything to fear (a further indication of the perceived redundancy of the sovereign). When the monster finally reveals itself, the only weapons they can produce include a net, electric prods, an improvised flamethrower, and a tracking device.[45] From peaceful citizens, unprepared for and unwilling to engage in combat, to soldiers fighting a war on behalf of the sovereign, the crew members are forced into a state of nature, forced to operate outside the law. Ripley, of all people, becomes a representative of the state in the moment that the state has been suspended. She wants to avoid the state of nature, but must still go through it in order to get out of it. That Ripley, in the end, more or less singlehandedly manages against all odds to defeat the monster makes her, paradoxically, an enemy of the state, even if it is the state itself that has forced her into this position.

Giorgio Agamben observes, at one point, that the sovereign and the figure of *homo sacer* constitute the two extreme positions along the political axis, two symmetrical figures mirroring each other: "the sovereign is the one with respect to whom all men are potentially *homines sacri*, and *homo sacer* is the one with respect to whom all men act as sovereigns" (*Homo Sacer* 84). *Alien* sets things in motion when the sovereign (represented by MUTHR and Ash) decides to sacrifice its citizens (thus turning them into *homines sacri*). Eventually, Ripley emerges as the sovereign slaying the Behemoth. Ripley is the citizen who unwillingly becomes the provisional sovereign in the state of nature, and thus, paradoxically, a *rival* to the state, making it superfluous by eliminating the monster.[46] Incidentally, this is why, throughout the four *Alien* films, an increasingly sympathetic relationship is established between Ripley and the alien, which culminates with Ripley becoming the mother of an alien, and finally an alien herself.[47] Power's real enemy is thus not the alien, but rather Ripley, whom the state, throughout the series, treats with increasing suspicion, in the sense that she elevates herself to the position of the sovereign (albeit in the liberal sense, the state as a machine).[48] With Ripley's defeat of the Behemoth, we return to the liberal social contract and to Earth, not with the hostile alien but with the friendly cat, thus challenging and ultimately making the Schmittian sovereign superfluous.

## Conclusion

The ending of the film begins with the explosion of MUTHR and the spaceship, while Ripley escapes in a shuttle with Jones and, as it turns out, the alien. That the alien secretly manages to crawl on board the shuttle underlines how the film operates with a geospatial notion that is different from that of the logic of the old city gate; that is to say, there is no longer an "outside" in this epoch of space travel. The surprise appearance of the alien demonstrates the potential omnipresence of the anomaly and thus the necessity of the sovereign's existence, even in the very moment we thought we were safe.

Overall, the film outlines two interpretations of state power: on the one hand, there is bureaucratic–mechanistic power—that is, the liberal interpretation of Hobbes's political theory of Leviathan as a machine. On the other hand, we find the Schmittian sovereign who has the right to declare a state of exception. As for the latter, the creation, production, and legality of power is fueled by the rational desire for security, whereas the former emphasizes the individual's rights in relation to the state as it governs collective life. When the objective of security has been achieved, Schmitt argues, individuals have an unfortunate tendency to forget the reasons why they originally agreed to give up their absolute individual rights and accept being ruled by an absolute sovereign, busy as they are with selfish and private concerns about money, food, and so on, as in the breakfast scene. Such a trajectory essentially makes the state as a mythical force redundant. As I have argued in this chapter, this constitutes the main reason why the Company must go about its plan in secret; power must re-establish a relation to the anomaly and redraw the boundaries, an ambition that goes directly against the interests of the citizens. In every little nook and cranny of this universe, power is obliged to reassert itself in relation to the state of nature, which constitutes its source of legitimization. The *Nostromo* crew is ordered to investigate the mysterious signal, not in order to *eliminate* any new life form, but rather to *establish a relation to it*—one that is dangerous and lethal, and which thus restores fear and the subsequent legitimization of the absolute sovereign.

Ripley attempts to sever this relation, refusing to let power have its way. In the subsequent films, power constantly attempts to re-establish this relation to the state of nature, the anomaly, while Ripley on every occasion is the fierce opponent, the citizen loyal to the principles of the liberal state. In fact, Ripley turns out to be such an extraordinary opponent of power that she herself eventually becomes the Behemoth. Thus, one could argue that Ripley ironically becomes a figure carrying out the secret project of the state as she turns into the monster that legitimizes power as a mythical force. Perhaps this is the reason why Ripley, in the third *Alien* film, commits suicide (which is "reversed" by the authorities through the resurrection of Ripley as a clone in the fourth installment).

In this chapter, I have attempted to present a reading of *Alien* that concentrates on the film's latent political conflict, which may be understood through the interpretation of Thomas Hobbes's *Leviathan* and, more specifically, Carl Schmitt's critique of the liberal interpretation of Hobbes's political theory. To Schmitt, power is ultimately justified through its right to rule over the exception, which is precisely what the liberal interpretation of Hobbes's *Leviathan* prevents. Power must, paradoxically, become a kind of anomaly in itself in order to deal with the anomaly or the state of nature or, in Schmittian terms, the state of exception. During this period of emergency, the sovereign may legally suspend the social contract or the constitution in order to protect, defend, and preserve it. In the absence of the anomaly, however, the state is constantly in danger of losing its power. To Schmitt, it is essential for a state to establish a relation to the anomaly in order to reassert itself. *Alien* envisions such a scenario, and it shows Ripley as a loyal citizen fighting against power's sinister attempt to restore fear and terror, even if she thereby simultaneously comes to personify the sovereign as well as the alien: that is, the outlawed, banned life, hero and enemy of the state—or friend and enemy—at one and the same time.

## Notes

1. That the feminist/psychoanalytic perspectives dominate, to an overwhelming extent, the reception of the film seems, in retrospect, to say more about the theoretical climate of the last two decades of the twentieth century than about the film itself. Examples of this theoretical dominance abound, including Ambrogio (1986), Barale (1997), Bell-Mettreau (1985a, 1985b), Carveth and Gold (1999), Creed (1993), Doherty (1996), Gallardo-C. and Smith (2004), Goode (1997), Greenberg (1986, 1988), Herman (1997), Jennings (1995), Melzer (2006), Penley (1991), Taubin (1993), Weinstock (1996), and Wood (1988).
2. In his philosophical reading of *Alien*, Mulhall describes the opening scene of the film as "a kind of rebirth" (16).
3. Quoting the contract verbatim, Ash says: "There is a clause in the contract which specifically states: any systematized transmission indicating a possible intelligent origin must be investigated. At penalty of total forfeiture."
4. As I will later show, the film may be divided into four parts: insemination (of Kane's body), scene of birth (the alien emerging from Kane's body), zone of exception (the fight against the alien monster), and finally victory (Ripley defeating the monster). What this development reveals is a penetration of the latent conflict during the breakfast scene in an attempt to make it manifest and explicit.
5. This is the main theme in Schmitt's *Leviathan in the State Theory of Thomas Hobbes*, but it is a concern that runs through many of his other publications, including *Political Theology* and *The Concept of the Political*. See Meierhenrich (2016) for a discussion of this issue.
6. Actually, Brett and Parker jeopardize the entire mission (because of their discontent with the salary conditions) when they deliberately and unnecessarily extend the time it takes to fix the engine. Their "antisocial" or selfish behavior thus threatens the stability and unity of the community.

7. It would be too simple here to read Parker and Brett as representatives of the working class only. What seems much more important is simply the fact that they are subordinates, employees: that is, ordinary—and supposedly obedient—citizens.
8. See Hobbes's "XIII: Of the Natural Conditions of Mankind as Concerning Their Felicity and Misery." *Leviathan* 76–88.
9. As McCormick writes in reference to Hobbes, "The state assures its subjects that private parties will never threaten their bodily integrity; in fact, neither will the state itself threaten the bodily integrity of subjects unless such subjects threaten the well-being of others or the stability of the state" (272).
10. In *The Leviathan in the State Theory of Thomas Hobbes*, Schmitt writes that the Leviathan is a mortal god "who transforms wolves into citizens and through this miracle proves himself to be a god" (31–2).
11. For liberal theorists of Thomas Hobbes, see in particular John Locke's *The Second Treatise of Government* (1689) and Rousseau's *The Social Contract* (1762); for more contemporary liberal theorists developing Hobbes's thoughts, see Leo Strauss (1952); and Ferdinand Tönnies (1971).
12. Or, as Rousseau formulates it in *The Social Contract*: "[The government] is an intermediate body set up between subjects and sovereign to ensure their mutual correspondence, and is entrusted with the execution of laws and with the maintenance of liberty, both social and political" (92).
13. To Rousseau, the social contract "is vain and contradictory if it stipulates absolute authority on one side and limitless obedience on the other" (50). Good governance is essentially about finding the right balance between the freedom of the individuals and sovereign power.
14. Behemoth is the monster referred to in Job 40:15–24. While Leviathan represents the social order, Behemoth stands for chaos and disorder.
15. See Schmitt, *The Leviathan* 36.
16. See Hobbes, *Leviathan* 76.
17. See Hobbes, *Leviathan* 78.
18. See Schmitt, *The Leviathan* 33.
19. Ash even plays on this humane motive a little later in the film, when he brushes aside Ripley's accusations that he broke the protocol, saying, "What would you have done with Kane? . . . His only chance at staying alive was to get into the infirmary." It is an odd argument coming from Ash—given the fact that, at the same time, he seems most eager to scientifically investigate the anatomy of the "tough little son of a bitch," as he calls it—which reveals his cynicism: to use humanism as a means to achieve an anti-humanistic objective.
20. To Schmitt, the political enemy is "the other, the stranger; and it is sufficient for his nature that he is, in a specially intense way, *existentially something different and alien*, so that in the extreme case conflicts with him are possible" (*Concept* 27; italics mine).
21. See Schmitt, *Political Theology* 65; and *Concept* 91–5.

22. When Ripley insists on getting rid of the small alien carcass, Ash responds, "For god's sake, Ripley, this is the first time we've encountered a species like this. It has to go back, all sorts of tests have to be made."
23. The cat Jones is precisely the other-as-friend, whereas the alien is the other-as-enemy. The state wants to distinguish clearly between friend and enemy, and this is why the film from time to time makes these juxtapositions of cat and alien. The state desperately wants the alien to be brought back to Earth, but Ripley obstructs this plan and instead brings back the cat.
24. On this issue, see in particular Agamben's chapter "The Paradox of Sovereignty" (15–29) in *Homo Sacer*.
25. As Schmitt observes in *The Leviathan in the State Theory of Thomas Hobbes*: "The starting point of Hobbes' construction of the state is fear of the state of nature; the goal and terminus is security of the civil, the stately (*staatlichen*) condition" (31). Writing during the tumultuous times of the Weimar Republic's defeat and the rise of Nazism, Schmitt saw himself as a twentieth-century Hobbes (who wrote *Leviathan* against the background of the English civil wars). See, in particular, Schmitt's *Ex Captivitate Salus* for reflections on the similarities between the epoch of Hobbes (and, more particularly, Hobbes's fear of parliamentarism, which he thought would lead to chaos due to a lack of a strong authority) and Schmitt's own time. Regarding Hobbes's fear of parliamentarism, see his *Behemoth or the Long Parliament*.
26. Some might argue that Schmitt's interpretation of Hobbes rather leads to war and destruction. As John Locke puts it (with reference to Hobbes): "[M]en are so foolish, that they take care to avoid what mischiefs may be done them by *pole-cats*, or *foxes*; but are content, nay, think it safety, to be devoured by *lions*" (50). The theme—that is, the difficulties of finding the right balance between human rights and security (or, the state as a guardian and as a demonic force)—is one that, more recently, has become popular in a number of Hollywood films, including the *Batman* trilogy by Christopher Nolan and the *Avengers* series.
27. Science Officer Ash is an ambiguous character, initially a friend but later revealing his true, hostile identity. Ash has been placed on board the spaceship with the specific purpose of convincing the crew to bring back the alien life form. (Dallas used to work with a different Science Officer, who was replaced with Ash a few days before the trip.) The fact that he is an android further underscores his affinity with power (and distance from the crew members, the citizens). He is, in a sense, a creation of power itself.
28. One reason why the Company sends a *commercial* ship to fetch the alien life form is perhaps that it wants the monster alive, and thus offers the helpless non-combat crew members as bait. While the crew seems to discover the alien life form by chance and is clearly ignorant about and surprised by its capacity, Ash's presence and MUTHR's behavior (as well as the inserted clause in the contract) suggest, on the other hand, that the Company had prior knowledge about this life form.

29. As the embodiment of the state of nature, the alien monster is, at one and the same time, something concrete, external—but also something inherent in the human psyche: the egotistic lust for power that threatens collective life.
30. And if we take into account the sequels—*Aliens* (1986), *Alien 3* (1992), and *Alien: Resurrection* (1997)—the attempt to eliminate the alien is evidently unsuccessful; that is to say, the Behemoth is potentially always present.
31. See Agamben, *Homo Sacer* 6–7.
32. As Agamben has observed, the state of nature paradoxically *survives in the sovereign* (see *Homo Sacer* 104–11).
33. In *The Leviathan in the State Theory of Thomas Hobbes*, Schmitt describes how the monstrous-demonic element of the image of Leviathan disappeared shortly before Hobbes felt compelled to restore it: "the essentially demonic content of the image vanishes between 1500 and 1600. The popular medieval belief in demons, which was still alive in Luther, disappears; the evil spirits change into grotesque or even humorous ghosts. The image of the leviathan experienced a similar fate in the literature of the sixteenth century, which can be seen in the rendition of the devil or the demons from the time of Hieronymus Bosch until the so-called hell of Bruegel" (24).
34. Ironic as the following lines from *The Concept of the Political* may seem in retrospect (written in the late 1920s, a few years before Schmitt became heavily involved with the Nazi Party), Schmitt was clearly aware of the difficulty of legitimizing a political cause: "the most terrible war is pursued only in the name of peace, the most terrible oppression only in the name of freedom, the most terrible inhumanity only in the name of humanity" (95).
35. Nietzsche's last man is the antithesis of the overman, a despicable person with no desire or ambition, apart from deriving as much material pleasure from existence as possible (see Nietzsche 254–63).
36. As Foucault writes: "For a long time, one of the characteristic privileges of sovereign power was the right to decide life and death" ("Right of Death", in *History of Sexuality* 135).
37. Biopolitics essentially involves the idea of optimizing life to its maximum potential. Once this life has reached or even exceeded its maximum potential, it turns into a monstrosity, and hence a biological danger: a life that knows no borders, limits, and hence a life that must be eliminated. Within a biopolitical perspective, *Alien* can be read as a film enacting a fantasy of the destruction of human life.
38. In *The Leviathan in the State Theory of Thomas Hobbes*, Schmitt observes that the state in the liberal epoch "was regarded as historically timebound, a transient affair, and at any rate it was expected that the state would make itself superfluous in time" (35).
39. This is a general theme regarding the dimension of power in all the *Alien* films: the desire to hold on to and to increase power—for the sake of power itself. By constantly teasing the alien creature into combat and confrontation,

it is an ambition that, on almost every occasion, threatens to destroy power—but also, at the same time, to intensify and revitalize it.

40. Here, one could also bring in the late work *Nomos of the Earth* (published in 1950), in which Schmitt reflects on the idea of a totally legalized space. Law, Schmitt argues, can exist only within a demarcated, controlled territory. He observes that "it was not the abolition of war, but rather its bracketing that has been the great, core problem of every legal order" (74). Schmitt is critical of universalist international orders that fail to take into account irresolvable political differences; to him, the world is a pluriverse, not a universe (see Schmitt, *Concept* 53). In other words, there will always be areas "outside" or "beyond" any given legal spaces—which may be the antitheses of the latter: that is, the state of nature, or simply different, albeit incompatible legal orders. One could argue that *Alien* envisions, as well as problematizes, precisely this universalist aspiration towards a totally uniform, homogenous, legalized space—even in the most remote corners of the universe.

41. In *Aliens* (the sequel), Ripley is sent back into the state of nature with a division of the Elite Colonial Marines; in *Alien 3*, the authorities attempt to capture Ripley as she is about to give birth to an alien queen; and in *Alien: Resurrection*, some 200 years later, Ripley has been cloned (partly with alien DNA), while the alien in her stomach—before she committed suicide—was captured and saved by the authorities.

42. MUTHR brutally informs Ripley that the crew is "expendable."

43. In *The Concept of the Political*, Schmitt criticizes the concept of a universal humanity because it eliminates the possibility of the friend/enemy distinction, and thus, by implication, leads to dehumanization of the Other. As Schmitt observes, "Humanity as such cannot wage war because it has no enemy, at least not on this planet" (54). Quite literally, *Alien* re-establishes the friend/enemy distinction in an age of universal humanity, albeit in outer space.

44. The alien form represents not only horror as such, but also, more specifically, a horror that we ourselves (or, more precisely, our predecessors—as Ridley Scott's prequel *Prometheus* (2012) reveals) have invented: a parasitic life created in an experiment that went horribly wrong.

45. One could make the argument that the crew is barred from using firearms because it would involve a high risk of damaging the spaceship (especially considering the fact that the alien's blood is extremely corrosive). Even so, there is no indication that the spaceship contains any combat weapons, such as ones to be used outside the spaceship.

46. From the perspective of power, the best thing that could have happened would, no doubt, have been if the ship returned with only the alien on board—as a pure, destructive form of life.

47. In this light, Jacques Derrida—in his essay on Carl Schmitt's friend/enemy distinction—makes the relevant point that the inherent instability of this axis eventually leads to a collapse, a breakdown. See "On Absolute Hostility:

The Cause of Philosophy and the Spectre of the Political" in *The Politics of Friendship* 112–37.
48. During the scene when Kane is brought back to the spaceship, Ripley, in fact, acts as the provisional captain of the *Nostromo* (because Captain Dallas is outside the spaceship): that is, the sovereign ruling over a state of emergency (while Captain Dallas, outside, demands that she open the hatch to let them in). Noticeably, as a provisional sovereign, Ripley insists on following protocol (that is, the constitution), rather than making an absolute decision (that is, a sovereign exception).

CHAPTER 2

# Monopolizing the Future: Steven Spielberg's *Minority Report* and Schmitt's Exception

## Introduction

Based on a short story by Philip K. Dick,[1] Steven Spielberg's 2002 film *Minority Report* tells the story of a future society (Washington, D.C., 2054) that has eliminated the occurrence of murder. At this point, it has become possible to predict murderous impulses in individuals via an innovative genetic technology called "precognition."[2] Law and order are executed by the so-called Precrime Unit, led by Tom Cruise's character, Chief Anderton, who is also the film's protagonist. In the opening scene, we see him busily organize some visual images produced by three individuals lying submerged semi-unconsciously in a pool of water (the "precogs") on a large screen; a murder will take place shortly, which may be prevented if Anderton's team manages to identify and neutralize the potential culprit before anything actually happens. When Anderton figures out the location, he immediately leaves the police headquarters with his men in order to arrest the suspect, Howard Marks, which he successfully does just before the precise moment when the man has raised his arm to stab his unfaithful wife with a pair of scissors. The man is arrested and paralyzed on the spot—"haloed," as the police officers euphemistically call it—and shortly afterwards brought to a facility at which his paralyzed body is kept indefinitely, without any possibility of explaining or defending himself and without actually having broken the law, at least not yet.

The long and detailed opening scene thus illustrates how the film's vision of a "normal" society in the year 2054 is based on a very literal fusion of the traditional tripartition of power. Anderton and his men represent, at one and the same time, the legislative, executive, and judicial powers.[3] The intention behind this tripartition was, of course, that these three dimensions separately would keep the others in check and thus prevent the abuse of power. However, the possibility of the latter seems minimal because of the new technology that detects murderous impulses in individuals even before the latter themselves are aware of them, and thus before they have any chance of reacting to them. Thereby, the tripartition of power equally becomes superfluous. The precog system constitutes a faultless, objective technology liberated from human errors of judgment that no longer needs this bureaucratic arrangement. In fact, the opening scene seems to insist that such a tripartition would slow down the reaction time necessary for the Precrime Unit to prevent something from happening in real time; had Anderton been merely a second slower, the opening scene suggests, the man would most likely have managed to kill his wife.

The ability to predict the future is the element that most conspicuously deviates from Darko Suvin's novum. To Suvin, a "novum of cognitive innovation is a totalizing phenomenon or relationship deviating from the author's and implied reader's norm of reality" (64), but, crucially, an innovation that can "be methodically developed against the background of a body of already existing cognitions, or at the very least as a 'mental experiment' following accepted scientific, that is, cognitive logic" (66). In other words, the novum is a cognitive innovation that grows "organically" or logically out of the present, and thus, to some extent, can be said to be predictable or at least imaginable. *Minority Report*, to a large extent, outlines a society developing logically—scientifically and cognitively—out of the present, *except* in relation to this ability to predict the future, a technological invention that almost seems like a miraculous intervention in the sense that it fundamentally displaces the ontological coordinates of the present.[4] It thus clears the way for the arrival of the future. It is a technological invention that should be understood as a *hegemonic* device, in the sense that it constitutes an event of such a radical character that it affects almost all other aspects in the present, the known world and thereby changes the latter's fabric of reality. We are not simply in a different place in a different time, but in a different normative world.

As a sci-fi film, *Minority Report* attempts to work through the political consequences of a technological event that changes reality's normative coordinates at a fundamental level. More precisely, the film asks this question: if we did actually possess this unique ability to predict the future, and more specifically the *violent* future, would this not lead to the elimination of the political? If power could guarantee the social contract—*protego ergo obligo*, in an absolute sense—would we not move beyond the political? *Minority Report* largely answers both questions in the affirmative. It is a work that intensely explores the intimate connection that has always existed between the sci-fi genre and the political. For the film's radical deviation from the novum is not simply any random departure; it is the event that suspends the future as such—that is, the radically unpredictable future. In *Minority Report*, the technological dimension has reached such an advanced stage and widespread use that the political no longer plays any significant role. The future emerges at the time when the technological has surpassed the importance of the political decision. My overall argument is that *Minority Report* articulates an extreme version of Fukuyama's liberal thesis of the end of history—that is, the radical *depoliticization* of social life. This has become possible precisely because of advanced technology in a way that was obviously not the case when Fukuyama wrote his book in the early 1990s. What exactly this involves is the total mechanization of legal discourse because the radically unpredictable future has by now been eliminated. Schmitt, as we have seen, defines the sovereign as the one who has the right to declare the state of exception—that is, the suspension of the constitution in order to protect and save it—from a radically unpredictable future, a future event that fundamentally changes and hence threatens the way we live in the present. Once this possibility of the emergence of a radical future event has been eliminated, the need for the sovereign would likewise seem to diminish. What happens in Spielberg's film, however, is that the sovereign returns in precisely that moment when the technological precog system is most vulnerable, the moment when it cannot protect itself against existential dangers. The film thus ends with the breakdown of technology and a return to the present—in other words, a return to the political.

## The End of History

In *Political Theology*, Schmitt observes that, since the political decision is *independent*, "the subject of the decision has an independent meaning, apart from the question of content. What matters for the reality of legal life is who decides" (34). That is to say, the concrete political decision carried out by the sovereign is precisely *not* something that can be depersonalized and thereby subsumed by a technological system.[5] However, the system's replacement of the sovereign decision is a tendency that Schmitt believes characterizes modern society. Thus, he writes in *The Concept of the Political* that

> Already in the nineteenth century technical progress proceeded at such an astonishing rate, even as did social and economic situations as a consequence, that all moral, political, social, and economic situations were affected. Given the overpowering suggestion of ever new and surprising inventions and achievements, there arose a religion of technical progress which promised all other problems would be solved by technological progress. This belief was self-evident to the great masses of the industrialized countries. They skipped all intermediary stages typical of the

thinking of intellectual vanguards and turned the belief in miracles and an afterlife—a religion without intermediary stages—into a religion of technical miracles, human achievements, and the domination of nature. A magical religiosity became an equally magical technicity. The twentieth century began as the age not only of technology but of a religious belief in technology. (84–5)

According to Schmitt, this semi-religious worship of technology blinds people in the same way as Marx, ironically, believed that religion blinded people. This blind faith in technology as a form of redemption constitutes a direct threat to the political, and, more specifically, is the reason why we need the political. Schmitt's tirade against technological modernity emerges against the background of a more general critique of liberal society, obsessed with ideas of rationality, reason, mechanical legality—the state as an administrative machine.[6] To Schmitt, what liberal society aims for is ultimately a world governed entirely by mechanical legality, the absolute constitution: that is, a predictable world in which the state of nature finally has been eliminated. This is a world, as Schmitt observes in *The Concept of the Political*, "in which the possibility of war is utterly eliminated, a completely pacified globe . . . a world without the distinction of friend and enemy and hence a world without politics" (35). In other words, it is an entirely peaceful world no longer in need of a sovereign making sovereign decisions.

And it is precisely here that we find *Minority Report*'s real political vision: the fulfilment of the dream of the end of history—and not simply in Fukuyama's normative formulation, but in a *descriptive* sense too:[7] that is to say, an absolutely risk-free society, now made possible due to the emergence of a new technology, which liberal society, in fact, always strived for—a complete and perfect mechanization of legal reality.[8] In the present, this is impossible, of course, although the desire is nonetheless evident in the emergence nowadays of ever more complex and advanced surveillance and security-enhancing technologies. However, the film's departure from the novum constitutes precisely this piece of fantasy, which turns the desire into reality, the ultimate dream of the end of history, the future as a perpetual, everlasting present. Although the critical reception of the film generally has circled around commonplace topics in connection with the sci-fi genre—namely, technology/determination versus individuality/free will—I argue that these subjects are largely subordinate to the film's political vision, the idea of the elimination of the future as radically unpredictable.[9] It is, at the same time, a vision that most radically and consistently articulates the *depoliticization* of social life; in such a society, there is quite simply no longer any space for the political any longer. The state of nature has, once and for all, been eliminated.[10]

## The State of Exception

When Carl Schmitt categorically insists on the sovereign's right to declare the state of exception, it is yet again important to recall that this argument is based on the premise that the future is radically unpredictable; no legal reality, however complex, detailed, or exact, will be able to predict all possible future events that may have the capacity to disturb and ultimately destroy the political coordinates of the present. This is the reason why liberalism, in Schmitt's view, presents a number of political challenges; it leaves society fatally vulnerable by mechanically translating everything into economic or legal terms. Liberalism as a political system creates an objective, anonymous, neutral state in which conflicts are solved rationally, competitively, or with reference to the norm—that is, the constitution. By radically *depoliticizing* the state, liberalism constitutes a dangerous form of regulative, mechanical, and predictable form of thinking.[11] To Schmitt, however, some human conflicts are of such an antagonistic nature that no rational discussion will be able to resolve them. It is within this context that Schmitt defines the political: the ability to distinguish friends from enemies.[12] Schmitt's political enemy cannot be determined substantially or "futurally," permanently, but only in the concrete situation: that is, in the present. These will always potentially change, depending on the political situation. It is thus impossible to predict who the political enemy will be; potentially, today's friend could be an enemy of the state in the future.

It is against this background that Schmitt believes sovereignty ultimately comes down to the right to declare the state of exception, which remains, by definition, radically unpredictable. At the same time, this means that sovereign authority—the state—can never limit itself to operate fully, always, and only within legal norms. In order to operate effectively, it *cannot always* be subordinated to a set of predetermined, constitutional laws. This does not mean dictatorship—that is, the sovereign's absolute right to act according to his or her will, at any time—but rather implies that the latter possesses this right in certain *exceptional* situations; in those situations, the sovereign holds the absolute decision monopoly. What is important in such situations is less whether the decision is the "right" one; what is important is *that the decision is made*, finally, unconditionally, by the sovereign, who thus, through the decision, not only confirms his or her sovereignty, but also guarantees the validity of the entire legal order. When a decision is made, the discussion ends. The validity of this decision is independent of the validity of the decision's content.[13] Schmitt writes:

> There exists no norm that is applicable to chaos. For a legal order to make sense, a normal situation must exist, and he is sovereign who definitely decides whether

> this normal situation actually exists. All law is "situational" law. The sovereign produces and guarantees the situation in its totality. He has the monopoly over the last decision. Therein resides the essence of the state's sovereignty, which must be juristically defined correctly, not as the monopoly to coerce or to rule, but as the monopoly to decide. (*Political Theology* 13)

This is why, as Schmitt observes in the same work, the "exception in jurisprudence is analogous to the miracle in theology" (36). The miracle is a phenomenon that escapes the rational, sensible, and logical, that which may appear implausible but also that which *saves* us from confusion and danger. In modern society, Schmitt argues, the political decision in the state of exception has been banished, just as the miracle has been banished in theology: "The rationalism of the Enlightenment rejected the exception in every form" (37). To Schmitt, however, the political cannot solely be explained rationally.

The sci-fi genre is, among other things, characterized by a bold, almost literal insistence on the creation of a hypothetical scenario in which ontological premises are fundamentally transformed. In *Minority Report*, the new premise is, of course, that we can now predict the future—which does not simply mean "more time plus new gadgets" but, on the contrary, refers to an event that radically changes the normative reality of the present: that is, the violent, disturbing act that potentially leads to the collapse of society and regression to the state of nature.

In fact, it is not only the violent future that these precogs can predict; in one of the film's many escape scenes, it seems clear that Agatha—the most talented precog—can see much more, such as how to escape those chasing after them. And when Agatha, in a particularly intense, almost cathartic, scene near the end of the film, tells Anderton and his wife what happened to their kidnapped son in the years during which the latter became an adult, it seems clear that this ability to predict the future is almost total.

In this scene, and more generally in those scenes involving an act of looking into the future, that which has not happened yet, we often find an aura of something obscene—a forbidden gaze on something that was never meant to be seen.[14] It is in this context that we must understand the exception, the concept Schmitt reserves for the sovereign alone. Schmitt's sovereign holds the right to declare the state of exception, which means the right to monopolize the future. No one, of course, can see the future and thereby decide it, not even the sovereign, at least not in a positive sense; what the sovereign's monopoly of the future involves is rather the right to *prevent others' access* to this obscene gaze. The sovereign's state of exception is empty: that is, it is negatively defined, in the sense that it serves the purpose of neutralizing any form of future event that may undermine current legal reality. Thus, Schmitt argues that the "exception, which is not codified in the existing legal order, can at best be characterized as a case of extreme peril, a danger to the existence of the state, or the like. But it cannot be circumscribed factually and made to conform to a preformed law," and a little later: "It is precisely the exception that makes relevant the subject of sovereignty . . . The precise details of an emergency cannot be anticipated" (*Political Theology* 6). The point here is that the sovereign holds the right to decide not only *when* the exception is to be declared, but also *what* it is, what it consists of, and what it contains. The only condition is that the exceptional situation constitutes an event dangerous enough to potentially destroy the current legal order. Lastly, the sovereign holds the sole right to decide when the normative situation has been *restored*.

*Minority Report*'s technological premise is, however, that this possibility is no longer the sole right of the sovereign, but something potentially accessible to anyone, a technology that allows for a different conceptualization of the problem of the future, its radical unpredictability, one that is not based on the sovereign's sole and negative right to declare the state of exception, and therefore no longer seems capable of being monopolized, at least not by the sovereign alone. What this means, more precisely, is that the normative situation at the outset of the film should be understood as a form of perverse intensification of what once constituted the sovereign's sole right to declare the state of exception. The latter has, in other words, been elevated to a *normative condition*, a permanent state of exception that has become the norm. People are arrested and neutralized despite their rights, precisely because technology has infallibly identified them as already guilty—albeit in a future that will never exist.

It is important to note here that this permanent state of exception, where individuals may be arrested and deprived of their freedom without the possibility of defending themselves, is precisely *not* the sovereign's state of exception; it should, rather, be understood as an intensification of a society conceptualized as *no longer having the space* for the sovereign's right to declare the state of exception. The sovereign is no longer the one who has the right to declare the state of exception; at this point, *no one other than the system* has the right to claim this "hole" in the law—or, the system now fully occupies this gap. What the new technology thus involves is the suspension of the radically unpredictable future—that is, the future as such, which likewise means that the sovereign has become superfluous as the individual or entity holding the sole right to declare the state of exception. For if no one needs to fear the violent, disturbing future, the need for the sovereign likewise disappears, and thereby in reality the need for the political. The political—that is, the ability to distinguish between friend and enemy—is here reduced to a form of absolute mechanical legality, a society in which the exception has become the norm because the future at this point, in a systematic–technological way, has been monopolized, and hence in reality terminated.

## Plot Discontinuities

As *Minority Report* eagerly underlines several times, the background for Precrime's existence and necessity is the violent past. In the time before Precrime, we hear, the murder rate was extremely high; the rate has now fallen to 0 percent. The film's plot begins around the time when the Precrime project is about to be implemented on a national level. The Precrime project essentially entails the normalization of what, in our present, would have been acceptable only during a period of emergency: the suspension of individual rights, incarceration without trial, and so on. Hence, FBI agent Danny Witwer, at the behest of the District Attorney, has been tasked with the investigation of the project's legality, obviously from a skeptical point of view.[15]

Anderton originally joined the Precrime project to prevent what happened to himself; his own son disappeared traumatically during a swimming trip and was never found again. Anderton is, in many ways, a person who, despite his professional focus on the future, is trapped in the past.[16] In the evenings, he compulsively watches—under the influence of drugs—old video clips in 3D with his son. Clearly, we are to understand, there is something pathological about this: a traumatized man trapped in the past, unable to move on to the open future. In a further sense, Anderton is, of course, the embodiment of the Precrime idea: a wounded society desperately trying to prevent something terrible from happening in the future. The film establishes a fairly direct connection between Anderton's personal repetition compulsion, the attempt to arrest time, and his professional job as a police officer trying to arrest people before they do anything bad. It is precisely the repetition compulsion that plays a significant temporal role in the film's plot; it is a plot driven by a futile, unproductive, static temporality.[17] Since Anderton's son was never found, and his fate therefore remains unclear, there is a minuscule possibility that he is still alive; the boy is theoretically still alive *as long as we do not yet know* whether anyone has hurt him. With the Precrime technology, this is, in fact, changed into a *positive* knowledge: that is, *knowing that no one has killed him yet*. It therefore makes sense for Anderton to arrest people before they have actually done anything, even if his son most likely died before the Precrime project began. It is in this way that Anderton manages to arrest time on a personal level, and further, to eliminate the future of an entire society.

This is essentially what the first part of the film is about: a man who, on a personal level, is trapped in the past while professionally engaged in eliminating or monopolizing the future in a systematic–technological way. However, the systematic–technological attempt to monopolize the future—to control time, the natural order of the world—involves a great risk. Signs of temporal disorder can be found throughout the film. What these temporal fractures indicate are the denaturalization or deformation of the temporal dimension, as if time in the film's plot can never quite find its natural form, constantly balancing between too little and too much.[18]

There is something melancholy about this corruption of temporality, a melancholy that lies deep within the film's plot. The Precrime project as a whole is legitimized on the basis of sorrow, as the commercials underline; if one could prevent sorrow, they ask, why not do it?[19] Anderton echoes this rhetorical question when he insists that Precrime is not about politics, but about pain—for example, the pain that constantly haunts Agatha, images of the murder of her mother. According to a precog technician, these images are moments of déjà vu: visuals of a murder that never took place, memories of something that never happened—which, of course, as we learn later in the film, is not the case.[20] There is, of course, something extremely unnatural about murder, a disruption of the natural course of life, and hence something melancholy, which Precrime prevents from happening.[21] But there is also a deep melancholy connected to the temporal disruption generated by the Precrime program itself—that is, the ability to predict a fixed and thereby determined and inevitable future trajectory (which should have contained infinite potentials of freedom), and to act accordingly to arrest this inevitable future trajectory before it happens. To know the future is thus a melancholy insight, perhaps even more so than the violent past. The latter evokes the sense of the irretrievable, the forever lost, whatever one does in the present. But to know something about what is destined to happen in the future—which, because one knows it, will not happen—seems to constitute an even more radical intervention, since it questions the very idea of free will. A genuinely free act seems possible in this universe only to the extent that the person in question is aware of the concrete details of their fixed and determined future trajectory.[22]

Premeditated murders, the film tells us, normally give the Precrime police unit up to four days before they happen, while the timeframe for impulsive murders is reduced to a few minutes (as in Howard Mark's case). Since people are *aware of this*, no one in their right mind will attempt to commit planned murders any longer. Anderton's name appears on a precog ball thirty-six hours before the event takes place, presumably because the intentions behind this murder lie somewhere between a premeditated and an impulsive murder. Anderton has no plans to kill anyone, and yet he always wanted, probably more unconsciously than consciously, to kill the man who kidnapped his son, at least in that unlikely situation of one day finding himself standing right in front of him, free to do anything. From this moment, the film's temporal dimension changes into a merciless countdown.[23] His colleague in the lab allows him a head start of two minutes before activating the alarm, which enables Anderton to make his escape. The rest of the film, all the way until Anderton's arrest, consists of action-packed escape scenes—as if the film is chased by time itself.[24] The film's title refers to an anomalous file produced every time the three precogs disagree about the outcome of a future event; the file thus refers to an alternative future that, however, as Dr Hineman reveals, is destroyed immediately since no doubt can exist within the system.[25] Yet, the file still exists inside the minds of the precogs, which is why Anderton decides to sneak back into Precrime and kidnap Agatha.

Here, things become seriously muddled in the film's plot. In his desperate search for a minority report, Anderton attempts to reopen a future trajectory that has now been fixed, and which culminates in murder. It turns out, however, that Anderton does not have a minority report because he has been framed by his boss, Lamar Burgess, the owner and creator of the Precrime project. Anderton has been set up because he has begun to suspect that a person who was once arrested by Precrime for the potential murder of a former drug addict, Ann Lively, was perhaps innocent after all. As we learn later, Ann Lively, Agatha's mother, was murdered by Burgess because she wanted her daughter back. Thus, it turns out that the entire existence of Precrime, whose overall purpose is, of course, the prevention of murder, was possible only insofar as a murder was committed without anyone being punished and which was later forgotten, repressed.

Why this plot twist, which seems to pull us out of the flawless, technological system and back into a cynical universe of evil, human intentions, exploitation, manipulation, and ultimately an argument about the impossibility of predicting the future? Burgess's murder of Ann Lively constitutes, on both a symbolic and a literal level, what Walter Benjamin calls founding violence—that is, a violent act that institutes a new law and, at the same time, eradicates the old law.[26] What is paradoxical about founding violence is precisely that its purpose is to break the law, commit a crime in order to create a new legal reality. Founding violence is that which creates the possibility of, and subsequently protects, the law, but which, at the same time, operates outside the legal sphere. The Schmittian sovereign's right to declare the state of exception is a remnant of this founding violence, which survives in the new legal sphere, a hole, a gap of a kind.[27] In reality, this is the problem that *Minority Report* identifies: that even in a society where it has become possible, in a systematic–technological way, to predict violent future acts, and thereby possible to eliminate the need for a sovereign, the frame of, and thus the conditions for, such a society *still* depend on the sovereign's exceptional decision in the dangerous situation. It is precisely against the background of the latter that we should understand what initially seems to be a somewhat random plot detail: the murder of Ann Lively.[28] To murder Ann Lively, Burgess conjures up an elaborate plan involving a hired killer, knowing that this person will be caught by the Precrime unit. It is the production of déjà vu memories (that is, a visual sequence of the murder that will never take place because the Precrime unit will prevent it), or "echoes," that enables Burgess to kill Ann Lively without getting caught; he dresses like the hired killer and, after the latter has been arrested, actually murders Agatha's mother. The possibility of exploiting this hole in the precog machinery, which Burgess has discovered, is in itself remarkable, implausible even—and which precisely, therefore, identifies Burgess as the one closest to the miraculous right of the sovereign, the one who understands the necessity of making the exceptional decision, identifies what it is, and is willing to carry it out.

We find a series of incredible, implausible aspects surrounding the story about this déjà vu memory, which not only leads to Anderton being framed, but also involves Detective Witwer's death. Is it, for example, plausible that Burgess managed to see this future sequence, which seems required since he must create an echo, an exact repetition, before he killed Ann Lively? For how could he otherwise have known how the hired killer was going to carry out the murder of Ann Lively down to the exact detail, so that it would look the same, except for the waves moving in the wrong direction? In the echo, Burgess is clearly on location; he comforts Ann Lively right after the hired killer has been arrested, and shortly after kills her. There is, in other words, a problem with timing, in the same way as there are temporal problems involving Burgess's framing of Anderton; when Burgess discovers that Anderton is about to unravel something suspicious about the Ann Lively episode, he apparently arranges the entire framing in just one night. Furthermore, the fact that Burgess decides to frame Anderton in this way seems equally strange, for Anderton has, in fact, not discovered very much at this point, not enough to suspect Burgess of anything. So, why does he react in this aggressive way at this early stage?

One explanation could be that Burgess had planned this long ago (including hiring the man who plays the kidnapper). Or, even more cynically, that Burgess was actually the man organizing the kidnapping of Anderton's son back then.[29] This, however, fails to explain why Burgess's name does not subsequently appear on one of the precog balls, since he obviously had the intention of killing Ann Lively *after* the Precrime project began. We find a similar inconsistency in connection with Anderton's murder scene, during which he decides *not* to kill Leo Crow, the supposed kidnapper, even if the latter ends up dead anyway. Likewise, the precogs fail to register the murder of Danny Witwer or Burgess's suicide near the end of the film.[30] All these examples raise the question: why did the precogs not revise their visions of the future? This points towards a temporal instability at the heart of the film's plot, suggesting that as soon as we *know* the concrete details of our future, it may be changed and manipulated and, notably, without the precogs revising their deterministic visions of the future.[31] In other words, we are back in the present again, or the determined future is annulled if one knows it.

## The Return of the Sovereign

The film illustrates that the problem with the new technology—to know the future, which thus opens the possibility of the complete and absolute mechanization of the legal reality—is that it has now become potentially available and applicable to everyone. If the right to declare the state of exception is a way of monopolizing the future negatively—that is, a right to decide what constitutes the dangerous event—the precog technology constitutes the positive definition. When Schmitt argues that the sovereign has the right to declare the state of exception, he is, at the same time, saying that the sovereign is the one who decides the future, albeit in a negative sense—that is, what the future is *not*. With the new, positive right enabled by a new and radical technology, this is no longer the case. Thus, both Anderton and Witwer discover independently that something suspicious is going on, precisely because they too have access to the precog technology.[32] Technology here makes it possible that the right to declare the state of exception, to identify the dangerous event, is no longer the sovereign's right alone. In other words, it is no longer a political issue; it is a purely mechanical matter, which potentially makes technology available to everyone. Anyone may be pulled into this system, and anyone may be replaced with someone else.

All this seems to indicate that the film is not really about the arrest of people who plan to commit murder; it is about this *right* to identify who is being arrested, and more specifically, *who* holds this right. The film's plot thus revolves around the question of who has access to Agatha, the physical embodiment of the ability to predict the future; Burgess kills her mother, who wants her back; Danny Witwer, on behalf of the DA, demands access to her; and Anderton kidnaps her. It turns out that if it was, in fact, possible to mechanize the entire legal discourse via a technology that enabled us to see the future, the negative definition of the future—that is, the sovereign's sole right to declare the state of exception—likewise dissolves: namely, what constitutes the state of exception, what it contains, what it is, and furthermore, when it ends. According to the positive definition of the right to declare the state of exception (that is, the technological ability to see the future), the system may identify dangerous threats to society but can no longer defend itself—for example, when it is being accused of abuse or corruption, or when it is being undermined from within. This is what Anderton and later Witwer inadvertently discover: a hole in the system undermining the aspect that the system initially was created to eliminate: namely, the state of exception. What they discover is that Burgess has exploited this hole, but they fail to understand that Burgess has done so because he realizes—as the only one—that *the system cannot protect itself*; Burgess does it because he wants to preserve the system. To Burgess, the problem is that technology makes the sovereign's exceptional right impossible. This is why Anderton's discovery constitutes such a threat to the system, and why Burgess so aggressively and so early activates the set-up.

A state that mechanically identifies and eliminates exceptional dangers in the future at the same time becomes predictable itself, and hence vulnerable. The film's plot twist—Burgess's set-up—thus consists of the old (and now superfluous) sovereign's attempt to protect the system, but crucially from a point that is *not* included in the system. How can the sovereign miraculously avoid a total system, a totally mechanized legal discourse? Burgess finds an exceptional way—exploiting the déjà vu memories—to do this, and thereby, through this hole in the precog system, he reclaims the sovereign's right to declare the state of exception, albeit in a minimal and perhaps implausible or incredible sense. Both Anderton and Witwer are caught up in this exceptional manipulation of the system; the latter is killed without the precogs registering it, while the former escapes *because he acts exceptionally*. At the beginning of the film, Anderton seems to be a representative of determinism, or the belief that whatever one does as an individual, it has already been decided in advance. It might seem tempting here to argue that this conviction changes when Anderton is identified by the precogs as the next murderer. However, this would be a misreading; Anderton still fundamentally believes in the correctness of the precog project, even after he has been identified as the next potential murderer, *except in his case*. That is, Anderton believes in the exception that confirms the rule.

It is only when Anderton discovers that he does not have a minority report that he seems to surrender to the idea of free will. Almost at the exact same time, Anderton realizes that he has been framed by Burgess, who acted *exceptionally* in order to protect the system that was created with the purpose of eliminating the need for the sovereign right to declare the state of exception. At this point, Anderton frames Burgess or, more precisely, forces the latter to reveal himself as the sovereign, the one who has the right to declare a state of exception by confronting him with a dilemma: if he kills Anderton, this will demonstrate that the system cannot prevent murder, but if he does not, the precogs are wrong, which thus shows that the system is fallible.[33] "What are you going to do now, Lamar?" Anderton asks. It is precisely in this exceptional situation that Anderton identifies the one who can make the sovereign decision, decide its content, when it happens, and when it ceases: Lamar Burgess. At the same time, of course, Burgess is, in this precise moment, paradoxically still the director of the Precrime project: that is, still a representative of the normative legal system. Burgess avoids committing murder, which would have undermined his Precrime project, but also avoids getting caught, which likewise would have been the end of his project. It is in this light that we should understand Burgess's final decision to commit suicide. Burgess kills himself, whereby he paradoxically *restores* the sovereign's right to declare the state of exception, the exceptional decision that eliminates the danger. The film ends with a reintroduction of natural temporality by returning to the present; the Precrime project is terminated, the prisoners are all released and pardoned (although kept on watch for many years), and the precogs are relocated to a peaceful, isolated house in the countryside, while Anderton and his wife get back together. The latter is pregnant, which suggests that they have moved beyond the trauma of their lost son, and thus once again are looking forward to the radically unpredictable future.

## Conclusion

In a strictly political sense, the film resolves very little; it merely postpones the realization of the absolute normalization of the state of exception.[34] The film's plot begins with a state of exception that has been elevated to a normative situation (potential future murderers are simply arrested, sedated, and imprisoned without trial). This normative state of exception is possible due to the invention of a radically new technology, which changes the basic political coordinates of society. What is paradoxical about this new technology—the ability to see the future—is precisely that it has been created with the purpose of eliminating the exceptional situation: that is, the radically unpredictable future.

Many of the film's technological gadgets are realistic in the sense that they are fundamentally thinkable, imaginable from our point of view; this is the film's novum. In fact, it is worth noticing that the context or frame around the film's novum in many ways constitutes a radical intensification of the present's technological potential; the film's technology, its amalgamation of advertisement and security technology in the form of face recognition, biometrical identification systems, retinal scanners, and wall-to-wall media, seems to grow organically out of the present.[35] The time we experience in *Minority Report* is thus, to a large extent, our own, albeit in an intensified form.

What radically departs from the film's novum is this almost magical ability to predict the future, and more specifically, the ability to prevent murder. We are not simply talking about an extreme form of probability calculation or ingeniously devised algorithms, but rather a strange, osmotic, inexplicable ability—almost a metaphysical miracle.[36] The miracle indicates a piece of technology that clearly constitutes the limit of what it is possible to imagine, think, and understand. This new radical technology ultimately creates a new political situation because it changes reality's basic coordinates and thereby opens up a space in which the future may emerge. In other words, it normalizes what, in the present, would have been limited to the state of exception.

*Minority Report* is a film that imagines the future as the state of emergency that has become a norm, a normative political system that operates within an exceptional space. Here, the future has been suspended, arrested, like the future murderers. It is a world devoid of temporality, trapped between an inaccessible past and an absent future (in the sense that it *is* the future). What happens in *Minority Report* is the collapse of technology via the revelation of Burgess as the sovereign, which leads to the breakdown of the entire Precrime project. Subsequently, a temporal dynamic is reintroduced, a time very similar to our own time. This is ultimately a return to the *political*, which thereby recreates a space for the proper state of exception as an always present potential in the normative society, and whose ultimate purpose is to bring back order. Thus, the film ends with the restoration of the ability to identify the utmost danger, which (yet again) is identified as the radically unpredictable future.

## Notes

1. Philip K. Dick's original story first came out in 1956. The film adaptation has changed several key aspects of the story. For a discussion of some of the differences, see Bond 35–7.
2. This technological ability seems to consist of an advanced form of brain-imaging technology, developed by the geneticist Iris Hineman, which allows certain neuramine-addicted individuals—the so-called "precogs"—to visualize situations involving future murders.
3. Dillman observes that what we see here is "the collapse of the legal and judicial branches into one system. Anderton, along with two 'witnesses', is detective, arresting officer, judge, jury, and executioner" (234).
4. In *The Discovery of the Future*, H. G. Wells suggests that the systematization of all existing knowledge and information may eventually enable scientists to predict the future (see 28). It is clear that the precog system in *Minority Report* operates on a very different assumption—not the total sum of knowledge but rather a kind of miraculous intervention.
5. Here, see in particular Schmitt, *Political Theology* 30–1.
6. Thus, in his book on Thomas Hobbes, *The Leviathan in the State Theory of Thomas Hobbes*, Schmitt argues that "the mechanization of the concept of the state thus completed the mechanization of the anthropological image of man" (99).
7. Fukuyama's Hegelian-inspired notion of the end of history is normative in the sense that it is based on the premise that "there would be no further progress in the development of underlying principles and institutions, because all of the really big questions had been settled" (xii), albeit not an end to "the occurrences of events, even large and grave events" (xii).
8. In this sense, one could argue that the tripartite division of power in the film is still operative; they simply work together in unison at an extreme speed.
9. See, for example, Kowalski's reading of free will/determinism in *Minority Report* 228–31; Huemer 104–13; and Rowlands 85–103.
10. In those cases where the film has been read politically, *Minority Report* is typically seen as a comment on the post-9/11 doctrine on preventive war: for example, Huiskamp's '*Minority Report* on the Bush Doctrine'; see also Seed's edited collection *Future Wars* for a general discussion of preventive war.
11. Schmitt particularly opposes the views of the legal positivist Hans Kelsen, who attempts to define the state as identical to the legal order itself. Thus, as Schmitt writes, to Kelsen, "The state, meaning legal order, is a system of ascriptions to a last point of ascription and to a last basic norm," and, a little later, "The basis for the validity of a norm can only be a norm; in juristic terms the state is therefore identical with its constitution, with the uniform basic norm" (*Concept of the Political* 19).
12. See Schmitt, *The Concept of the Political* 26.

13. In *Political Theology*, Schmitt thus argues that the sovereign's "decision becomes instantly independent of argumentative substantiation and receives an autonomous value" (31).
14. The precogs are able to detect murderous instincts within the neurological fabric of the human mind and, on this basis, create visuals that match what will happen. The film thus suggests that the ability to predict the future is particularly related, albeit not limited, to something specifically violent. But there is a sense in which the film is also suggesting that the act of looking into the future *per se* is violent, that it is connected to some form of extreme danger as such, regardless of the future vision's content. At no point in the film does the act of looking into the future involve something positive, happy, or good, not even when Agatha recounts the future story of Anderton and his wife's son—it merely seems to deepen their sense of loss.
15. When the plot begins, the Precrime project is about to become nationalized if approved by a popular referendum to be held two weeks later. For six years, it has operated as a successful experiment that has kept the murder rate at zero. In other words, the Precrime project is an *exception about to become a legal norm*.
16. At one point in the film, Anderton dreams about Sean, his son; the latter tests how long he can hold his breath under water in the swimming pool. Anderton does the same, the stopwatch falls into the water, and when he re-emerges to the surface the boy is gone—symbolically suggesting that time has frozen.
17. The vast number of repetitive elements in the film underlines this static temporality: for example, the pre-visual sequence of Ann Lively's murder is repeated five times, a visual which is supposed to be merely an "echo" of something that was meant to happen, but did not (but which, of course, turns out to be a visual of something that really did happen). Further repetitive instances include Ann Lively's daughter, who is kidnapped—like Anderton's son. And Ann Lively was framed by Burgess involving a third, unknown murderer, also as in Anderton's case.
18. This denaturalization of time is quite literally illustrated in those scenes during which people are working in front of the glass screen, analyzing, rearranging, manipulating—and thus creating a narrative out of—the precog visuals within a timeframe that can be accelerated or decelerated at will.
19. The commercials show a society in which the murder rate was extremely high, thus stressing the failure of a state to protect its citizens.
20. That is, Burgess did really kill Ann Lively.
21. As Dr Hineman says, "there is nothing more destructive to the metaphysical fabric that binds us than the untimely murder of one human being by another."
22. The precogs can see and identify a real intention to kill; apparently, however, they cannot see whether someone else has planted or "activated" this intention in them in the first place. For a discussion of the philosophical implications of this issue in the film, see Kowalski 228–31.

23. For example, Anderton at this point literally starts a stopwatch.
24. The rest of the film largely consists of escape scenes: Anderton escaping the Precrime building; Anderton narrowly escaping after the eye operation; Anderton (and Agatha) making their escape in the shopping center; Anderton being pursued by Burgess in the film's penultimate scene.
25. The fact that Anderton—as the chief police officer of the Precrime project—does not know this ("Jesus Christ—why didn't I know about this?") seems a little strange, but it underlines the fact that Anderton is not related to—and is, in fact, ignorant of—the notion of the exceptional.
26. See Benjamin, "Critique of Violence" 278–87.
27. Sava describes Schmitt's state of exception as a gap, which "emerges between the particular, the social and political reality, on the one hand, and the general, which is established by the abstract legal norm. We can see this gap as a place in which the decision can be and, actually, is inserted" (26).
28. One of the unanswered questions here is why Ann Lively is the only one insisting on getting back her daughter, Agatha, who also happens to be the most talented precog?
29. The kidnapper, Leo Crow, seems to have been involved in this plot for some time. For example, the pictures—showing Sean at the age he would have been if he was still alive—indicate that a lot of time and effort has gone into this (even if the photos are fake). Crow, as it turns out, had agreed to let himself be killed by Anderton to receive an insurance sum for his family. That all this should have been planned during just one night seems highly unlikely. Lamar Burgess plays an odd role in the plan; we know that he is the person framing Anderton via Leo Crow, but the film also vaguely suggests that he may have had a part in the actual kidnapping of Anderton's son (for example, Burgess and Anderton knew each other before the Precrime project began; Burgess eagerly wanted Anderton to join the Precrime project; he is worried that Anderton's grief might affect his work). It is even possible that Burgess initially hired Crow to kidnap Sean before Anderton joined the Precrime project. More likely, however, Burgess hired Leo Crow to play the *role* of the kidnapper, probably, the only person Anderton would want to kill, regardless of the consequences. As Dillman observes, "John Anderton's story contains gaps and unresolved issues. He lost his child at the swimming pool and Sean disappears without a trace, which the narrative fails to resolve" (234–5).
30. As Kowalski points out, this seems to suggest that "once Anderton or Burgess discovers the contents of the original prevision, it becomes obsolete" (246n).
31. As the film demonstrates on several occasions, if people are actually aware of what they are destined to do, they can change the future. One could ask if it might not have been better—from both a legal and a moral point of view—to apprehend these future murderers, show them the previsuals, and then give them the freedom to change their future act? What seems to be the case here is less the freedom of the individual than the prevention of any form of

violence in the form of deterrence; the people arrested become examples of what will happen if we give in to our murderous desires.

32. Witwer discovers that what was supposed to be an echo is, in fact, a different event. Anderton likewise discovers that something is wrong, since there is no record of it (the record has been erased because the technicians believed it was an echo).

33. Nor is letting himself be arrested and "haloed"—like Howard Marks—an option for Lamar Burgess, since this can only happen insofar as he harbors an intention of killing Anderton.

34. As Bond observes, "Despite all of its imaginativeness, the film fails to imagine a positive legal future capable of progressing beyond our historical moment" (39).

35. For a list of technological gadgets—including electronic gloves, holographic displays, voice recognition, optimal tomography, talking billboards, thermal scanning, electronic spiders, magnetic levitation and "halos"—used in *Minority Report*, see Wright (483). The point is that, today, many of these technologies seem a lot less "science fictional" than in 2002.

36. Hence the religious references surrounding the precog project (for example, the basin in which the precogs are submerged is called "the temple").

CHAPTER 3

# The Anomalous World: *Elysium* and the Invention of the Med-Bay Machine

## Introduction

Neill Blomkamp's dystopian sci-fi film *Elysium* (2013) tells a story in which Earth has been transformed into a gigantic ghetto, inhabited by an impoverished, disease-ridden, and disheveled crowd, while a small percentage—the rich and privileged—live, like Dante's blessed pagans, in comfortable surroundings outside Earth's hemisphere on a rotating space wheel, Elysium.[1] The film ends, perhaps somewhat predictably, with the destruction and collapse of this political situation, which at the same time articulates the promise of a new beginning—namely, that everyone now automatically gains citizenship in Elysium, and thereby, in a further sense, all the privileges belonging to the middle class: security, clean air, health guarantee, welfare.

*Elysium* thus lends itself to a traditional, class-critical narrative about the way in which the present's political arrangement—the wealthy West versus the rest—in intensified form eventually will reach beyond the boundaries of Earth. When Earth's natural resources have been used up, the affluent West simply reproduces the same political arrangement in space. The space station's physical distance thus establishes a new kind of ultimate border. Those who attempt to illegally cross this border automatically risk being deported or destroyed. Whereas one could say that Fukuyama imagined the normative end of history as Elysium (that is, realized everywhere on Earth), this space paradise clearly constitutes the *exception* in the film; in this future scenario, the *norm* is a burned-out, exhausted, and overpopulated Earth.

This is also why the film's perspective is centered around the main character, Max, who represents the average Earth resident haunted by the dream of Elysium—that is, the pure, secure, and healthy life—without hope of a better future, while desperately fighting for mere survival in the present. In other words, there are no obvious signs indicating any impending change in Max's present life. Thus, it is indicative that the plot is initiated by a random accident: Max is fatally injured at the weapons factory, after which a chain of different events subsequently leads to revolution and the downfall of the system. Without this accident, we are to understand, things could have continued in the same way indefinitely.

More generally, the film's plot narrates the story of a totalitarian, unjust, and *exceptional* political situation that eventually erupts into a violent revolution culminating in a utopian ending, at which point the many now possess the same rights as the few. In other words, the film's plot ends with a utopian solution, a sort of fantasy *Ersatz* for an irresolvable political problem, which, of course, was the very occasion for the initial unjust political arrangement: the construction of the gigantic space station, Elysium.

The political problem that the film addresses is the point at which a radical, new technology demands a fundamental change in the political coordinates of the present—that is, the point at which the future arrives. My argument is that *Elysium* tells the story of a future scenario, which precisely constitutes the *future* because the emergence of a radical, new technological invention has disturbed the political coordinates of the present; with the invention of the so-called Med-Bay machine, it is now possible to cure almost anything, which thus creates a wholly new and potentially uncontrollable biopolitical situation. More concretely, what this entails regarding the political is the emergence of the possibility of a radical and extreme form of equality, a kind of state of nature in which everyone is fundamentally equal.[2] In such a society, the political collapses—that is, power's ability to provide control and security. What we see in the film is thus power's *reintroduction* of difference. This occurs through the restoration of a premodern political construction, the city gate, which serves the purpose of preventing access to the Med-Bay machines in the form of Elysium's architectural nature, a floating space paradise physically distanced from Earth. The entire population of Earth (those who do not have access to the Med-Bay machine) is thereby transformed into a gigantic concentration camp—an *anomaly*, which, however, because of its disproportionality, becomes the *norm*. Thus, we return to a premodern political situation in which the city or civilization, as represented by Elysium, constitutes an *exception*, now surrounded by vast swathes of states of nature. In this new political landscape, the concentration camp or Earth no longer constitutes the anomaly, the exception; it is, rather, Elysium that has become the exception, even if its politicians stubbornly, perhaps hypocritically, believe in a liberal–humanistic constitution that momentarily, in peaceful times, allows them to sustain the illusion that they still represent civilization.[3] This is precisely the paradox of the film's articulation of the future: a world that, due to a radical new technological invention, has fundamentally changed, but is still dominated by a liberal fantasy (similar to our present) of a civilized society, albeit with a few unpleasant exceptions or anomalies, like the camp. That this civilized world can exist only to the extent that it elevates itself to an exception, which thereby turns the condition of Earth's miserable and lost population into the norm, constitutes a political conundrum that the film never fully manages to resolve.

## The Exceptional Med-Bay Machine

*Elysium*'s sci-fi world largely builds on what Suvin calls the novum: that is, a future that it does not seem impossible to have developed at some point from within the horizon of the present, and, more specifically, the *normative* present. What departs from this vision in the film—that is, its radical impossibility, the absolute limit of imagination, a form of absurd technology that questions the genre's sci-fi realism and that potentially thrusts it into the realm of fantasy—is the Med-Bay machine. A crucial scene thus appears at the beginning of the film, involving a woman (whose age is difficult to determine, although she is clearly healthy and fit), dressed in a swimsuit—as if she had just emerged from a swimming pool—entering the Med-Bay machine. Her skin is wrinkled in a slightly unnatural way, although she does not appear especially aged. The scene is quite short and inconspicuous—almost as if we are not supposed to dwell on it; it involves no central characters (we never see the woman again), and no meaningful event seems to occur. And yet the scene is important precisely because it *normalizes*, in such a spectacularly casual, careless, and inconspicuous way, something monstrous and exceptional.

The scene is immediately contrasted with—perhaps, to some extent, overwritten by—another scene that takes place on Earth: a large, disorderly group of sick people desperately try to board one of the spaceships that are about to force their way illegally into Elysium to access the Med-Bay machine. It is the juxtaposition of these two scenes that frames the central conflict in the film—those holding the right to access the Med-Bay machine, and thereby the right to everlasting health, beauty, and happiness, and those denied access. For the Med-Bay machine—which, in a sense, constitutes a *pars pro toto* figure for the entire aesthetic design of Elysium (resembling a gigantic sunbed)—is a kind of miracle machine that can cure almost anything, such as aging, injuries, diseases, even death.[4] It is in this sense that the Med-Bay machine represents the fulfilment of the biopolitical promise in its most radical sense: the ultimate maximization of life.

At the same time, there is something brutally simplistic about this machine, a form of aggressive literalness that testifies to an acute inventive meltdown, an absolute zero point of imagination, or a traumatic failure in our imaginative ability. In other words, the machine represents the *limit* of our imagination. Beyond this limit there is quite simply nothing concrete to relate to. It is precisely at this limit that the film locates the exceptional space. The radically new technology opens the gap through which the future slips, and which thereby necessitates the emergence of the state of exception.[5] Or, more precisely, this state of exception has now become the norm due to the invention of a technology that is so radical that it creates *a new political situation*. Thus, the entire existence of Elysium, this gigantic wheel floating effortlessly and apathetically just outside Earth's hemisphere, seems to serve the sole purpose of separating these Med-Bay machines *physically* from Earth's population. In other words, the emergence of the Med-Bay machines has led to a political situation demanding the creation of an entirely new world, a new reality. There is literally no place for such machines in the old world.[6]

It is in this sense that the future arrives in a similar way to Stanley Kubrick's mysterious monoliths in *2001: A Space Odyssey* (1968), which always appear like an inexplicable gap in reality—although the Med-Bay machine is not really mysterious at all; if anything, it is *overinvested* with meaning, with all the objects of desire one could possibly imagine within the biopolitical register. What the Med-Bay machine promises is nothing short of a miracle: the everlasting young, healthy life in its maximum form.

As the highest object of desire, the Med-Bay machine defines all the characters and their motivations in the film. Thus, at the beginning of *Elysium*, we see three dilapidated spaceships under the guidance of the rebel Spider and his people, being filled up with diseased, aging people desperately trying to reach Elysium, even though they risk being arrested, deported, and killed. Max da Costa and Frey already dreamed about reaching Elysium as kids (that is, they dreamed of a middle-class life), while as adults they simply dream about the cure offered by the Med-Bay machine: Max because he is fatally injured after a factory accident, and Frey due to her dying daughter. Meanwhile, Delacourt, Elysium's defense minister, and Carlyle, the weapons manufacturer for the space station, represent two characters tasked with the job of defending the Med-Bay machines, which, more specifically, means preventing the masses from achieving access at all costs.

The film indicates that if everyone, in fact, had access to this machine, Earth's population would rise uncontrollably, thus potentially leading to the draining of natural resources and hence the collapse of civilization. If everyone could maximize life to the fullest, this would not lead to paradise, but to a Hobbesian state of nature. At least this is what Elysium's government fears, a fear reflected in the physical *distance* between Earth and Elysium's position in outer space. As Hobbes observes in *Leviathan*, what characterizes the state of nature is precisely a negative notion of equality—that is, a situation in which everyone, because of equal strength and intelligence, is a threat to everyone else's security. All individuals have the same rights to everything, and furthermore, everyone can kill or be killed in equal measure. In such a situation, power is created through reestablishing a dynamic of difference legitimizing a politics of separation, a *hierarchy* to justify why some have access to the maximum life while others do not, and thus to justify why some may live while others must die. It is in this sense that the film formulates a central problem: what happens when technology has made it possible to realize the ultimate aim of biopolitics, the total maximization of life? More precisely, how does power articulate itself in such a situation? The big question the film raises is thus not only who has the right to live, but also, and perhaps in particular, who must die—that is, how to legitimize the choice between those who must be sacrificed so that others may live. The Med-Bay machine is, at one and the same time, a machine that creates total life, but also brings about a political situation that necessitates death and, more precisely, the death penalty. If no one needs to die naturally any longer, it becomes necessary to install death unnaturally.

## The Sovereign

At first, it may seem that the biggest threat to Elysium's security is Spider and his army of rebels, who lead a brave resistance fight on behalf of the sick and poor inhabiting Earth.[7] But in another sense, it is clear that the real threat is not posed by Spider or the people on Earth, but rather by the radical technological invention of the Med-Bay machine itself. The Med-Bay machine would potentially make the political superfluous, unnecessary—at least to the extent that everyone has access to the machine. The machine epitomizes biopolitics as forever striving towards the maximization of life as such. In reaching this aim, however, the biopolitical becomes obsessed with death and destruction.

Whereas Hobbes's social contract, *protego ergo obligo*, outlined a scenario in which power would offer protection in return for obedience, the new radical technology has led to an imbalance—quite literally, since the space world of Elysium seems to have been created for precisely this purpose—in terms of the relationship between the people and power. To the people, the main concern is no longer protection, for what does protection against violence mean if violence's destructive effects ultimately can be cured by a miracle machine? On the other hand, to power, the main objective is no longer obedience, but rather the implementation of an extremely oppressive political structure as the most efficient way of securing the sole ownership of and access to the Med-Bay machine.[8] This is why the tension between the people on Earth and Elysium's brutal military is so intense; the former do not want protection but access, while the latter do not want obedience but rather to ensure sole control over the limited access to the Med-Bay machine. Neither entity really needs the other in this situation. In other words, it is not possible for a social contract to exist under these circumstances. There is, quite simply, no real balance here, since both entities want the same thing: access to and control over a machine that promises the perfect life.[9]

The only political solution to this problem—the invention of a machine that can cure everything, and which, in case universal access was granted, would lead to problems of overpopulation, depletion of resources, and so on, but whose real threat is the undermining of the concept of the political, and thereby any form of power—is to *physically* separate the machine from the masses and protect access to the machine zealously. This is the raison d'être of Elysium: restriction, separation, limitation—that is, physical borders in an otherwise potentially borderless and infinitely equal world. It is in this connection that the political enemy may be recreated as the figure denied access.

Delacourt, Elysium's defense minister, is acutely aware of the task at hand. Already from the beginning of the film, she initiates an exceptional procedure to deal with the political enemy. Her explicit contempt for Elysium's politicians underlines that she does not care primarily about the liberal middle-class values so intensely cultivated among Elysium's privileged citizens; she is, first and foremost, interested in protecting this world from external threats. Delacourt represents in this sense the traditional sovereign power, who staunchly believes in the right to declare the exception as the only proper basis of this power and the unlimited freedom to act with which such a right would endow her.

Delacourt's government, on the other hand, is explicitly portrayed as a group of liberal, peace-seeking politicians insisting on the validity of the legal order at all times, and who are sharply opposed to her exceptional methods. Thus, when Delacourt orders the destruction of Spider's intruding spaceships, she is harshly reprimanded for not following legal procedures. What upsets the politicians is that Delacourt has used a so-called sleeper agent to deal with the threat—an exceptional method that was apparently used before, but which now has been removed from Elysium's constitution because it was deemed too brutal and inhuman.[10] However, on closer inspection it remains ambiguous as to why exactly the politicians are so upset; either because Delacourt broke the constitutional law, or because Delacourt failed to prevent one of the rebel spaceships actually penetrating the security sphere surrounding Elysium, which thus forced its inhabitants to face an ugly but necessary truth about their existence: that it can exist only because others are brutally oppressed and excluded—a truth they would have preferred to ignore or, even better, to have remained completely ignorant of.[11] Clearly contemptuous of her government, Delacourt carries out the dirty work that no one wants to acknowledge but which is absolutely central to Elysium's political construction; her function is precisely to ensure that Elysium's population may live safely in ignorance, convinced that they are not only healthy and powerful, but also morally superior.

This minor collision between Delacourt and Elysium's political leadership at the beginning of the film seems to convince the former of the necessity of planning a *coup d'état*. She makes a secret deal with Carlyle, the person in charge of Elysium's weapons manufacturing and, more generally, security technology, all of which is produced on Earth.[12] Carlyle agrees to help her, while she, as the future leader, promises him and his company, Armadyne, a 200-year contract. Armadyne is the company whose technology may secure the exceptional political situation required after the invention of the Med-Bay machine.[13] This plan coincides with Spider's attempt to hack the system via the fatally injured Max, who is desperate to reach Elysium, and more specifically, one of the Med-Bay machines. Together, they manage to steal Carlyle's data, which is stored in his mind, before the latter is killed by an accident. With this data now in the hands of the rebels, Elysium's defense system suddenly becomes extremely vulnerable, which eventually leads to Delacourt declaring a state of emergency, whereby she suspends the constitution and takes upon herself the role of sovereign in Elysium. Spider's plot thus, in fact, paradoxically seems to underpin or assist Delacourt's plan, since she had already intended to take over Elysium before she knew anything about Spider's plans, albeit in a different and perhaps more controlled way. It merely confirms what she was always acutely aware of: that Elysium cannot defend itself without relying on exceptional, extra-legal measures. Ironically, Delacourt is later killed by one of her own exceptional weapons, the uncontrollable sleeper agent Kruger, after which Max and Spider manage to reboot the entire system, meaning that everyone, including the masses on Earth, now become official citizens of Elysium and thus automatically acquire the right to treatment in the Med-Bay machine.

## The Camp

In *Elysium*, it is thus clear that Delacourt represents the figure who most clearly understands the new political situation that the Med-Bay machine has created: the concrete, new danger that this technology has brought into the world. Fittingly, Delacourt, like Carlyle, does *not* end up in a Med-Bay machine when she is fatally injured, but instead bleeds to death.[14] Spider's real purpose is, in fact, not to overthrow Elysium's regime, but rather something which is evident already in the first scene of the film: to access the Med-Bay machine.[15] However, the very idea of universal access to the machine creates a dangerous situation, which potentially would involve the elimination of the political. The political, or the ability to distinguish friend from enemy, is precisely the identification of borders within a space whose natural borders and limits are about to be, or have been, eradicated. If the future is that event that breaks down these borders, the political aim consists in re-establishing and resecuring those borders.[16]

It is in this sense that a premodern conception of power re-emerges as an attempt to contain this radical, new technology: the city gate.[17] Delacourt's job is that of the gatekeeper, the nature of which is already underlined in the opening sequence of the film, during which she overrules the constitution by ordering Kruger to shoot down and eliminate Spider's illegally incoming spaceships. Like Ridley Scott's *Alien*, Blomkamp's film circulates around the city gate as a topos, the threshold dividing the inside from the outside.

That this exceptional act—the elimination of Spider's spaceships—is considered entirely unacceptable to the political establishment in Elysium points toward the paradoxical conflict in which this floating space paradise is situated. One could argue that Elysium's construction is a desperate attempt to create an artificial "outside" in a world that no longer permits any natural notion of an "outside." The latter becomes the case when the natural state of nature—the enormous territories of lawlessness surrounding the city—have been eradicated. It is at this point that the camp emerges. According to Giorgio Agamben, the emergence of the camp signals precisely that situation in which there no longer is an outside or, rather, the outside has now been included as exclusion.[18] When the state of nature has permanently been eliminated outside the city walls and territorial–national borders have been established, which makes the city walls unnecessary and impractical, the state of nature emerges as a form of necessary *anomaly* within civil society—namely, in the form of a logic of the exception. The latter serves the purpose of legitimizing and defending the city's identity, its civility, against barbarism and chaos. The political here re-establishes itself as a form of *a-nomos*, a form of vacuum that precisely enables the protection of the law, or the constitution. Agamben's further point is that the exception is necessarily built into the norm's ground of existence, its constitution, as two sides of the same thing. The exception, as Agamben observes, is a power without norm, while the norm is right without power.[19]

How does one legitimize a norm, as the one we find in Elysium—at least according to its politicians—which apparently is based on a constitution that allows a small group of people access to everything, and the rest nothing? That this arrangement is necessary seems initially beyond discussion; thus, as mentioned, the film's beginning indicates problems such as overpopulation, destruction of Earth's natural resources, and so on—whereas the ending simply ignores this problematic and leaps into a utopian scenario where all humans (minus the evil people) are granted access to the Med-Bay machines.

The legitimization is articulated and manifested in Elysium's architectonic construction as well as its location, in space, just outside Earth's hemisphere. Earth, on the other hand, has been transformed into a gigantic camp. In his reading of Schmitt, Agamben argues that Hobbes's concept of the state of nature paradoxically survives in the sovereign. This is what Agamben calls a "zone of indistinction," a legal vacuum that emerges after the state of nature has been conquered and eradicated.[20] The state of exception is a security mechanism whose existence testifies to the system's vulnerability; it is introduced in vulnerable situations during which the city's order and the citizens' lives are under threat. The exception's security mechanism is activated by the suspension of the validity of those paragraphs in the constitution that should have protected the citizens' civil rights. Borrowing Schmitt's idea that the normative law is dependent on the exception, Agamben argues that it is within this "zone of indistinction" that the transition between the human and the bestial, the cultural and the natural, is revived. In the state of exception, the state—and, in a further sense, civilization—re-establishes and reaffirms the close connection to the state of nature. The sovereign in the state of exception banishes dangerous elements, and thus protects the law, but operates at the same time outside the law. Thus, the state of exception is neither inside nor outside the law, but rather—like Kafka's gatekeeper—constitutes a zone of indistinction. It is a zone traversed by force, but not rights.

In this zone, there is no longer any sharp distinction between the (almost-)dead and the surviving. These are inhabitants that have been banished from the city to a place that is neither sacred nor secular: that is, they occupy the space of the exception. The sovereign, as the figure who continuously returns to the essence of the political, attempts to fill the gaps and holes within the normative legal system: that is, those instances where the latter breaks down or no longer makes sense. The future is precisely such an instance. *Elysium* envisions a scenario in which the future has arrived in the form of a radical technological invention. This has created a situation in which the anomaly has grown so large (Earth's entire population) that we seem to have returned to a premodern political situation: the isolated city, the civilized life, placed in the midst of enormous territories of the state of nature. In this world, the camp, or Earth, no longer constitutes the anomaly; it is rather Elysium, this floating space paradise, that constitutes the anomaly, the exception. This is precisely the paradox of the film's vision of the future: a world that, due to a radical technological invention is still essentially ruled by a familiar, well-known, and present liberal notion of the civilized society, punctuated by a few unpleasant exceptions or anomalies such as the camp. It is a world that can exist only in terms of the logic of the exception, even if a large part of humanity is thereby sentenced to death. Ultimately, this is a political problem that the film never entirely manages to resolve.

## The Death Penalty

According to Agamben, the camp's logic does not consist in punishing the figure of the muselman as a criminal, but in dissolving his or her status as a legal subject, and in a further sense, as a human being. The camp is thus a zone in which the sovereign decides whose life is worthy and whose life is unworthy. A human being without rights is at the same time a dehumanized being, halfway a non-human, like the muselman.[21] The muselman, Agamben observes, possesses no form of life, only bare life: a life that inhabits a human shell, one that balances between the human and the non-human. It is a life that is paradoxically included and excluded at the same time; or, to put it differently, to be properly excluded, this figure must be *included-as-excluded*. What the camp produces is bare life that is no longer considered worthy of the rights that, under normal circumstances, would have been attributed to a human being. Agamben connects bare life to the werewolf, a being that is neither human nor animal. The werewolf lives in the gap between nature and culture, nomos and physis. The task of biopolitics essentially consists of the attempt to protect life from this being, the animalistic, the enemy. To Agamben, the biopolitical is constituted through the original, natural threat from the animalistic human—that is, the banishing of the latter in the attempt to create a pure city, a pure human being. The camp's purpose is to purify civilization's life for remnants of the animalistic human.

Why is it the case that some people in *Elysium* have access to the perfect life while others do not? In the film's rather explicit attempt to insert a present political context, we see the poor lower class represented by a Spanish-speaking community; the affluent citizens in Elysium speak French, while the main characters all use American English. The coarse and cynical Kruger speaks South African English. In other words, there seems to be no real, meaningful justification as to who has access and who does not. This lack of justification is, furthermore, underlined by the simple fact that the only thing that seems to separate one group's access from another group's denial of access to the Med-Bay machine is *physical* distance. The establishment of this physical distance indicates that there is a political problem that has not been solved, but simply postponed indefinitely.[22] In Elysium, people have ceased becoming old, and therefore, in a sense, no longer need time or temporal development; they live in an eternal present. The only form of politics these people need is the politics of exclusion—that is, the exclusion of anything that might remind them of the circumstances making this exceptional situation possible (which, of course, is Delacourt's job).

On the other hand, people on Earth are clearly aging, dying, and, in a sense, are already dead. The only promise of redemption that these people seem to possess is the microscopic chance of reaching the Med-Bay machine, albeit only after an extremely dangerous and near-impossible journey in one of Spider's small and worn-out spaceships. After his fatal accident, Max represents this collective desire in intensified-individualized, concrete form. This also means that there is something "impure" about the character of Max; he is not a tragic hero, by any means—or rather, it is only at the very end of the film that he becomes representative of a wider cause, something that stretches beyond his own interest.[23] Until his accident, Max lives a quiet, ordinary life on Earth. Clearly working-class (with a criminal past), Max stoically goes about his everyday business, from time to time harassed by the authorities (now entirely robotized), without much affiliation with or sense of community. In fact, on several occasions we see him shy away from the communal, while clearly harboring little sympathy for Spider and his cause—in other words, a defeated, reclusive person. What sets him on a revolutionary path is a fatal accident, which initiates a desperate attempt to reach Elysium.

Occasionally, we see Max's childhood memories in flashback; back then, he wanted to take the same-aged Frey to Elysium, where they would live the perfect and healthy middle-class life. The desire to reach Elysium and the perfect life was thus once important to Max; now, in the present, Max simply wants to reach Elysium to be cured and thus survive.[24] Even after he re-encounters Frey and her chronically ill daughter, Max's only goal is to reach one of the Med-Bay machines to cure himself. It is only when he actually reaches Elysium that he chooses to sacrifice himself for Frey's daughter, and for humans more generally, so that everyone may have access to the machines.

In a wider perspective, the Med-Bay machines introduce not simply the possibility of maximizing life, but also, indirectly, the sovereign's right to kill—that is, the death penalty. The moment that biopolitics reaches its ultimate expression thus coincides, paradoxically, with the moment that biological life is condemned to death. Michel Foucault observes at one point that there is something paradoxical about biopolitics, in the sense that it focuses on life on the one hand, but on the other hand involves an obsession with death on a scale never seen before in history; biopolitics kills in faster and more unprecedented ways than ever before, in order to promote life.[25]

The reason behind this obsession with death is that when biopolitics reaches its ultimate expression, the distinction between pure and impure life becomes all the more evident; the latter potentially constitutes a direct danger to the former. The point here, however, is that with the Med-Bay machine such distinctions can no longer be made. At this juncture, the distinction and its justification have become impossible. The only solution to this insurmountable problem is the creation of physical distance in the form of a border, which divides a group of people (the dying) from another group (the ones granted eternal life). Those inhabiting Earth are, simply in terms of being denied access to the Med-Bay machine, instantly sentenced to death in the form of either natural death, disease, or accidents. They are the living dead who may die at any time, and actually already are submerged in a process of dying. When the biopolitical is manifested in absolute form, the body itself constitutes a threat, a repository for all sorts of ailments, unpleasant surprises, dangers, and natural processes; life becomes a countdown to the inevitable end. Biological life as such hence becomes a death sentence. *Elysium* thus imagines a time during which the ultimate biopolitical machine now exists, which instantly transforms the natural–biological life into a death sentence. Thereby, the entire planet as represented by Los Angeles, has become transformed into a gigantic concentration camp.

## Zones of Indistinction

The real reason why power cannot grant everyone—all human life, or perhaps any form of life—access to the Med-Bay machine is, therefore, less related to problems of overpopulation, at least not to begin with. It is, rather, the fact that political power would no longer be able to distinguish itself, precisely because power is legitimized in the form of protection and preservation of this very distinction, even if this has been reduced to an anomaly or exception. If everyone actually had access to the Med-Bay machine, we would have potentially returned to a form of state of nature in which everyone would have been *radically equal*. It is in this connection that power redefines itself as an attempt to introduce and establish a dynamic of difference that legitimizes a politics of inclusion–exclusion: to legitimize why some people have access to the healthy, perfect life—and why others do not. In *Elysium*, we thus find ourselves in a future in which technology has created a situation that potentially allows us to return to the radical and extreme anarchy that Hobbes fearfully envisioned as the state of nature.

The paradoxical situation in the film is, however, that this zone of indistinction that creates the anomaly or the exceptional space—for example, the camp—at the same time elevates this anomaly to the norm. Earth, the exception, this gigantic concentration camp, is not simply an invisible, distant, and repressed anomaly, but rather the norm as such, whereas power, Elysium, constitutes the exception. The denial of this fact is precisely the aspect that Delacourt, Elysium's defense minister, despises so much: that Elysium's politicians keep pretending that it is the other way around. To the politicians, there are no longer any enemies—*except*, of course, when they accidentally force their way through the protective barriers of Elysium.

In fact, one could argue that Elysium allegorically represents the Urscene that Hobbes presents in *Leviathan*'s famous scene during which he imagines the state of nature and the creation of the social contract, the transition from the state of nature to civilized life, or the time when humans are miraculously pulled out of the swamp of the state of nature and into the normative life of the state. That this transition does not occur naturally on its own, peacefully and passively, is something Hobbes repeatedly stresses.[26] This is why the sovereign, especially during this transitional phase, necessarily must rule and exercise his or her authority with absolute power—that is, as a lawless beast fighting against other lawless beasts in a lawless world. That this exceptional power eventually is included in the constitutional framework, and thereby the norm, is a sign indicating that we have moved away from the fear of returning to the Hobbesian state of nature. However, what we find in *Elysium* is a paradoxical situation in which the floating space paradise is still reliant on an illusion of the civilized world as a norm, an illusion maintained by way of physical distance, whose purpose is to create both physical safety *and* blindness, willful ignorance, all of which allows its inhabitants to continue believing that the reality of the state of nature is still the exception, not the norm. As Schmitt argues, the real sovereign is the one who decides when the exception occurs, when it ends, and what it consists of. Delacourt, aided by the weapons manufacturer Carlyle, has identified the state of exception as a permanent situation or, rather, has determined that there is no other way than to maintain and sustain this temporary situation. The exception constitutes the very possibility of Elysium's existence, which, at the same time, represents the civilized life's potential survival in a world in which the state of nature has become the norm.

In the liberal vision of Elysium, there are no longer any enemies, only civilized humans, Elysium's citizens, and then exceptional forms of life—that is, Earth's population fighting for the right to access the Med-Bay machines. The film does not really provide any sensible answers as to how this distinction is legitimized, which thus indirectly gives us an answer: there is no rational or moral explanation behind this distinction whatsoever. In reality, the Med-Bay machine has created a fundamental collapse of borders and distinctions, and it is because of this absolute confusion that the containment of the anomaly, the exception, has spread to the entire planet. Elysium constitutes, via its physical location, an exception to this future scenario.

## Conclusion

This is the reason why the film's ending constitutes such a strange form of wishful thinking. It obviously attempts to articulate a vision that basically continues the illusion already propagated by Elysium: the belief that Elysium, as a political vision, could be more and something else than an exception. The most radical solution the film seems to reach is thus to reboot the entire system in order to give all humans on Earth citizenship to Elysium, and thereby the right to treatment in the Med-Bay machine. Max sacrifices himself to reboot the system, but importantly not to change the system, not to destroy the Med-Bay machine (which, of course, was the device creating the totalitarian political situation in the first place). To reboot the system here simply means to transform the political problem to a moral solution that allows everyone, minus the evil people, to win.[27]

The film articulates the political problem thus: if the biopolitical reaches a stage during which age, disease, and even death no longer pose a concern for the population, how does power articulate itself in such a situation? *Elysium* rejects this concern as ultimately immoral (that is, the biopolitical question of who has the right to decide who may live and who may die). The film's ending suggests that no one has the right to decide this, even during conditions so grotesque and miraculous as those created by the Med-Bay machine. Thus, the film ends with a *moralizing* vision about Elysium, not only in a limited, exceptional, and exclusive sense, but also as a place now elevated to a universal principle of rights, in both an ideal and a practical sense. A moral solution to a political problem is also, however, the rejection of a political solution. As Vardoulakis has observed, such a reformulation of a political problem into a moral one would potentially create an uncontrollable challenge regarding overpopulation and a possible infrastructural collapse; furthermore, it might possibly lead to an even more violent, totalitarian, and dangerous situation—an even more restrictive form of sovereignty and distribution of power.[28]

The film's ending thus, at the same time, constitutes its ideological limit; *Elysium* cannot think beyond this horizon of desire. And it is precisely this limit, I would argue, that constitutes the limit of the imagination of the future: the radically unpredictable future. This is why the film's moral solution never seems entirely satisfactory, which thus questions the entire premise of the film. It is precisely here that we begin to sense that the film simply cannot imagine a point at which we actually could organize ourselves politically beyond the invention of the Med-Bay machine, except in the form of an exceptional political arrangement. The Med-Bay machine arrives before the story begins and transforms the political situation into a monstrosity; when this monstrosity has been destroyed (the film's ending), the Med-Bay machine nonetheless still constitutes the highest object of desire for everyone. That is, when the film ends, we find ourselves in a potential déjà vu situation, in which we face the problem of organizing ourselves politically in a radically changed world yet again, perhaps like the situation that preceded the beginning of the film, and which led to the creation of Elysium.

The Med-Bay machine represents a caesura, an event that forces the political to rethink itself. The film, however, postpones the problem indefinitely by way of moralization. Thus, perhaps the most interesting aspect of the film's plot structure is the fact that it ultimately suggests that nothing can really be changed on a fundamental level, and that we are doomed to repeat the same violent cycle of hierarchization. This perhaps explains, in a more narrow aesthetic sense, why the film is caught in a web of clichés, as if we have seen everything before; almost every scene consists of a rehash of elements seen in previous films and TV series, a degradation of something done before elsewhere, as if the film deliberately refuses to reinvent itself.[29] The film's banal emancipation plot articulates a story about good, poor, and excluded people versus evil, wealthy, and privileged people—a political arrangement that is overturned at the end of the film. That the film cannot think beyond this social–liberal fantasy (according to which everyone has equal access to the Med-Bay machine) is neither surprising nor interesting. The interesting aspect of the film is that it explores this limit so thoroughly, as if the film suggests that the future and its radical unpredictability can be expressed only in the form of clichés and wishful thinking, or the present minus aging, disease, and death.

As science fiction, *Elysium* is characterized by and centered around the event that changes the political coordinates of the present. It is in this sense that the genre constantly raises the ghost of the political; in the imagination of the future, we return again and again to the problem of the political. Precisely because the future is radically unpredictable and is the future only to the extent that it arrives in the form of a radically unpredictable event, the sci-fi genre, almost by default, generates unrealistic emancipatory thoughts that are impossible within the political paradigm of the present. *Elysium*'s clichéd ending outlines, in fact, not really a genuine future vision of the political, but rather the negative limit of the political imagination of the present. Most of the film's world is thus recognizable, even Elysium itself, this floating *ancien régime*, home of the rich, the few, and the privileged. The only political progress this film seems to be able to imagine is that this space Eden is spread to the entire Earth—to let everyone become a lawful citizen of Elysium, thus excluding the other possibility, the very premise of Elysium's separation from Earth in the first place—namely, that the entire universe, including Elysium and Earth, would be transformed into a Hobbesian state of nature. It is precisely in this limit of the political imagination that we grasp the contours of the future, albeit in negative form, as a limit that reminds us of the dangerous illusion that the present may last forever.

# Notes

1. As the name suggests (in Greek mythology, Elysium is the place where blessed heroes went after life), this is a place of perfect comfort, security, welfare and healthiness.

2. To Hobbes, the state of nature is precisely characterized by a destabilizing, anarchic notion of equality that potentially enables everyone to kill or be killed. See *Leviathan* 76.
3. In that sense, the political situation in *Elysium* is almost diametrically opposite to that in Blomkamp's perhaps better-known film, *District 9*; in the latter, the camp is still the exception, surrounded by a normative society.
4. For example, when sleeper agent Kruger is blown to pieces, the Med-Bay machine performs nothing short of a miracle; in a matter of seconds, Kruger's body is completely fixed and brought back to life.
5. We are never told who invented the Med-Bay machine, although it was most likely created by the Weapons and Security Facility, run by Carlyle. In other words, it is a technological invention closely connected to the military.
6. The film operates with a spatial—rather than temporal—logic; we do not know how long this political arrangement has gone on, how old Elysium is, or when the Med-Bay machine was invented. Indeed, since the Med-Bay machine cures aging, anyone inhabiting Elysium could, in fact, be much older than they look.
7. Spider's political motivation—what legitimizes his struggle—is the misery of Earth's population, apparently because they are being denied access to the Med-Bay machine (although not ordinary hospitals, welfare, and so on).
8. It seems that Elysium—apart from human contractors, like Kruger and his men—is solely reliant on highly advanced robot soldiers for protection.
9. A series of parallel acts and scenes—which, at first sight, seem a little odd, like technical glitches—underlines the uncomfortable relationship between the political and the moral within the plot. For example, Delacourt plans a coup at the same time as Spider plans a data heist; Max, a former felon, wants to remain on the right side of the law, while Carlyle, his boss, wants to break it; Max loses his job at the same time as Kruger loses his. The parallels indicate something unstable, but also the fact that there is commonality, a common set of interests circling around the same political problem: namely, the existence of the Med-Bay machine.
10. At first, President Patel reprimands Delacourt for having failed to deal with the situation (involving the destruction of two shuttles, killing forty-six civilians) "quietly"; secondly, Patel reprimands her for using a sleeper agent, which he previously ordered her not to—not, apparently, because this method is inhuman or immoral, but rather because it is too explicit. In other words, President Patel wants the problem solved, albeit unnoticeably.
11. Tellingly, no one—neither politicians nor others—attempts at any point to question or justify the fact that Elysium's population has the sole right to the Med-Bay machines.
12. Carlyle is a representative of ruthless capitalism; his few comments are all limited to issues concerning business and productivity. A curious personality trait of his is a hysterical fear of germs—underlining the associations to the camp and Earth's population as vermin.

13. Similar to the Tyrell corporation in *Blade Runner*, Armadyne's production facilities and headquarters are located on Earth. The company apparently needs people on Earth to provide raw material, and its people to do the hard, physical labor; this reality, furthermore, needs to be distanced physically from Elysium and its population.
14. Most of the characters in the film dream about having access to the Med-Bay machine, except, of course, the characters whose mission is to protect Elysium (since they already have access): Delacourt, Carlyle, and Kruger. However, Delacourt and Carlyle both die without getting a chance to be saved by the Med-Bay machine, while Kruger is being put in the machine by his men after his head is blown off—and only so that he can continue his self-destructive mission to kill Max.
15. Paradoxically, the most subversive forces in the film—represented by Spider and his gang—seem to be driven by nothing more than dreams of accessing the Med-Bay machine. The film thus explicitly suggests that if everyone had access to the Med-Bay machine, there would be no revolution, no political upheaval, no forceful removal of the sovereign—that is, an entirely *a-political* solution to what essentially comes down to an irresolvable, political conflict.
16. This furthermore underlines Schmitt's famous dictum that the "concept of the state presupposes the concept of the political" (*Concept* 19).
17. Here, I particularly draw on Virilio's reflections on territory, security, and the city gate; see Virilio (1977, 1993, 1994).
18. See Agamben, *Homo Sacer* 40. While Earth's population is excluded from Elysium (and hence denied access to the Med-Bay machine), people are, at the same time, clearly registered in the system (which is controlled by Elysium)—as exemplified during the scene where Max is interrogated at the detention center.
19. Agamben, *Homo Sacer* 49–62.
20. See Agamben, *State of Exception* 15.
21. See Agamben, *Homo Sacer* 62.
22. Thus, it is, in essence, similar to that of a wall, suggesting a spatial solution (or, rather, postponement) of what seems to be an insoluble political situation.
23. At one point, Frey's daughter tells Max a story about a hippo helping a meerkat; Max interrupts her and says that it does not end well for the hippo. It is only near the end, when he is about to die, that he finally seems to understand what the banal story is about—that is, not himself, but others.
24. It is never entirely clear what Max as a character wants—that is, until the moment he is injured. Before this, we have the sense that he no longer believes in his childhood dream of entering Elysium (that is, the flashbacks), or the conversations he had with a nun (who told him that all people are special).
25. See Foucault, *History of Sexuality, vol. 1* 137.
26. See Hobbes, *Leviathan* 88–98.
27. At the beginning of the film, there is an imbalance, in the sense that people on Earth need the Med-Bay to survive; people in Elysium need the Med-Bay

machine to keep fit and healthy, and to stop aging—like the lady emerging from the swimming pool in the first scene. Eventually, however, it becomes clear that the real purpose of Elysium is to prevent sick, already-dying people from getting better. The reboot presents itself as a solution to the former imbalance, but not the latter problem.
28. Vardoulakis 42. In the same way as Arendt criticized the notion of universal human rights for essentially being meaningless unless actually protected and guaranteed by particular nation-states, one could say that the universal right that seems to manifest itself near the end of *Elysium* is problematic because it is guaranteed by no one. See Arendt, *The Origins of Totalitarianism* 267–302.
29. In interviews, the director, Neill Blomkamp, has expressed dissatisfaction with the final version of *Elysium*, or more precisely with the story, which he felt was not entirely satisfactory (see Ryan (2015)).

## CHAPTER 4

# *Blade Runner* and the Right to Life

### Introduction

One of the most debated issues in connection with Ridley Scott's sci-fi classic *Blade Runner* (1982) is whether Deckard—the protagonist, played by Harrison Ford—is a replicant or not. Allegedly, Ford was strongly opposed to Scott's decision to include the famous unicorn scene in the film, which apparently confirms that Deckard, like Rachael, Tyrell's replicant, possesses "implants," synthetic memories in a scene anticipating the film's ending, during which Deckard finds an origami unicorn left by detective Gaff, who thus reveals that he knows about Deckard's real identity, that he is, in fact, a replicant.[1]

In this chapter, I suggest that, although much of the criticism on *Blade Runner* tends to focus on this particular issue, it largely serves the purpose of a decoy, the real function of which is to blur a far more traumatic issue, which Michel Foucault, in the first volume of *History of Sexuality*, addresses thus: "The 'right' to life, to one's body, to health, to happiness, to the satisfactions of needs, and beyond all the oppressions or 'alienations,' the 'right' to rediscover what one is and all that one can be" (145).

The struggle for this right takes place in a strangely somber, majestically gloomy universe, intent on conspiring against life itself. The film's ill-boding opening crawl introduces the concept of the replicant, and more specifically, the Nexus-6 battle model, as well as its "negation," the blade runner agents. Their job description goes like this: "This was not called execution. It was called retirement." Already, here, one starts wondering what kind of monstrous being lurks underneath the term "replicant"—a monstrosity apparently in need of three negative words ("not," "execution," and "retirement") to verbally contain or neutralize it.

Initially, the replicants inspire so much fear because of a bloody mutiny in the off-world colonies initiated by the Nexus-6 battle model, as the opening text informs us. After this mutiny, all replicants have been banned from Earth, while those violating this injunction have been outlawed. Upon reflection, however, the question emerges as to why the replicants are, in fact, banished from Earth. Throughout the film, we have the impression that anyone capable of leaving Earth has already done so, and that those left are there more or less against their will, a disparate lumpenproletariat of impoverished people, punks, perverts, and religious fanatics—and, of course, J. F. Sebastian, who does not pass "the medical test" due to his health condition.[2] One reason behind the ban may be the fact that the Tyrell Corporation, led by the "God of Biomechanics," Eldon Tyrell, still resides on Earth. Indeed, the Tyrell Corporation is the reason why the Nexus-6 replicants return to Earth; they want more life (and to avoid death), and Dr Tyrell, their maker, is probably the only one who can possibly grant their wish.[3]

One of the premises that viewers easily accept is that these replicants are inherently dangerous. Initially, this seems easy to confirm; in the first scene of the film, the replicant Leon brutally assassinates blade runner Holden, after which the semi-retired Deckard is summoned back. On closer inspection, however, the replicants seem neither particularly dangerous nor murderous—that is to say, no more dangerous than any human being would have been in similar situations. The replicants easily blend into the heterogeneous crowd: that is, they *pass* the Turing Test as humans.[4] Thus, the police ironically need a *machine*—the so-called Voight-Kampff—to distinguish them from humans. They become dangerous, of course, when chased by people with murderous intent—for example, Leon in the interrogation room, Zhora in the nightclub, and Pris and Roy in J. F. Sebastian's apartment complex. In all these cases, the replicants' undoubtedly violent reactions seem hard to distinguish from those of human behavior in similar circumstances. So why is it absolutely crucial to hunt down and kill these beings, who, after all, soon will die—in fact, throughout the entire film, are in the process of dying, and in the end actually die on the roof of the Bradbury Building as "naturally" as may be possible for a replicant?

In several scenes, we encounter the following questions: When will I die? How old am I? Have you seen my classified file? That these files actually do exist is visually illustrated during the scene in police Captain Bryant's office. The files, one may assume, contain data relating the replicants' life expectancy and thus reveal that all of them are facing imminent extinction: a few days, a couple of years, no more. Leon, for example, was "born" on April 10, 2017, which means that his "date of expiration," or death, would be around April 10, 2021, one-and-a-half years later.[5]

But even if Leon may live a bit longer than someone like Roy Batty (who seems to have only a few days left when Deckard starts searching for him), it nonetheless remains an indisputable fact that *his* moment of death has also been determined in advance.

Thus, there is a sense in which it seems entirely superfluous to send out a group of professional killers to eliminate the escaped replicants when these beings already have a "fail-safe device" built into their operative systems: the four-year life span.[6] Detective Gaff's last words (repeated in Deckard's thoughts when he finds the origami unicorn in the last scene) are: "Too bad she won't live—but then again, who does?" Initially, Gaff's comment seems to suggest that Rachael, qua replicant, will eventually "expire" due to the built-in fail-safe. The comment may also indicate that Deckard is a replicant as well, and thus likewise lives on borrowed time.[7] Finally, Gaff's comment might be understood in a more sinister way: that is, as a threat—that Rachael, qua replicant, sooner or later will be hunted down and killed by the blade runners (or, in the language of the film, "retired").

The raison d'être of the blade runners is the enforcement of the death penalty. However, given the fact that the enforcers of this death penalty *know* that these replicants will die a "natural" death within a foreseeable future, one of the riddles this film presents is that the *enforcement* of this violent law seems far more important than the simple fact of death. So, to repeat the question: why is it so important to liquidate these beings, when, in fact, they will die very soon anyway? Since the photo IDs of the escaped replicants actually exist in the files, and furthermore, since the police eventually discover that the replicants have returned to Earth to prolong their lives, why not simply increase security measures around the Tyrell Corporation (which seems strangely vulnerable and open), and wait until the replicants expire? In Roy Batty's case, the expiration date almost coincides with the moment of his possible liquidation; Deckard could not possibly have reached him any sooner. In any case, in their desperate pursuit of more life the replicants are hard pressed for time, as Roy mentions to Sebastian in an attempt to persuade the latter to introduce them to Tyrell. More specifically, the in-built four-year life span seems in itself to constitute a brutal death penalty, one that ought to have made the blade runner squad superfluous, at least as a *death squad*.[8] One might have imagined a security force, perhaps an anti-terrorism corps, but a professional team of executioners seems like a sinister redundancy that has gone strangely unnoticed in the critical reception of the film. I argue, however, that it is precisely this redundancy that constitutes the ideological blind spot of *Blade Runner*: the legitimization and activation of the death penalty as a response to a situation in which a certain kind of life is perceived as a biological danger to others.

## Biopower

"The norm," Schmitt observes in *Political Theology*, "requires a homogenous medium" (13). This is the normal space—a "normal, every day frame of life" (13)—which the sovereign seeks to protect via the exceptional decision, and which ultimately involves the biopolitical exclusion of heterogeneous elements. "For a long time, one of the characteristic privileges of sovereign power was the right to decide life and death" (135), writes Foucault in *History of Sexuality*, a text outlining the emergence of a new form of power that articulates itself in two forms related to the body: discipline and biopower. This power is—if not opposed to—at least different from the previous kind of power embodied by the sovereign, whose power in the end, writes Foucault, "was essentially a right of seizure: of things, time, bodies, and ultimately life itself; it culminated in the privilege to seize hold of life in order to suppress it" (136). The sovereign's power is, according to Foucault, basically the right to demand the subject's life insofar as the sovereign's power is threatened, internally or externally.

This right to take life and let live gradually changes during the seventeenth century to "a power to *foster* life or *disallow* it to the point of death" (138). Foucault describes this change that occurs in the power structure as "nothing less than the entry of life into history, that is, the entry of phenomena peculiar to the life of the human species into the order of knowledge and power, into the sphere of political techniques" (141–2). What power "demanded and what served as an objective was life, understood as the basic needs, man's concrete essence, the realization of his potential, a plenitude of the possible" (145). On the one hand, there is a disciplining of life that is "centered on the body as a machine [and] its integration into systems of efficient and economic controls" (139). On the other hand, there is a biopolitics aiming at the population: "the species of the body, the body imbued with the mechanics of life and serving as the basis of the biological processes: propagation, births and mortality, the level of health, life expectancy and longevity" (139). What is at stake here is a relatively new dynamic of power in history, according to Foucault, which basically involves a political redefinition of the subject or biological existence. Life is no longer controlled simply in terms of punishment or death, but rather a process that becomes the object of a radical transformation with far-reaching consequences.[9]

*Blade Runner* is, in many ways, a film that envisions the furthest consequences of this transformation. To Foucault, the inscription of life itself into political history represents a provisional culmination: "The atomic situation is now at the end point of this process; the power to expose a whole population to death is the underside of the power to guarantee an individual's continued existence" (137). The film can be seen as an articulation of this atomic situation that Foucault describes—in its most fatal extremity.[10] *Blade Runner*'s apocalyptic universe thus contains the story of life after biohistory has come to a culminating end point, at which stage the replicant embodies the most pregnant expression of biopower's subject, its most passionate dream.[11] As Dr Eldon Tyrell tells Roy Batty, the leader of the escaped Nexus-6 replicants, "You were made as well as we could make you . . . you have burned so very, very brightly, Roy."

## The Sovereign and the Death Penalty

Foucault's genealogy of power is not a chronological linear process; that is, the sovereign society is not chronologically replaced with the disciplinary society, which subsequently is replaced by the governmental society. Rather, the elements of all three forms of power are present simultaneously, although increasingly dominated by the latter two.[12] However, in the symbolically charged scene during which the "prodigal son," Roy Batty, returns to the father, Tyrell, we see a remarkable celebration of the old sovereign. It is true that Tyrell, at one point, says that death is "a little out of my jurisdiction," although this is, in fact, the only thing of which he is a master in this particular context—more life, as we know, he cannot give Roy. To the contrary, Tyrell seems surrounded by death: as the maker of the replicants, he is the one who implanted the fail-safe device (the four-year life span), and furthermore—one may assume—is responsible for the excommunication of the escaped replicants, and thus ultimately responsible for the blade runner death squad. In other words, Tyrell embodies the one who can issue the death penalty over those challenging his power, the survival of his sovereignty.

Why do we find a passionate celebration of the sovereign, these multiple references to this particular kind of power, one that Foucault clearly *dissociates* from the intensification of biopolitics?[13] Why does the figure of the sovereign emerge at this point? Initially, one could argue that the film ironically plays on the Enlightenment theme of man's rebellion against the Creator[14]—or, as quite a number of critics have done, one could read the film in terms of an Oedipal dynamic, with Roy Batty committing patricide.[15] In a biopolitical reading of *Blade Runner*, however, when biopower reaches its purest expression in the form of life as replicant, an ironic reversal occurs, after which life itself becomes a monstrosity, something uncontrollable that threatens power, and which subsequently must be eliminated.

It is in this light that one should understand the death penalty, which the film latently and manifestly struggles to legitimize: the legitimization of excommunicating a life that must be liquidated, gotten rid of at any cost. As Foucault writes, the death penalty as a characteristic of the sovereign's power does not disappear entirely within the new forms of power. Since the sovereign's power gradually changes to a dynamic that increasingly aims toward the optimization and complete administration of life, the death penalty becomes more difficult to legitimize. Foucault writes: "How could power exercise its highest prerogatives by putting people to death, when its main role was to ensure, sustain and multiply life, to put this life in order?" (*History* 138). Within the new forms of power, death becomes a kind of scandal, a contradiction, the most radical expression of power's limit. Thus, the death penalty is enforced only in those cases where the issue is related less to the monstrosity of the crime, but more to "the monstrosity of the criminal, his incorrigibility, and the safeguard of society" (138).

In *Blade Runner*, this monstrous criminal arrives in the shape of the replicant, which, at the same time, epitomizes the culmination of the biopolitical life.[16] The replicant is excommunicated less because of a monstrous act, but more because its very *being* is monstrous. The replicant is, at one and the same time, the most perfect[17] and the most perverse human;[18] it is on the basis of its extreme being that the replicant is outlawed and sentenced to death.

Never before, writes Foucault, have so many wars been fought "in order to go on living" (137)—wars fought

> on behalf of the existence of everyone; entire populations are mobilized for the purpose of wholesale slaughter in the name of life necessity: massacres have become vital. It is as managers of life and survival, of bodies and the race, that so many regimes have been able to wage so many wars, causing so many men to be killed. (137)

It is against this background that murder on a collective level finds its most concrete expression: "One had the right to kill those who represented a kind of biological danger to others" (138). However, the ironic reversal that takes place in *Blade Runner* is that it is *not* the replicants who constitute an immediate biological danger from a biopolitical perspective;

it is, to the contrary, the imperfect human beings. The film explores the irony of the moment when the Tyrell Corporation's motto, "More Human Than Human," literally becomes true—that is, the creation of a *perfect* human being without flaws or imperfections (that is, all that which, in a sense, makes human beings *human*): a stronger, more intelligent, noble, beautiful, and ironically, more passionate and emotional creature. By contrast, the humans in *Blade Runner* are portrayed as clearly inferior, suffering from all kinds of maladies and defects, such as alcoholism (Deckard), aging (J. F. Sebastian), poor eyesight (Tyrell), decadence (Taffey Lewis, owner of the Snake Pit), and lack of emotion.[19] Even the world they inhabit seems to be in a state of shutdown, as if having survived a major climate catastrophe: a postmodern world no longer *progressing* but *deteriorating*.[20] The paradox of this motto—"More Human Than Human"—becoming literally true constitutes the entire raison d'être of the blade runner squad, the sovereign's sword; indeed, one could argue, the *re-emergence* of the sovereign.

## Replicants and Sex

"Perhaps one day people will wonder at this," Foucault writes in *History of Sexuality*; "They will not be able to understand how a civilization so intent on developing enormous instruments of production and destruction found the time and the infinite patience to inquire so anxiously concerning the actual state of sex" (157–8). Foucault's argument is that sex throughout the nineteenth century becomes a crucial tool in the creation and understanding of what it means to be a subject. Far from being a concept in response to which power exerts prohibitive measures, sex is the history of a creative, productive force, a crucial part of power's operative dynamic.[21]

As a pivotal component of biopolitical power, the concept of sex replaces the metaphysics of the soul. It becomes the *essence* of what makes up personal identity—"all that we are":

> Sex—that agency which appears to dominate us and that secret which seems to underlie all that we are . . . sex is the most speculative, most ideal, and most internal element in a deployment of sexuality organized by power in its grip on bodies and their materiality, their forces, energies, sensations, and pleasures. (155)

What Foucault emphasizes here is that "sex" constitutes an important tool for power, whose efficiency consists in the dynamic by which the subject is induced to manifest its sex in an attempt to *avoid* power, understood here as a discourse of denial or prohibition, in order to reach itself, the innermost secret of one's self:

> It is through sex—in fact, an imaginary point determined by the deployment of sexuality—that each individual has to pass in order to have access to his own intelligibility . . . to the whole of his body . . . to his identity. (155–6)

In the perspective evolving around *Blade Runner*, what Foucault outlines in the paragraph above is that elusive category of "human being"—a being capable of feeling and recalling authentic memories—that is to say, the being that, according to the Voight-Kampff test, should be distinguished from the replicant. It is the Cartesian *cogito*—as the name "Deckard" possibly refers to—that stands sharply demarcated from the mechanical clockwork of the animal's inner life.[22] The story of the film (as well as the critical discussion of it) seems, at times, to deteriorate into an ideological debate as to whether Deckard really is a replicant, whether he himself has ever taken the Voight-Kampff test,[23] why his eyes gleam strangely (which, apparently, only the replicants' eyes do).[24] In other words, the story of the film persistently pursues the idea of difference (which, at the same time, it attempts to undermine). If one replaces the word "sex" with "human" in the above quotations from Foucault, it becomes clear why this issue is so problematic.

The film as a whole is, however, one long movement towards the effacement of differences: the radical collapse of time, distinct places, histories, ethnicities, styles, languages, sounds, and light. *Blade Runner* envisions a universe in the process of an acute meltdown, a gigantic, compelling black hole that erases and devours differences, contrasts, dualisms between the self and the other, culture and nature, meaning and meaninglessness, masculine and feminine, civilized and primitive, cooked and raw, real and unreal, the total and the particular. Photos have no real references and yet contain bottomless worlds;[25] as an instrument of the law, the Voight-Kampff machine creates more terror than it restores order;[26] the files are misleading or classified, or contain information not used; all the animals are artificial, dead and yet alive like never before;[27] Pris is recognized by Deckard among the mechanical dolls ironically because she looks too human (at one point she even says to Sebastian: "I think, therefore I am," *cogito ergo sum*—which Rachael, in her dialogue with Deckard, inverts: "You think I am a replicant"). One is never quite sure whether it is night or day; the authority acts in immoral, unsportsmanlike ways (such as when Deckard fires upon the unarmed Roy Batty); the criminal shows magnanimity (such as when Roy Batty saves Deckard on the roof of the Bradbury Building); the machines have warm feelings; the humans are cold, heartless; young people look old and vice versa;[28] even the film (or its many versions) seems to be in radical disagreement with itself.[29]

## The Confession

Even if the dominant formal figure of the film seems to be that of effacement, one should distinguish *Blade Runner*'s main concern—the radical question it poses—from post-humanist ideas arguing that the sharp border between the human and the artificial now has been erased, while exploring the consequences of such an erasure. The problem with these arguments in this particular context is the underlying premise that the essential issue refers to the relation between human and replicant—that is, difference or the dissolution of difference.

From the biopolitical perspective, the present and future potential of humanity is simply everything that goes into and is absorbed by the concept of the replicant. The replicant as a theoretical concept is the culmination of biopower, its deepest consequences, its most distant border, its final ecstasy. It is in this way that the actual question of the film refers to quite a different aspect of the Voight-Kampff machine: not the question of who is human and who is replicant, or whether it is possible to find any essential difference at all, but rather the question of why the Voight-Kampff machine, in *certain suspicious* situations, is used to legitimize and activate the death penalty, the right to kill. The access to this right to power, to kill, and in a further sense, the right to meaning, identity, humanity, sex, moral, and one's self, is here reduced to an arbitrary technological instrument of confession, a kind of perverse Turing test. Whereas, in the Turing test, humans are the ones deciding who should pass as humans, in *Blade Runner*, ironically, only a machine is capable of making such a judgment.

In the article "About the Concept of the 'Dangerous Individual' in Nineteenth-Century Legal Psychiatry," Foucault tells the following anecdote: "I would like to begin by relating a brief exchange which took place the other day in the Paris criminal courts. A man who was accused of five rapes and six attempted rapes, between February and June 1975, was being tried. The accused hardly spoke at all." Foucault continues:

> "Questions from the presiding judge":
>
> "Have you tried to reflect upon your case?"
>
> –Silence
>
> "Why, at twenty-two years of age, do such violent urges overtake you? You must make an effort to analyze yourself. You are the one who has the keys to your own actions. Explain yourself."

–Silence

"Why would you do it again?"

–Silence

Then a juror took over and cried out, "For heaven's sake, defend yourself!" (176)

Foucault comments:

> It happens that the machinery jams, the gears seize up. Why? Because the accused remains silent. Remains silent about what? About the facts? About circumstances? About the way in which they occurred? About the immediate cause of the events? Not at all. The accused evades a question which is essential in the eyes of a modern tribunal, but which would have had a strange ring to it 150 years ago: "Who are you?" (176)

Foucault's point is that it is not enough to merely confess that one has committed a certain act; one must also explain why, so that power may examine, control, evaluate, and ultimately sentence the subject within its own frames. Power must know who you are according to its own norms, terms, and parameters; and power knows who you are insofar as you answer its questions, which already contain their own answers. The man before the court is the subject that escapes power's mechanisms and thus becomes *particularly suspicious* or, in *Blade Runner*, the subject put in front of the Voight-Kampff machine, whose real function is less about the registration of feelings (or other arbitrarily chosen humanistic concepts)[30] in order to determine whether one really is a human, but more that the person is now placed in front of the machine and forced to confess: who are you? If one already is placed before the machine, one is already sentenced (no one in the film passes the Voight-Kampff test as a human).

In the end, the replicant chooses irreconcilability rather than confession. "I have seen things you people wouldn't believe," says Roy Batty during the last moments of his life, which ends with the words: "Time to die." Death itself constitutes the limit of power, as Foucault writes;[31] whereas suicide was a crime during the rule of the sovereign, it now becomes an individual and private right.[32] The individual right to die, this strange determination to command one's own death, constitutes one of the few moments during which life's autonomy may manifest itself, where it may momentarily escape the smothering hands of power. We experience a glimpse of this freedom through Roy Batty's kitschy–poetic soliloquy of the things only he has seen: "attack ships on fire off the shoulder of Orion, I watched c-beams glitter in the dark near the Tannhäuser Gate"—strange, alluring memories of sublime moments, with no references attached, freed from time, places, and persons, floating briefly before disappearing forever "like tears in the rain"—along with Roy himself as he *chooses* to die. This is less a *confession* than a defiant expression of life manifesting itself in its most potent, intense, and momentary being, a *right* to live beyond the narrow confines and regulations of power.

## Conclusion

One could argue that *Blade Runner* as a sci-fi film is one long journey towards the end of the night,[33] the moment when Deckard becomes a witness to the future itself, Roy Batty, who has seen things no one else has seen, a future mirror image of himself (and, literally, Deckard is excommunicated when he escapes with Rachael at the end of the film). In this mirror image of the future that *Blade Runner* visually explores, we see the culmination of biopower in a being whose absolute perfection is, at the same time, an expression of absolute monstrosity, a being that is so infinitely far from life itself, and yet so close that they become indistinguishable.

Here, in this world of indistinguishable shapes and things, where everything seems to collapse in a crucible of fire, rain, dust, fog, and darkness, we constantly return to the question: what legitimizes the reappearance of the sovereign and his or her sword, the death penalty enforced by the blade runner squad? One is tempted here to paraphrase Foucault: it happens that the machinery jams, the gears seize up. Why? Because the accused remain silent. Remain silent about what? About tortoises lying on their backs? About their mothers? About crawling wasps? Not at all. The subject refuses to give an affirmative response to power, and through the silence, the violence, the alienation, defiantly expressing the "'right' to life, to one's body, to health, to happiness, and to the satisfactions of needs, and beyond all the oppressions or 'alienations,' the 'right' to rediscover what one is and all that one can be" (Foucault, *History* 145).

## Notes

1. See Sammon 362.
2. J. F. Sebastian suffers from the Methuselah syndrome (accelerating aging), which makes him look a lot older than he actually is.
3. Somewhat strangely, however, the replicants' motives initially confuse the police. Thus, at the beginning of the film, Deckard asks Captain Bryant, "Why did they come down here?"—to which Captain Bryant responds, "You tell me pal, that's what you're here for."

4. In the 1950 paper "Computing Machinery and Intelligence," Alan Turing argued that if a machine can have a conversation with a person, without this person realizing it is a machine, the machine has passed the test of thinking. See Turing 448. For an extended discussion of artificial intelligence and *Blade Runner*, see Littmann's "What's Wrong with Building Replicants?"
5. As the opening crawl points out, the film takes place in November, 2019.
6. Strangely, Deckard does not seem to know anything about this four-year life span when Captain Bryant tells him—strange, taking into account that Deckard is an experienced blade runner. One must assume that the previous, less sophisticated, models (such as Nexus-5 and so on) had no "fail-safe device." The "fail-safe device" was created to prevent the replicants from developing real emotions, and subsequently self-consciousness, free will, and autonomy. It is thus a counter-measure to the "implants," fake memories, which originally were a counter-measure to what Dr Tyrell observes as the replicants' "strange obsession" with their emotions ("a cushion or pillow for their emotions").
7. At one point, Gaff tells Deckard that "You've done a man's job," indicating, possibly, that the latter is not a real human being.
8. See Captain Bryant's comment after Deckard's assassination of Zhora: "[H]e's a goddam one man slaughterhouse!"
9. See Foucault, *History* 143.
10. To paraphrase Rachael's words: life is not "*in* the business, I *am* the business."
11. See Tyrell's comment about Roy Batty: "You're quite a prize!"
12. On this issue, see Lazzarato (2002).
13. The film conjures up an aura of sovereignty not only in this specific scene, but throughout its universe: for example, the solemn, temple-like pyramid, the chess game, the numerous appearances of semi-religious rituals, and the general atmosphere of a state of nature.
14. For a reading along these lines, see Desser (1997).
15. For discussions of *Blade Runner* in terms of the Oedipal Complex, see Harvey (1990); Silverman (1991); and Pope (2010).
16. This situation comes close to Schmitt's ominous description of the possibility of transcending the framework of the specifically political; in a world where the friend/enemy distinction has been dissolved, Schmitt observes, the only war justifiable becomes the war against those intent on destroying humanity as a universal concept. "Such a war is necessarily unusually intense and inhuman because . . . it simultaneously degrades the enemy into moral and other categories and is forced to make of him a monster that must not only be defeated but also utterly destroyed. In other words, he is an enemy who no longer must be compelled to retreat into his border only" (*Concept* 36).
17. See Tyrell's comment to Roy Batty: "You were made as well as we could make you."
18. See Roy's response to Tyrell—"I've done questionable things"—after which Roy kills him, with his bare hands, in a gesture that could almost be described as tender and affectionate.

19. This is characteristic of almost everyone in the film, in particular Deckard (until he falls in love with Rachael), whose ex-wife called him "a cold fish" (in one of the many deleted scenes from the *Director's Cut* version). Ironically, the exceptions are the replicants, as well as J. F. Sebastian—surrounded by all his cute, mechanical friends, as he welcomes strangers into his house. J. F. Sebastian suffers from accelerating aging, and thus, in a sense, shares the same fate (of imminent death) as the replicants.
20. Drawing on Fredric Jameson's *Postmodernism*, Giuliana Bruno's analysis of *Blade Runner* (as an archetypical postmodern film) remains one of the most dominant readings of it; see Bruno (1987). At the same time, one could argue that the tendency to read it as an archetypical postmodern film (partly inevitable, given the visual spectacles) has marginalized a more latent issue in it: namely, the legitimization of the death penalty.
21. As a concept, the notion of "sex" is productive, Foucault argues, because it creates a fiction that people come to believe in and act upon: the notion "made it possible to group together, in an artificial unity, anatomical elements, biological functions, conducts, sensations, and pleasures, and it enabled one to make use of this fictitious unity as a causal principle, an omnipresent meaning, a secret to be discovered everywhere: sex was thus able to function as a unique signifier and as a universal signified" (154).
22. Descartes writes in *Discourse on Method*: "[Animals] are not rational, and . . . nature makes them behave as they do according to the disposition of their organs; just as a clock, composed only of wheels and weights and springs, can count the hours and measure the time more accurately than we can with all our intelligence" (43).
23. When Rachael directly asks Deckard whether he has ever taken the test himself, he dodges the question.
24. See Sammon 362.
25. Rachael's personal photos are fake; Deckard displays his family photos on the piano, but nothing in the film indicates that he actually has any family (thus, perhaps, suggesting that his portraits have no real references either, or depict real people unrelated to Deckard); when Deckard investigates Leon's photos while using the Esper machine, he discovers a three-dimensional world hidden below the photo's surface.
26. The machine is used in the first scene, when Leon kills blade runner Holden; the second time occurs when Deckard exposes Rachael as a replicant, after which she runs away, deeply depressed upon discovering that her treasured childhood memories are, in fact, those of Tyrell's niece.
27. When Deckard sees Tyrell's owl, he does not know whether it is real; the same goes for Zhora's snake—yet they *look* real. Similarly, Rachael genuinely *remembers* the spiders hatching the egg, just as Deckard *remembers* a unicorn running through a forest.
28. Due to his illness, J. F. Sebastian *looks* a lot older than he is, whereas Deckard—as a semi-retired police officer—*looks* younger than he probably is.

29. The "Director's Cut" was released in 1992 and a "Final Cut" in 2007 (as the two most important edited versions, among several, since the film's release in 1982). The 1992 version, along with the 2007 version, in particular seems to indicate that Deckard is a replicant. For a detailed history of the many rewrites and edits of the film manuscript, see Sammon 51–70.
30. Ironically, Deckard must suppress his feelings in order to kill (this is probably why he is so good at it—as Captain Bryant points out); when he starts to develop feelings, he is no longer capable of killing.
31. See Foucault, *History* 138.
32. As Foucault further observes, "This determination to die, strange and yet so persistent and constant in its manifestations, and consequently so difficult to explain as being due to particular circumstances or individual accidents, was one of the first astonishments of a society in which political power had assigned itself the task of administering life" (*History* 139).
33. For example, in the last scene (included in the US theatrical release in 1982), during which Rachael and Deckard escape, the urban night atmosphere has changed into natural, bright daylight.

CHAPTER 5

# Terminating the State of Exception: *Oblivion* and the Problem of Exceptional Being

## Introduction

Joseph Kosinski's *Oblivion* (2013) tells the story of humanity's survival after a total catastrophe. This is, at least, the film's starting point, told through a voiceover belonging to the protagonist, Jack Harper, whose mission consists of maintaining large machines draining Earth's last natural resources. When the film begins, Harper and his partner are about to depart for a new planet where the rest of the world's population has relocated after the catastrophic war. This is the background story: Earth was attacked by hostile aliens half a century ago. They destroyed the moon, which led to the collapse of Earth's gravitational pull and, eventually, the collapse of the ecosystems. To counter this attack, humans deployed nuclear weapons and in the end won the war, but Earth consequently became uninhabitable.

Within a political perspective, the film's opening situation thus constitutes the last phase of the state of exception; the worst of the crisis is over, the enemy has been defeated, the danger eliminated—and we are about to return to the *normal situation*. This is what Jack Harper firmly believes. In reality, however, things are very different. It turns out that the past event— the war against the hostile aliens—was so drastic and extreme that nothing, quite literally, is the same any longer; everything has changed. What the film focuses on, though, is the fact that Jack Harper is *entirely ignorant* of this fact; to him, it was the humans who won the war, and now they are about to return to the normal situation, the same as before, albeit on a different planet. The turning point in the film occurs when Jack discovers that something is fundamentally wrong; not only did the hostile aliens win the war, but the enemies (referred to as "scavs"—scavengers) are, in fact, the remaining human population. Most disturbingly, Jack Harper realizes that he himself is not himself; he is a clone created by the aliens, whose mission, in reality, consists of draining Earth's natural resources before they move on to colonize another planet.

Initially, this is the story of how Jack Harper comes to fight the aliens because he is still able to remember and identify with an essence of humanity buried deep inside him, even though he is, in fact, a clone. At the same time, however, the film offers a more challenging and, ultimately, more problematic narrative about *self-consciousness in the state of exception*. One of the indirect questions that the film's plot raises is that of why the aliens *need* human clones. Why this almost perverse deception, this massive theater? What is the function of this intimate self-consciousness (embodied, first and foremost, in Harper's voiceover—that is, homo-diegetic first-person focalization) that we encounter in the first and the last parts of the film?

In answering this question, it is crucial to look at the ways in which *Oblivion* addresses the temporal paradox of the state of exception. The state of exception is so *radical* that it presents a concrete problem, in that we are incapable of comprehending quite how drastic it is. This is essentially because the "we" is always necessarily situated within the normal situation; there is, quite simply, no unproblematic position from which this "we"—who are supposed to do the "comprehending"—can exist within the exceptional situation. In the state of exception, everything is potentially turned upside down, to such an extent that it is no longer possible to fully comprehend its scale, implications, consequences—and, most crucially, how to terminate and escape from it: in other words, how to return to the normal situation, the same as before the catastrophe. This is the great danger of *being in* the state of exception *after* the sovereign's decision on the exception has been made. In *Oblivion*, the war continues—we just do not know it; we no longer understand which side we are on, and in the end, who we ourselves are. What the film thus attempts to articulate is a paradoxical self-consciousness that is created, born, and shaped *within* the space of the exceptional situation. When Carl Schmitt insists that the sovereign is the one who decides on the exception, what he is arguing is that the figure of the sovereign claims the right to decide what it consists of, what it is, when it begins, and how to end it. In an interesting and partly speculative intellectual exchange between Schmitt and Walter Benjamin, the latter objects that the force and nature of this decision can be understood only within the context of the normal situation; once this situation has been *suspended* by the sovereign, the latter can no longer make the sovereign decision. In other words, the sovereign can no longer identify the exceptional situation within an already suspended space. In the following, I want to read this problematic alongside some of the issues explored in Kosinski's film. The sovereign is the one who identifies what the exceptional situation is and decides what to do about it. But once we are *in* the state of exception, it is difficult, if not impossible, to understand what it is, to recognize it for what it is and what it is not, and to know what to do in order to terminate it and return to normality.[1]

## The Present: 2077

*Oblivion* begins with a dream. We see some gray moving images accompanied by a voiceover that addresses a "you," a woman on top of the Empire State Building:

> "Before the war, New York, before I was born. The place I've only seen pictures of. I know you. But we've never met. I'm with you. But I don't know your name. I know I'm dreaming. But it feels like more than that. It feels like a memory. How can that be?"

It is unclear whether the voice is part of the dream. Eventually, it becomes clear that the dream is everything that is left from the normal situation, the time before the state of exception, the only connection; these are images from before the catastrophe.

The film's diegetic tense is framed in exact language, as if to solidify its present temporality: March 14, 2077, five years after the obligatory "memory wipe," and half a century since the aliens destroyed the moon, which initiated the great war leading to the destruction of Earth. Jack Harper is a maintenance and repair guy, Tech-49, who administers a control platform along with his partner, Victoria (or Vica, as Jack calls her), a communications officer. Their task is to maintain the drones and to ensure that the oxygen pumps, the hydraulics, are running efficiently. The very survival of humanity, as Jack at one point observes, depends on their work. The big machines generate energy to be consumed in the new space colonies, where the human population has relocated after the war against the aliens. The scattered remainders of the latter apparently continue the fight, disparately and disjointly, destroying the drones and stealing their batteries.

Jack's task consists of repairing these drones, changing batteries, and freeing them when they are stuck in debris. The first part of the film describes this daily routine, which seems to have gone on for some time. It is a period that is coming to an end; Jack and Vica are about to join the rest of the human population and end their work on Earth. This is the plan. In two weeks their turn is over, and Vica is clearly afraid that something might go wrong before they join the new space colony on Titan, Saturn's biggest moon, while, at the same time, dreaming about enjoying a drink and socializing with other people. In other words, the present constitutes the last point in time before Jack and Vica return to the normal situation—and in a further sense, normality: the last days of the state of exception.

On several occasions, we see how Jack, in contrast to Vica, is not particularly keen on the idea of leaving Earth and finding a new home on a different planet; he is nostalgically connected to Earth in a rather irrational, inexplicable way. For example, when he arrives at the ruins of an old football stadium, he immerses himself in an imagined game, the last Superbowl played in 2017—which he has only read about.[2] A little later, he waters a small flower, even though nature has apparently become toxic after the nuclear war. Finally, Jack collects old books and other human artefacts, and brings them back to a secret hut he has built near an idyllic, peaceful lake.

The film's present thus constitutes the time after the future event that changed the political coordinates of the present, quite literally: Earth became uninhabitable. The existential threat is apparently over, survival has been secured, and thereby, also the road back to normality. But the costs are enormous. The victory effectively entails a farewell to the old world, which Jack finds difficult to accept. As he observes at one point, there is something wrong with the fact that humans won the war for Earth and yet are bound to leave it. What he fundamentally does not understand is why they cannot recreate the normal situation on Earth, since they were victorious.

## The Problem of Temporality in the State of Exception

From a political perspective, *Oblivion* thus addresses one of the biggest challenges in Schmitt's *Political Theology* and, more generally, in the discussions on the state of exception: how does one get out of it again? Schmitt writes in *Political Theology* that since

> the exception is different from anarchy and chaos, order in the juristic sense still prevails even if it is not of the ordinary kind. The existence of the state is undoubted proof of its superiority over the validity of the norm. The decision frees itself from all normative ties and becomes in the true sense absolute. The state suspends the law in the exception on the basis of its right of self-preservation. (12)

It is one thing is to declare the state of exception in the attempt to prevent the existential threat, and thereby save the state, civilization, and humanity, but when this goal has been achieved, how do we find our way back to normality? The problem is that when the state of exception has been declared, everything is potentially thrown up into the air. There is, in other words, a potential paradox in Schmitt's concept of the sovereign: namely, that if the decision is conditioned by the norm, it is difficult to understand, when this norm has been suspended, how the decision on the exception can legitimize itself—that is, maintain a real and legitimate connection to the normative and not be transformed into a total fiction, an imagined connection to the normative law. The latter is potentially so distantly situated from the state of exception that it becomes a challenge to identify any real connections.

This is a problem that Giorgio Agamben and others have identified in a reading of the fascinating, albeit somewhat speculative, relationship between Carl Schmitt and Walter Benjamin.[3] Agamben returns to Benjamin's essay "The Critique of Violence" (1921), in which Benjamin describes what he calls "pure violence" that does not relate to the law in the form of foundation or preservation. Schmitt's theory of sovereignty in *Political Theology* (from 1922), Agamben argues, "can be read as a precise response to Benjamin's essay" (*State of Exception* 54).[4] More specifically, Schmitt's state of exception, as decided by the sovereign, is a concept designed to contain and deal with Benjamin's notion of pure violence, to bring it back into a legal and juridical context.[5]

To Schmitt, the sovereign's decision constitutes a limit concept, in the sense that he or she—in contrast to (representatives within) normative law—is able to create a space *outside* the law, while at the same time remaining legally connected to the latter.[6] The sovereign's decision to declare the state of exception constitutes a kind of *Frist*: that is, a *katechon* or a "Restrainer"—the figure that prevents the arrival of the Antichrist.[7] Without this *Frist*—that is, a temporal clause that suspends normal time, or time within the normative, legal framework—Schmitt's theological concept of sovereignty would degenerate into a simple defense of dictatorship.[8]

When read together, the two works essentially raise the question of whether the sovereign is capable of preserving control, power, in the state of exception—that is to say, whether the sovereign can still decide on the exception *in the state of exception*. According to Agamben, it is clear that Schmitt's definition of the sovereign as the one who makes the decision on the exception is supposed to involve the idea that the sovereign can, indeed, control and contain pure violence once the normal situation has been suspended. It is in this connection that Agamben reads Benjamin's response to Schmitt's argument about the sovereign in *Political Theology*—in Benjamin's *The Origin of German Tragic Drama* (1928).[9] Benjamin was clearly inspired by Schmitt's concept of the sovereign for his work on German Baroque drama and developed some fascinating connections, as well as a subtle critique of Schmitt's concept.[10] One of Benjamin's main points concerns "the indecisiveness of the tyrant.

The prince, who is responsible for making the decision to proclaim the state of exception, reveals, at the first opportunity, that he is incapable of making a decision" (*Origin* 71). While Schmitt, as we have seen, defines the figure of the sovereign in terms of his or her right to make the decision, Benjamin's notion of indecision here refers, on the one hand, to the normative legal framework, which is precisely characterized by the sovereign's *lack of decision*, an *in-decision* or a negative force that conditions the possibility of the normal situation—that is, that it has *not yet* been suspended—a "not yet" that potentially calls into question the figure of the sovereign; peaceful, normal times threaten to turn the sovereign into a powerless, unwanted, and invisible figure. On the other hand, Benjamin's sovereign indecision refers to the state of exception itself; once the normal situation has been suspended, once the sovereign is in the exceptional situation, the decisiveness potentially loses its force, since the essence of the sovereign decision consists of the suspension of the normal situation. In other words, once there is no longer any normal situation, the sovereign can no longer *become* the sovereign by making the sovereign decision; all he or she can do is to fight the anomalous, which, at the same time, risks deepening the exceptional situation, not bring it back to normality. This is essentially what Benjamin sees as "the indecisiveness of the tyrant." The risk of deepening of the state of exception is, according to Agamben, what Benjamin refers to in the famous paragraph in the essay "Theses on the Concept of History," in which he writes that "The history of the oppressed teaches us that the state of exception in which we live is the rule" (392). If the sovereign has already once suspended the normal situation—that is, the point at which we find ourselves in the state of exception—there is no longer any normal point of reference to evaluate and measure the abnormality of the exceptional situation, how far from or close to the normal situation we are. In other words, we have lost the connection to this preceding normality. Thus, to Benjamin, there is something fundamentally paradoxical about Schmitt's concept of sovereignty, which leads to even greater problems in distinguishing clearly between the state of exception and the normal situation once the decision has already been made, and the dangers of normalizing the state of exception. Kosinski's film, I argue, addresses this problematic of the sovereign (in)decision in the state of exception and, more specifically, how to return to normality.[11]

## The Permanent State of Exception

In *Oblivion*, we witness a world ravaged by a war against enemies, aliens; the film is about the aftermath of this event. The war is over; it was won but everything was destroyed. Throughout the film, we constantly see images of well-known buildings now destroyed, half-buried in sand, submerged in the ground—for example, iconic monuments like the Pentagon building, White House, Empire State Building, Washington Monument, Statue of Liberty, and many other structures. All of America—which in Hollywood, of course, means civilization as such—has collapsed. Earth's atmosphere seems peaceful on the ground, but the stratosphere is ravaged by a layer of intense thunderstorms. Vica and Jack Harper's post is built on a large and very tall metal pole high above this layer of thunderstorms. The design of their platform is clean and neat, almost in direct contrast to Earth's organic form. As mentioned, Vica viscerally abhors nature, while Jack, on the other hand, is longing for anything organic; thus, he tends to his little earthly hut next to a lake with fish, surrounded idyllically by flowers and trees. Here, he brings all the human traces he finds scattered around as he carries out his daily missions: records, a toy gorilla, a cap, sunglasses, and so on. Many of these are, in fact, objects appearing in the dream sequence, the last scene that Jack remembers from the normal world.

That the well-known world has been ruined seems to make the deception—that is, the story of humans fighting against the aliens, destroying Earth in order to win the war—more credible. The destruction illustrates, in this sense, precisely what Schmitt's exceptional state entails: survival, preservation at any cost, even if the price is the total destruction of everything well known.[12] This is, in reality, what the legitimacy of the sovereign decision comes down to: to save the reality of the norm, even if it entails total and permanent suspension.

In the attempt to articulate this peculiar dynamic, it is crucial to notice here that the film, in fact, presents two competing narratives: one that articulates the triumph of humans, and one that articulates the exact opposite.[13] In the false story, Jack Harper believes, along with the audience for much of the film, that he is a drone maintenance and repair guy on Earth. He and Vica are among the last people on Earth before they leave for Titan, where the rest of the human population has relocated. But in what is supposed to be the true story, Vica and Jack are, in fact, clones of the last and bravest human soldiers before they were defeated and presumably killed by the aliens; they were created by aliens, while the scavs, in reality, are the humans who lost the war. Jack is thus already dead but does not know it. His self-consciousness survived as a clone, implanted in a new body that replaced the original one.

There is something perverse in this plot twist, for not only did the humans lose the war over the right to Earth's resources; the aliens also cloned them and made those clones believe that humans actually won the war, and that the scavs are the last few soldiers of the defeated alien army. Jack wonders why these scavs are still fighting when the war is evidently lost, which only further underlines the perversity of this deceptive situation. A crucial question here is why it is necessary to create this deceptive narrative, this plot twist: why is it important that Jack and Vica (along with all the other identical clones) believe they are humans, fighting for humanity and not the aliens? Initially, we are led to think that these clones will *work* better than enslaved humans. The work is important; this is the entire reason, the film suggests, why the aliens chose to attack Earth—they need the natural resources. But it would also have been possible to imagine, perhaps more plausibly, that one of their "own" could have carried out this mission with equal enthusiasm and competence, and with less risk of potential disobedience. Why go to the extent of cloning humans to carry out work on Earth, and simultaneously endow them with the *same* story in reverse form? Why not give them an entirely new narrative, or no narrative at all? And why use not only cloned human self-consciousness, but the *same* cloned self-consciousness?

The practical answer here is that cloned humans would be familiar with the once normative situation on Earth—for example, the climate. At the same time, it is this familiarity that, ironically, situates them in an imaginary relation to that which once constituted the normal situation. The deceptive structure raises a number of issues in terms of an implausible or questionable plot structure, suggesting that we should examine this problem from a different angle. What seems to be important here is that there is no simple, straightforward way back from Jack Harper 49 to the original Jack (and thereby the normal situation, before the nuclear war against the aliens). Rather, this road back has become deeply problematic, imaginary if not impossible. There is no longer any organic continuity or causality. At this point, the real question is no longer who won the war. The race war, in the Foucauldian sense, is over, even if the film (via the subplot with Beech, leader of the human resistance army) enthusiastically attempts to convince us of the opposite, and even if it does end with images of human victory and the return to normality.[14] The point is that in the state of exception, it becomes increasingly difficult to distinguish friends from enemies, or rather friends can be enemies and vice versa, since the coordinates underlying these categories have, likewise, been turned upside down in the state of exception.

## The Ideological Core of the "Human"

The event that disrupts Jack's everyday routine is a large explosion on one of the enormous hydro rig core platforms in the middle of the night.

Horrified, Jack flies off to inspect the accident. He discovers that someone has attempted to set up an old code system by the half-sunken Empire State Building in order to receive a rogue signal coming from what seems to be outer space. At this point, there are only a few weeks before Jack and Vica are due to leave, in order to join the rest of the human population on Titan. What Jack eventually discovers is that this short period, the remainder of the exceptional period about to come to an end, is an illusion—a *Frist*, one could say. Perhaps it was always an illusion: there is no time or, rather, this *Frist* is all the time there is and perhaps ever was. The point is that once we are in the exceptional situation, the idea of time in the normal sense likewise becomes anomalous. In fact, Jack suspects that something strange and illusory is going on, even before this major explosion occurs; he has strange, clear, and recurring dreams, and he is nostalgically attached to Earth in a deeper and more emotional way than Vica. And when he—on the same day as the explosion—is ambushed but not killed by the scavs, Jack begins to speculate whether there is something possibly deeper going on. After he has been ambushed by the scavs, Jack flies back to his secret little, off-grid place, the idyllic hut by the lake, where he has collected all sorts of human remnants and objects from the time before the catastrophe. He falls asleep, and upon waking up, witnesses a strange object with a parachute crashing towards Earth. Back in the control tower, Vica receives strict instructions from TET, the alien headquarters, to stay away from the crash, which apparently is located close to a border, a zone that Jack Harper is not allowed to enter, seemingly because of nuclear radiation—which, however, turns out to be another deception. Driven by curiosity, Jack nonetheless goes to the place, where he discovers humans in what look like prewar capsules that the drones are now trying to destroy. It is at this point that he realizes that something is fundamentally wrong, and, in a wider sense, that what looks like an exceptional situation coming to an end is, in fact, far more exceptional. For the person in the capsule is none other than the same woman who appears in his recurrent dreams. When a drone attempts to destroy the capsule, Jack heroically protects her with his body. Here, Kosinski's film seems to comment on the critique of the use of drones in wars.[15] In a straightforward allegorical reading, the film suggests that, by inhumanely using drones during war, we lose our humanity—and not only that: while we still believe that we are humans, we have become something else. The moral here is that when we fight against monsters using monstrous means, we risk becoming monsters ourselves. Jack Harper believes he is human, fighting on behalf of humans. When he discovers that the opposite is the case—that he is not a human, and that he is actually fighting against humans—he agrees to embark on a suicide mission: that is, ironically, in a sense *acting like* or even *becoming* a drone himself.

In fact, the film seems to suggest several things at this point. There is no doubt that the large, round, flying objects armed with lethal machine-guns and precision military equipment constitute something morally reprehensible in the film; at times error-prone (this is why Jack is there—to fix them), the drones follow orders blindly and kill ruthlessly. Even though Jack Harper is a clone, he is still human, or at least humane enough to understand this difference. But on the other hand, the film suggests that there is no real, substantial difference, except that one has a human face while the other takes the form of an anonymous, indistinct killing machine. Does the film not thereby imply that as long as we possess the *illusion* of the human, then everything is as it should be? What is actually the real difference between Jack and the drone?[16]

The film does not really present any new answers to this question, perhaps because this is not the essential issue it addresses. *Oblivion* half-heartedly hints at memory, books, love, love of nature, and other clichéd references that not even the film itself seems very convinced of. Its passion seems to be concentrated on the problem of the paradoxical self-consciousness emerging within the state of exception. It is precisely in the state of exception that we are no longer substantially capable of determining who is a friend and who is an enemy.[17] This is because we no longer know who "we" is, what it consists of, its essence, its purpose. The "we" is precisely that which can be conceived only within a normal situation. It is ultimately this aspect that the title of the film addresses. Oblivion refers less to the fact that we have forgotten our humanity (we have not; Jack clearly understands himself as a human) because we are using drones or other forms of deceptive modern technology. The notion of oblivion in Kosinski's film is far more radical; it refers to the fact that the "we," on the one hand, no longer remembers who or what it was in the normal situation, and on the other hand, *continues* acting as if it did. The characters still act as if there were a straight line back to normalization, which is no longer the case. The film is essentially about becoming aware of this fact.

We find this problematic precisely in connection with Jack and Vica's memory of their humanity. After Jack has saved the woman from the wreck and brought her home, he begins to speculate about the strange fact that they remember nothing from before the mission—that is, apart from the figure of the woman, who hitherto has been nothing but a strange, recurrent dream but who now turns out to have an actual connection to his reality. The next day, Jack and Julia (who has been in delta-sleep for at least sixty years) return to the wreck in order to find the flight recorder;

here, they are ambushed by the scavs and taken prisoners. Horrified, Vica watches everything from the control tower, albeit remaining calm and asking TET for drones to save them; ironically, this is also the moment when Vica's possible humanity, or rather struggle against her non-humanity, begins to reveal itself. Julia's reappearance seems to awaken something deep inside Vica's memories: namely, the time when she loved Jack, unhappily because he was with Julia. It is almost in the same moment that Jack, now one of the scavs' prisoners, discovers that the scavs are not aliens, but humans. After he has been convinced of the truth of their story and agrees to carry out their plan to mount a nuclear bomb on one of the drones and bring it to TET, he and Julia are released. On their way back, they end up at the Empire State Building, the exact same place as in the dream. Here, Julia reveals that she was Jack's wife before the catastrophe, and in the precise instant that they embrace (and thereby, in a sense, resume the temporal line that was disrupted by the alien invasion), the signal returns, and Vica watches them on the screen—at which point her human memories seem to break through her cloned consciousness, as she shouts "It was always her!" Her reaction is, one could say, *human*. She subsequently declares that they are no longer "an effective team," after which TET activates a destruction mechanism, a robot that attempts to kill them. In other words, here we find an actual exceptional situation that disrupts the (false) permanent state of exception in the precise moment when the human dimension resurfaces.

## Jack Harper and the Human

As we have observed, there are numerous examples throughout the film of Jack Harper's nostalgic attachment to the human. Later, when Jack is captured by the scavs, Beech tells him that he once observed Jack reading a book and that he thought there might be a core of humanity buried somewhere deep inside the clone.[18] This theme of rediscovering humanity runs throughout the entire film.[19] It is a human core that may be radically changed in biological form, but which still possesses an essence strong enough to survive a total physical transformation. Jack's dreams feel like a fragmented memory from the past—from the time before the war against the aliens—on top of the Empire State Building, where he asked Julia to marry him: that is, a crucial memory from the time everything was still normal, when the world was still normal, and Jack was still a normal, biological person.[20] "It feels like a memory; but how can it be?" asks Jack at one point, while he wonders why he keeps dreaming this same dream again and again.

The film thus presents a problematic related to self-consciousness; a narrating "I," Jack Harper, who gradually becomes conscious of the fact that the "I" that speaks to a "you"—that is, Julia, the woman in his dream, who later turns out to be his wife—is not the "I" who originally loved this woman: "I know you, but we've never met," as he melancholically reflects. It is the recognition of being infinitely reproducible, and at the same time possessing the self-conscious feeling of being unique. The voice we hear and instinctively associate with Jack Harper, who comes across as a unique individual, is actually a machine, a clone with what seems like a ROM self-consciousness of something that no longer exists. Here, we come back to the initial questions: why is this illusion created through the focalization of Jack Harper 49—and, in a further sense, why do the aliens really need to employ this structure of deception?

Here we need to ask another question: who are these aliens? We never actually see them, with the exception of a video image of Sally, a woman who is, however, likewise a clone of an original human being, now dead. Thus, we only ever see ourselves, not the real enemy. This does not, of course, mean that the enemy, in fact, does not exist, that the enemy, and thereby the existential threat, is only a figment of our imagination. The enemy is real and the danger is overwhelming. The point here is, rather, that the actual identification of the enemy—and, by implication, the identification of the real danger—*is something that can be done only within the normal situation*. In the state of exception, on the contrary, the figure of the enemy is confusing, ambiguous, perhaps even meaningless. It is from this perspective that one could argue that it might be misleading to assume that the aliens intentionally created the deceptive structure, that it is the alien consciousness that has deceived us humans, and that they needed to do so in order to achieve their goal. In the state of exception, the boundary between deception and reality becomes blurred. At this point, we can no longer make moral judgments based on who we are because we simply do not know who we are or what we fight for. At best, we might come to realize this conundrum—that who we think we are and what we fight against is misleading and deceptive.[21] The deceptive structure in *Oblivion* does not so much reveal an actual form of deception underneath which we find the truth; the truth of the deception is, rather, that the very coordinates for assessing *truth as such* have disappeared.

Within the film's zone of indistinction, we thus find a much more fascinating problematic: namely, that Jack's self-consciousness in reality is the one that emerges within the state of exception itself. It is the becoming-conscious of the exceptional situation itself—what it means, its radical consequences in reality. The deceptive structure is a way of articulating what self-consciousness might look like in the exceptional situation *as if* we were still inhabiting the normal world, although only to the extent that we delude ourselves. The more we start to wonder about the inconsistencies, gaps, and discrepancies, the more the fatal truth emerges: that the connection to the normal situation, the end of the exceptional time, is just as porous, artificial, and problematic as Jack's connection to his own humanity.

Jack wonders occasionally why they do not remember more than they do, whether they, in fact, remember anything real, and whether the memories he does seem to remember are actually his own. His self is an impossible "I," one that cannot be articulated within the framework of the exception. In the exceptional situation he has become someone else, one who perhaps, in the best-case scenario, vaguely remembers something from before, but only in the form of a fragmented dream that no longer seems to belong to himself entirely, or perhaps something ultimately dreamed by someone else. The problem surrounding self-consciousness and the issues of focalization are furthermore externalized in the film; the characters are generally separated, spending most of the time on their own in different rooms while communicating with each other: Vica in the control tower, Sally in TET, Jack flying around in the landscape or visiting his secret hut, while the scavs are tacitly there, watching them secretly at a distance. Constantly, the film underlines how the characters can see each other, and often communicate or hold information about each other, but cannot see what each is thinking, if they are thinking at all.[22]

It is in connection with the film's focalization through Jack Harper's self-consciousness that something very strange emerges: a thinking consciousness that appears absolutely normal, and yet at the same time, given the circumstances, a thinking consciousness that represents a form of absolute anomaly or otherness. The hut, which represents Jack's internal, private fantasy, is identical to the scenario that the original Jack dreams about and which Julia, his real wife, recognizes; it was this hut that Jack was always talking about, where they would grow old and die.[23] In the present situation, it exists like a secret, hidden miracle, an *exception* surrounded by vast oceans of abnormal territories. The hut quite simply represents the normal situation, while at the same time constituting a *pure fantasy*—that is, the fantasy of life before the state of exception. In the end, it is this kitschy–idyllic, unreal, enigmatic piece of fantasy that reconnects us to an idea of the normal situation. The problem is, however, that there is no place of return in this world; the normal situation—Earth before it was destroyed by the nuclear war against the aliens—simply no longer exists.

That the plot against the aliens thus, in reality, seems somewhat secondary is precisely due to the film's focus on Jack Harper's self-deception and his way back to humanity, which here simply represents the normal situation. Ultimately, it is the normal situation that defines what constitutes humanity, and hence the coordinates underlying the friend/enemy distinction: the self versus the existential other. Once we are in the state of exception, these coordinates become increasingly ambiguous and confusing. Thus, when Jack Harper 49 encounters Jack Harper 52 in a surreal scene in the desert, we find an illustration of this problematic: a mirror situation in which the possibility of distinguishing between friend and enemy is entirely dissolved. The other has become oneself. That both Jacks, in fact, fight for the aliens (and are unaware of this fact) is thus, in a sense, accidental; they could have fought for anyone or anything, and this is precisely the problem within the state of exception. In a literal sense, Jack is fighting against himself. It is in this moment, as Jack Harper 49 later tells Julia, that he discovers that he is already dead.[24] It is also in this very moment that he becomes self-conscious of the fact that the situation he lives in is a permanent state of exception.

## Repetition and Suicide

It is thus in relation to this problem that we must understand the famous eighth thesis of the history fragments, where Benjamin writes that the "tradition of the oppressed teaches us that the 'state of emergency' in which we live is not the exception but the rule" ("On the Concept" 392). History, to Benjamin, in the form it has been delivered to us, is written by the ones who won the wars; thus, "all rulers are the heirs of prior conquerors" (391). According to Benjamin, the critical task consists in breaking this false continuum of history, this empty homogeneous time, to wrestle the actual (broken, fragmented, repressed, or forgotten) truth from history—and thereby, as he writes, to encourage and hasten "a real state of emergency" (392). This comes about by blasting "open the continuum of history" (396), to "blast a specific era out of the homogeneous course of history" (396). Both Schmitt and Benjamin talk about a real state of exception, to be distinguished from the permanent state of exception in the form of an explosive moment blasting the empty, linear time that tells only the story of the "heirs of prior conquerors."[25]

In *Oblivion*, we see an almost literal illustration of this explosivity regarding the permanent state of exception, during the scene where Jack embarks on his last mission to detonate a nuclear bomb at TET. To destroy TET is thus a paradoxical form of remembering; to remember the time before the state of exception, Jack must destroy the false history created by TET, which essentially means destroying himself. During the suicide mission, Jack listens to the original flight recorder, 3–8–2019, and the scene visually changes into the scenes from the original mission. The goal of the original mission was to travel to Titan to investigate the possibilities of habitation. On the way, the travelers were ambushed by the aliens. Earth's moon must, at this point, have already been destroyed, which led to serious atmospheric disturbances. This is why people on Earth have come to the conclusion that they need a new home, and why the astronauts—including Jack, Julia, and Vica—have been sent on a mission to Titan. At this point, however, they have no clue about the impending alien invasion.[26]

Listening to the flight recorder, Jack Harper 49 remembers the original mission: how he communicated with the real Sally on the screen, how Vica always loved him unhappily, and that he was in love with Julia. While remembering the original mission, the scene visually—almost unnoticeably—slides back into the present, the present mission, the destruction of TET, but also, importantly, the destruction of Jack Harper 49 himself. In order to regain individuality, uniqueness, and, in the end, humanity, Jack Harper 49 must eliminate his own self, not simply as an individual, but as a concept. In the floating TET pyramid, Jack Harper 49 strangely witnesses the truth about himself: a horror cabinet of clones, thousands of Jack Harpers and Vicas—the best and brightest among the humans, now endlessly reproduced. That TET, in a physical sense, seems to consist of little else than these two clones (no aliens, no alien world) testifies to the future that awaits; this is, in a sense, the inner chamber of the permanent state of exception.[27] It is only when this permanent state of exception has been destroyed that Jack Harper can re-emerge as a normal human in the form of Jack Harper 52, now unique since his clone siblings have all been destroyed.

That Jack Harper 49 can get free access to TET is because the aliens want Julia's body, presumably so that they can clone her as well. However, Jack—without Julia being aware of this—replaces her with Beech, who, at this point, is mortally wounded. Jack's purpose is thus deceptive; he deceives the aliens in a similar way to how they deceived him.[28] We thus find a series of parallels during this final sequence, which together underlines the increasingly complex temporal problematic emerging during the final attempt to break out of the permanent state of exception, and rediscover the lost thread back to the normal situation. The mission is a kind of repetition, albeit not with the purpose of finding a new future (like the original mission), but rather to break out of the false continuum, the permanent state of exception, to create the conditions for a possible return to normality.

## Conclusion

*Oblivion* illustrates how the permanent state of exception in the future creates a paradoxical consciousness, in the sense that this consciousness can properly be understood only within a normal situation. It is fundamentally impossible to discern what it is in the actual permanent state of exception. Furthermore, the film illustrates one of the biggest challenges of the state of exception: how do we get out of it, how do we avoid its becoming permanent—*how does one return*? There are essentially three moments in the sovereign's decision on the exception: the decision as to what actually *constitutes* an exception; the decision as to what *exceptional measures* need to be implemented in order to preserve and protect the state; and finally, when it is *over*. The possibility of this tripartite structure of the decision lies deep within every legal constitution like an ahistorical premise, a necessity that can never fully be removed, although in stable times perhaps forgotten.[29] Benjamin would agree with the first two moments, although he would radically question the possibility of the third—the ability to decide when the state of exception is over—precisely because the sovereign decision possesses force only within a space that has not already been suspended. More specifically, the problem is that such a decision has already been made by the sovereign, who, in a constitutive sense, has been endowed with exceptional powers, to the extent that they may follow their own system of norms, one created by themselves. This problematic thus comes very close to the situation that runs parallel to the sovereign act of founding—for example, a new order (instead of returning to the old one).[30] It is in connection with this point that Benjamin observes—against the historical background of the 1930s rise of fascism—that the history of the oppressed teaches us that the state of exception has now become permanent.

Near the end of the film, Julia wakes up, hearing the explosion of TET, and to her great surprise, finds herself in Jack's idyllic little hut. She is, in other words, back in the normal situation. The normality of the latter is underlined by the fact that we immediately skip three years (that is, nothing significant happens in a political sense), at which point we see her with a little child (probably Jack Harper 49's child) playing with a toy gorilla (the same as in the dream sequence) while she works in the garden, a prehistoric tableau of peace and harmony, far removed from the horrors of the state of exception. In the scene, a group of human survivors approaches the hut. The first among them is a child. Although this is, in reality, a state of nature (since there is no government, no recognizable authorities), any sense of danger is absent. On the contrary, this is a prelapsarian state of nature, in which humans seem to be united in a community of fate after having survived a war against a monstrous enemy. Among the humans is Jack Harper 52. The film ends with his voice: "For three years I have searched for the house he built. I know him, I am him." The little girl, Julia's (and Jack Harper 49's) daughter, asks who he is: "I am Jack Harper, and I am home," he says, suggesting that Jack Harper 52's "I" merges with Jack Harper 49—and, ultimately, with the original Jack.

In a further sense, where does this voice come from, and who is actually speaking? Initially, the voice seems to confirm the very survival of human beings. However, from the perspective emphasized here, one could argue that this is the consciousness that emerges from within the state of exception—and *returns*. It is one that never fully returns to the normal situation before the exception because the "I" is now different, at least to the extent that Jack Harper 52 is different from the original Jack. But as the ending of the film suggests, it is a return that, at least, presents the possibility of believing that everything is or will be the same again as before, however fictional and deceptive this belief might be.

## Notes

1. As Meierhenrich observes, the declaration of the state of exception is justified "because its purpose was the preservation and re-equilibration of an existing political order, *not* the creation of a new order" (185)—yet this, of course, is precisely the dangerous possibility of the exceptional state.
2. This imaginary game might be a reference to the scene in which Jack Harper listens to the original flight recorder during the suicide mission to TET, the alien headquarters; here, Sally, the NASA mission director, at one point tells him that he had "a hell of a game last night"—which would have been played in 2017, fifty years ago.
3. See Agamben, *State* 52–64; Bredekamp 247–51; Heil 1–9; Weigel 110–11.
4. Benjamin's "pure violence" is a form of violence that does not preserve or found the law, but rather underpins a revolutionary force that seeks to emancipate the state from itself, the evil circle in which it is caught—the endless cycle of violence either founding or preserving the state. In Agamben's reading, Schmitt rejects any notion of violence occurring entirely outside the realm of law (for example, chaos, disorder). The state of exception is—Agamben claims—precisely the concept that Schmitt develops to bring back Benjamin's pure violence to the realm of the law: a violence "included in the law through its very exclusion" (Agamben, *State* 54).

5. As Agamben observes, "While the strategy of 'Critique of Violence' was aimed at ensuring the existence of a pure and anomic violence, Schmitt instead seeks to lead such a violence back to a juridical context. The state of exception is the space in which he tries to capture Benjamin's idea of pure violence and to inscribe anomie within the very body of the nomos" (*State of Exception* 54).
6. See Schmitt, *Political Theology* 5.
7. Schmitt derives this concept from the second letter to the Thessalonians in the New Testament (2 Thess. 2:7). See also Hell's article "*Katechon*"; Meuter's *Der Katechon*; and Balakrishnan's *The Enemy* 221–5.
8. After the danger has been averted, exceptional sovereignty must make itself redundant. If not, Schmitt observes, it becomes equivalent to "arbitrary despotism" (*Dictatorship* xlii).
9. See Agamben, *State of Exception* 52–64.
10. Bredekamp makes the point that Schmitt, later in his life (in 1973), claimed that his 1938 book on Hobbes was a response to Benjamin's *Trauerspiel*: "'Unfortunately, my attempt to respond to Benjamin by examining a great political symbol (the Leviathan in the political thought of Thomas Hobbes, 1938) went unnoticed'" (Schmitt cited in Bredekamp 261). When Benjamin first sent a copy of the *Trauerspiel* to Schmitt in 1925, the latter apparently never responded. In the 1970s, Benjamin's writings had become famous, especially among left-wing critics, and it is possible—as Bredekamp suggests—that Schmitt was simply "seeking some share in Benjamin's fame. He may have viewed this as a welcome opportunity to disguise the book's open anti-Semitism by describing it as a veiled answer to a Jewish emigrant" (Bredekamp 261).
11. While Delany no doubt has an important point when he argues that "Sf is not about the future; it uses the future as a narrative convention to present distortions of the present" (*Starboard* 48)—it might, in certain cases (especially works from the period that I discuss in this book), be more accurate to make the claim that sci-fi is one long attempt to *return* to the present—and, in a further sense, normality: that is to say, returning from the future as the state of exception.
12. This is, of course, Agamben's main criticism of Schmitt: that the sovereign's exceptional right to ensure the state's survival reduces life to "bare life." See Agamben, *Homo Sacer* 15–29. I will discuss this point further in Chapter 6.
13. As Geduld writes, science fiction has generally tended to subscribe to the humanist tradition, "insofar as it has usually assumed the primacy of man and his values, and insofar as it has expressed confidence and conviction concerning man's ability and need to survive any confrontation with the forces of a hostile or inscrutable universe" (142). *Oblivion* adheres to this tradition, while at the same time radically undermining it. See also Telotte (35–8) for further discussion of sci-fi as a humanist genre.
14. Foucault's notion of "race war" refers to a historical situation in which two—or more—groups of individuals come to perceive themselves as

ontologically different and fundamentally opposed to each other (although not necessarily in a biological sense); the other's existence is a threat to one's own existence (see Foucault, "*Society*" 77). This comes close to Schmitt's definition of the political, which likewise excludes references to biological racism (see, in particular, *Concept* 26).

15. On this issue, see Derek Gregory's "Drone Geographies" 7–9. While the title of the film, *Oblivion*, obviously refers to Jack's "memory swipe," it also emphasizes the importance of remembering something forgotten: namely, humanity. In a similar way, the drone functions like "memory swipes," allowing us to forget the war's inhuman dimensions, its monstrosity. The war of drones adds a dimension of unreality to war, in the sense that we never confront the enemy or see our victim with our own eyes; the drone destroys the enemy without our direct participation. The drone sees and kills for us, and thus allows us to ignore or forget the horror it causes.
16. Near the end of the film, Jack Harper programs the drone and observes that it is "just a machine." The irony is, of course, that Beech and his band of surviving humans need Jack to program the drone: that is, they need a machine, or at least a non-human being, to program another machine.
17. That the scavs wear metal helmets—to confuse the drones, but which also makes them look inhuman, alien—reinforces the illusion of their otherness.
18. This, again, raises the problematic of temporality. Is Beech here referring specifically to Jack Harper 49 or the generic model of Jack Harper? Is it the same book (by the lyric poet Horatius) or a different one? Did Jack Harper 49 build the hut or was it someone else, such as a previous model? Perhaps the hut was always there, all the way back to the original Jack Harper? What we *do* know is that it is when Jack Harper 49 meets Beech—a human—that he first starts to realize who or what he is: that is, a non-human.
19. Thus, the film refers, positively, to Andrew Wyeth's *Christina's World*, which reminds Julia of home: that is, the normal situation. The painting is essentially about the physical entrapment of the body, the autonomy of the mind, and the striving towards home. The analogy is clear: Jack Harper 49 is trapped within a cloned body, but his mind and memories are still in there, longing for home, or the normal situation.
20. In the grainy dream sequences, we see Jack asking Julia to look through the binoculars to see the future, while holding up a wedding ring. Later, Julia still has the wedding ring in her possession. What cannot be erased or forgotten, the film suggests, is human love.
21. Thus, we come very close to Hobbes's description of the state of nature—that is, a place of absolute negation: "In such conditions there is . . . no knowledge of the face of the earth; no account of time; no arts; no letters; no society" (*Leviathan* 78).
22. Beech, for example, secretly watches Jack in the early parts of the film; it is through this observation that Beech—in contrast to his men, who remain skeptical until the last part of the film—becomes convinced that the real

human Jack is buried somewhere inside the clone body. As Beech says: "You were in there, somewhere, I just had to find a way to bring you back"—even though it is unclear which "you" Beech is actually referring to.

23. After Jack Harper 49 has met Jack Harper 52 and realized that he is not the real Jack Harper, he flies back to the hut with the injured Julia. The latter tells Jack that "I've loved you for as long as I can remember. When the war is all over you'd built me a house on the lake, we'd grow old and fat together, and then die. And the world would forget about us, but we would always have each other." Jack tells her that he will come back to this place and live out the rest of his life here, with her. In a sense, this is true, but in order to do so, Jack will need to destroy TET and all the thousands of other Jack Harper copies, including himself.

24. Julia is initially repelled by this horrible discovery, but quickly comes around to the idea that Jack Harper 49 (and later Jack Harper 52) is the real Jack Harper. Jack Harper 49 is recognizable due to the scar on his nose. He flies to Jack Harper 52's control station in order to seek medicine for the injured Julia. Here, he meets Vica 52, who clearly believes that Jack Harper 49 is Jack Harper 52 (despite the scar on his nose). Somewhat oddly, he asks her to come with him but Vica reminds him of the regulations. Why does he ask her to come with him? Where would they go? And when Jack Harper 49 returns, Jack Harper 52 is gone. Where did he go? Would the original Jack Harper have done so, without the injured Julia? The doubling here raises a number of questions that the film leaves unanswered.

25. As Schmitt writes in *Political Theology*: "The rule proves nothing; the exception proves everything: It confirms not only the rule but also its existence, which derives only from the exception. In the exception the power of real life breaks through the crust of a mechanism that has become torpid by repetition" (15). For a discussion of this issue, see Bredekamp 264; and Wolin 433.

26. Originally, Jack Harper, Vica, Julia, and others were sent on a research trip to Titan. Six weeks before the crew arrives, they discover an alien object, TET, and Sally reassigns them to a different mission (probably combat engagement). This is why they are in delta sleep. Jack and Vica are the first to wake up, but right in that moment they are attacked and hijacked by the aliens. However, they manage to ejaculate the delta sleep capsules—which are the same ones Jack discovers sixty years later, now as a clone. There is a strange, and somewhat implausible, coincidence here between Jack Harper 49 discovering these capsules at this particular moment, and Beech simultaneously discovering something human inside Jack Harper 49's clone personality—which eventually leads to the revolution.

27. As Beech tells Jack Harper 49, the alien invasion consisted of thousands of Jack Harper clones, which, again, raises the whole question about the necessity of the deceptive structure.

28. When Sally tests Jack Harper 49's voice and tells him, bluntly, that he is lying—Jack responds by telling a story from Horatius about martyrium, and

about dying a good death against fearful odds. Jack Harper 49 is essentially repeating what he—or, rather, the original Jack Harper—did the first time around: namely, fight against a technologically superior enemy. This time, though, he is supposed to be on their side (hence Sally's desperate statement, "I created you Jack, I am your God," to which Jack responds "F*** you, Sally," before detonating the nuclear bomb.)

29. See Schmitt, *Political Theology* 7.
30. On this issue, see Kalyvas 1533; and Bussolini 64–9.

CHAPTER 6

# Escaping the Production of Bare Life: *Blade Runner 2049* and the Miracle of Birth

## Introduction

If one of the most intensely discussed issues in Ridley Scott's 1982 film *Blade Runner* centers around the question of whether Deckard is a replicant, and if this question, in reality, is a bit of a decoy, since the real question was always directed at the re-emergence of the traditional sovereign and his or her right to kill in the exceptional situation—that is, the death penalty implemented in those situations during which it would no longer be possible to clearly distinguish the human from the non-human—Denis Villeneuve's *Blade Runner 2049* (2017) is primarily about the right to *create life*. As the title suggests, the year is 2049, around thirty years after the first *Blade Runner* ended. It is essentially the same post-industrial, ravaged world, only less exotic and exciting, and more everyday and older—a *post-world* drained of all the adventurous and mysterious energy of the first film. The light is gray, indistinct, dull, feeble, creating a monotonous atmosphere, although clearly daylight, in contrast to the permanently dark atmosphere shrouding the first film. The central incident in the sequel is, in some sense, a natural development of the events from the first film—namely, the two lovers, Deckard and Rachael, having a child together. "Natural," that is, if it were not for the fact that this birth apparently constitutes a physical impossibility. It is an event that, even more radically than in the first film, questions the distinctions between the natural and the artificial, the human and the replicant.

While Scott's *Blade Runner* explored the idea of a sacred, human essence and eventually found this issue to be irresolvable (which was why the death penalty was activated as a way of containing this problematic), the sequel is, in many ways, about the same thing,[1] but also something fundamentally different: the circumstances surrounding who has the right to give and create life—rather than the right to live as a human, and thereby the right to kill those who are not defined as humans. That replicants are now able to give birth, something hitherto believed to be impossible, is thus the scandal in the sequel—the event that threatens to destabilize the status quo. Birth—whether biological or artificial, or a mixture of the two—suggests something beyond the control of a creator, and hence beyond the control of power. In the first *Blade Runner*, Tyrell clearly held the monopoly on this right, just as he held the monopoly on the right to kill. In the sequel, this monopoly is being challenged; here, we have a life that, for the first time in history, is born beyond the reach of power. But what does it mean that something is born outside the monopoly of power? This question ultimately relates to the idea of life beyond the grip of the political, a life created and lived outside the sovereign's definition of what constitutes a legitimate life form. It is here that the intimacy of the relationship between the sovereign and life as such is finally revealed. What we find in *Blade Runner 2049* is, in many ways, a further development of the problematic in the first film: namely, the replicant as the culmination of the biopolitical, which, at the same time, coincides with the eradication of the sharp border, not so much between human and non-human, since this border was transgressed long ago (or, more exactly, in the first film), but rather, between the sovereign decision to protect civilization and life, and the production of bare life.

According to Carl Schmitt, the sovereign's legitimacy basically stems from the exception, and the purpose of the latter: the elimination of chaos in order to ensure that life may survive. To Agamben, however, by reducing the ultimate aim of life to mere survival as the primary objective, Schmitt's sovereign effectively transforms life into bare life, the *homo sacer*. The replicant represents, in many ways, the absolute culmination of the biopolitical production of bare life, and thereby the ultimate expression of the sovereign's power. *Blade Runner 2049*, I argue, attempts to articulate something that escapes this sphere of sovereign power: the miracle of birth.

## Opening Crawl

Like the first film, *Blade Runner 2049* begins with an apocalyptic opening crawl, a green, blinking cursor on a black screen, writing out lines whose author is similarly unknown. Where do these words come from? Who writes them? It is as if the opening crawl, in both the original and the sequel, attempts to create a neutral, invisible, and thus, in a sense, *impossible* point of articulation, a machine-like, telegraphic, objective voice, like an omniscient perspective floating somewhere above the film's diegesis. At the same time, the text anchors the film's fictional diegesis to its background history—that is, the first film and everything in between.

We learn that Earth's ecosystems have collapsed, presumably as the result of overpopulation, resource depletion, and pollution. Global famine was averted due to the artificial farming programs invented by the industrialist Niander Wallace, who thus becomes the *de facto* savior and guardian of Earth's population, the new biopolitical god figure. It is a role he has further consolidated by taking over the Tyrell Company, which went bankrupt after the production of replicants was outlawed due to an increase in rebellions. Wallace continues the production of replicants, albeit a newer kind; different from Tyrell's Nexus-6, these new models do not have a built-in limited life span. Whereas the Tyrell Company was eventually derailed by the state authorities, Niander Wallace is evidently in such a powerful position that he can ignore the state ban on producing replicants. His company thus constitutes a state within the state; in fact, throughout most of the film, Wallace's company is directly antagonistic to the police and the authorities.[2] Wallace's new replicants are different in the sense that they simply obey; their task is to hunt down and kill the old Nexus models.

One of the important things to keep in mind regarding a political reading of *Blade Runner 2049* is that its futuristic world does not relate directly to our present. In a temporal perspective, the film locates itself *in extension* of the first film's temporality (which, of course, operated with a future temporality in relation to our present time). This is essentially what the opening crawl establishes: a *pre-history* from the first film (just as the opening crawl in the first film did in relation to our present).[3] In Scott's *Blade Runner*, the opening crawl indicated that the film was merely a fragment of a much larger story, a supplement to a larger plot. In the sequel, the words directly comment on the story from the first film; it thus transforms the latter's mythological universe into a genuine *original* (whereby we forget that the first film likewise defined itself as a "sequel"), which perhaps explains the many flashbacks and direct visuals from the first film. In this sense, there is a thematic connection between the sequel's major event, the birth, and the fact that the first film "gave birth," so to speak, to the sequel; the latter literally originates from the first film's story. As a sequel, *Blade Runner 2049* precisely asks questions on a thematic level about the idea of coming after something, to have an origin, the problematic of something preceding oneself. Thus, it deviates from many other sci-fi films, including those we have discussed here. Although the sequel articulates a similar problematic to those we have seen in other films—namely, the permanent state of exception within the imagination of the future—what *Blade Runner 2049* essentially attempts to do is not to return to the present, to our time, but rather to imagine a future within the horizon of the future itself.

Whereas the major problem in *Blade Runner* was the culmination of the biopolitical, the total separation of bare life from its form of meaning, in the shape of replicants—which, at the same time, articulated a vision of perfect being and thereby emerged as a *threat* to the very concept of the human—what we find in the sequel is a further development of this problematic. To make replicant life as efficient as possible, the Tyrell Company inserted "implants," artificial memories, which apparently made them more emotionally robust. The first film's emancipatory project involved the liberation from these artificial memories and the attempt to create new, authentic memories.[4] In the sequel, these new memories have now become real, in a literal sense, via the birth of the child.[5] The entire film is essentially about this transgression of the physically impossible—that is, the fact that a replicant not only believes that she is "human," but actually proves it through giving birth, regardless of any Voight-Kampff machine. Birth here articulates the defiant struggle to bring together bare life and its form of meaning once again, and the fight against those forces represented by the figure of Wallace, the sovereign, and his henchmen attempting to keep them separate.

## Agamben's *Homo Sacer*

To Giorgio Agamben, bare life, or zoé, designates the notion of life as such in its stark and brutal, biological sense, entirely separated from or devoid of any other form of meaning. To capture the exact implications of this extremely reduced notion of life, Agamben refers to the archaic Roman concept of the *homo sacer* ("sacred man" or "accursed").[6] One of the crucial points about the *homo sacer* figure in Agamben's use is that it is not a naturally occurring phenomenon; someone, something, will have to directly intervene in the circumstances of life in order to create a biological human being entirely devoid of any other form of meaning. Although the concept of the *homo sacer* is no longer used in legal contexts, Agamben identifies a similar structure within political societies today: the "unnatural" production of bare life is intimately linked to the legitimacy of sovereignty, even in contemporary politics.

As the guardian of the law, the sovereign is the entity supposed to ensure the safety and security of citizens, and the punishment of those citizens who harm others. When a life is no longer protected by the law, the sovereign will no longer punish those harming this life: *homo sacer* is a person whose killing entails no punishment. But at the same time, the *homo sacer* figure also entails the rather strange notion of a person who cannot be sacrificed to the gods.[7] There is a double ban involved in the figure of the *homo sacer*, whereby a life form is excluded from both the human law and the divine law at the same time.

Agamben argues that the *homer sacer* figure is intimately connected to the very premise of sovereign power. If life, even in its most reduced biological sense, is nonetheless still the highest priority, there is a danger of potentially reducing the politics of life to a question of mere survival at any cost, and which, in turn, must be protected at any cost by the sovereign. What is forgotten at the same time is the *form* of life. To Agamben—and it is in this connection that he (following Arendt) criticizes discourses on human rights—life is never in itself simply bare life, the *homo sacer*. Life is always-already understood as something more than simply "biologically alive": what it is doing, what it can be, rather than simply what it is (that is, alive). In the case of the latter, the "it" is elevated to something "sacred," at which point we come to accept the possibility of bare life, or life entirely separated from or devoid of any other form of meaning.

The purpose of the legal realm is typically to ensure that life and its meaning, its form, are not separated—that life, in its many forms, may unfold meaningfully within a sphere of peace, safety, and regularity. The sovereign will punish those who disturb this sphere of peace, "those" being criminal individuals whose lives are "cleansed" through punishment, and hence prepared for inclusion in the legal sphere of peace or society again (albeit, in the case of capital punishment, typically in the very moment they are executed, or rather because they are executed in that very moment). To Agamben, the sovereign thus becomes the figure who guarantees that life and form are never separated—but also, paradoxically, the figure who, in fact, insists on this possibility of separation in the first place. Hence the figure of the *homo sacer*: being excluded from both the human and the divine world, the *homo sacer* occupies what Agamben calls a "zone of indistinction."[8] The point is that this figure is so far beyond any possibility of redemption or cleansing that there is no way this person could ever be given even a minimal chance of returning to human society, even in the moment of death.

To Carl Schmitt, the sovereign comes into existence through the decision on the exception. More specifically, the sovereign may, under certain exceptional circumstances—that is, times of existential danger, suspend what is otherwise the norm. In peaceful times the sovereign lies dormant, inactive. In the normal situation it is quite simply difficult to identify and decide what constitutes an exception; there are no specific predefined rules that may help us here. In other words, no normative framework—such as a constitution—can make this decision. This is why the sovereign, in Schmitt's view, steps into being in the very moment of decision;

sovereignty is precisely revealed in this act of making a decision.[9] The sovereign is outside the law in the sense that he or she may suspend it; but the sovereign is also directly connected to the law, and hence in a sense inside it—precisely because he or she may legally suspend it. The sovereign's decision constitutes, in fact, the very possibility of the law or, rather, the fact that the sovereign decides *not* to decide, to remain *indecisive*; this is what constitutes the possibility of the normal situation. Agamben's point here is that the sovereign's paradoxical relation to the law is that of *included exclusion*; the sovereign is included as the one who has not made the exclusive decision (yet).[10]

If sovereignty, to Agamben, ultimately is included exclusion, the figure of *homo sacer* is, paradoxically, included in a more or less identical way.[11] Agamben's sovereign is the one who has the right to produce bare life as included exclusion in the normative legal realm. To Schmitt, the legitimacy of the sovereign—his or her right to suspend the constitution *in toto*—is ultimately grounded in the fight against the state of nature. Without this right to suspend the constitution, the state would be unable to defend itself against all kinds of imaginable and unimaginable threats. Agamben's point is that Schmitt thereby legitimizes sovereign power on the basis of the notion of life as sacred, and hence on the basis of the survival of life in whatever form as the highest priority. This, then, leads to ever more extreme forms of biopolitical situations or, more precisely, the production of the *homo sacer* figure.

Agamben's *Homo Sacer* is essentially a warning against the sovereign act of reducing life's highest purpose to a brute, biological fact. As such, the latter becomes indistinguishable from the life in the state of nature—life reduced to brute survival. Sovereignty legitimizes itself as the guardian of life and its biological survival, but thereby also includes exclusion, the figure of the *homo sacer*. To Agamben, the sovereign's original task is thus not simply to prevent the state of nature, but rather to reproduce it within the normative realm of the state in the form of the *homo sacer* figure.[12]

## Replicant and Pregnancy

What *Blade Runner 2049* attempts to envision is a point after this stage, during which the total or maximum production of bare life has become not only a distinct possibility, but, in fact, the norm—that is, a *normal situation* during which bare life is included in the law in the most intensive ways—as excluded. What does it mean in this connection to create a life outside the monopoly of power? What consequences result from challenging power's monopoly on producing and creating life?

One of the most central passages in the film is the scene during which the police and the medical doctors investigate Rachael's bones. At this stage, they are not aware that she is a replicant; however, they quickly discover that she was young and died while giving birth. It is K, the blade runner replicant who found the skeleton, who discovers the serial number, indicating that Rachael was unquestionably a replicant. Why can the doctors see that Rachael died while giving birth, but not that she is a replicant? What is entailed in this difference? It is possible that K has supernatural sight (something illustrated in a later scene during which he goes through microfilm images of DNA sequences at extreme speed), but it once again emphasizes that the difference between replicants and human bodies is ambiguous; it is so minimal that even medical specialists are unable to tell the difference, but at the same time significant enough since K is the only one to make the discovery.

Joshi, the police superintendent and K's boss, is utterly perplexed by this discovery and insists that K must remain silent about it. It is a dangerous moment because it possibly redefines the political field; no one at this stage knows how anyone will react to the discovery. In other words, we are talking about a scandal with potentially catastrophic consequences, the scope of which no one at this point clearly understands. But the police understand enough to activate the death penalty. It is thus after this discovery that Joshi reacts in the usual way in the exceptional situation: she orders K to get rid of the child, to make it disappear so that the status quo may be maintained.

To kill older replicants is not a problem for K, even if he himself is a replicant. This is his job and, in the wider sense, his raison d'être. Literally, K is in sleep mode the first time we meet him; he wakes up only when a radio sound indicates that he has arrived at the place where he is about to liquidate Morton Saper, or at least arrest him (and probably then kill him). The blade runner job is the executive element of the sovereign's gesture, the execution of the death penalty.[13] As Morton, an older model, says when K arrives: how does it feel to kill one's own?[14] K responds dryly that the newer models do not run away, and probably not just because there are simply no longer places to escape to (as in the first film), but rather because the new models have no illusions of living a normal life as humans.[15] But killing a child, even a child who has been miraculously, impossibly, born to a replicant, leads K, perhaps for the first time, to speculate on the idea of being, of having a soul, and, in the wider sense, being unique and original—everything that is monopolized and concentrated in the concept of the human.

In the first film, replicants were built with a four-year life span. That is why Roy and the others were so desperate to come to Earth; they thought

Tyrell could give them a longer life. In the sequel's opening crawl, we hear that the subsequent models, the Nexus 8s, do not have such a fixed life span. These replicants survived when the Tyrell Group collapsed, and these are the ones that K, in his job as a blade runner, hunts down to kill and exterminate. That Nexus 8 and all subsequent models, including K, have no built-in fixed life span means that they can potentially live longer than humans. The fact that Nexus 6s had a four-year life span but, at the same time, were hunted and killed before they died was always one of the strange things about the plot in the first film, which seemed to emphasize that it was not death in itself that constituted the problem, but rather the right to decide on death.

In the sequel, we have a further development of this right, albeit in a very different form. Here, the right applies not only to the decision on death, but also to the reproduction of life. Whereas, in the first film, there appeared to be a ban on the individual's right to die in his or her own way, in the sequel there exists a further ban on individual reproduction. This ban is not explicit but rather a construction built into the replicant's body structure. It ought to be impossible for them to reproduce, physically, individually, and autonomously, just as it was impossible for Roy and the other replicants to exceed the four-year life span.[16]

The fact that Deckard and Rachael were able to have a child thus indicates a transgression of the frames within which humans, and more specifically Tyrell, created their inventions. The point here is that it was a possibility that, via Rachael and Deckard as parents, was already present in the first film.[17] If this possibility were not already present in the first film, the sequel quite simply would not have existed. At this point, people are no longer just creators of passive robot slaves; they are creators of beings who have now become creators themselves. What we find here is, in fact, a difference that, in many ways, illustrates the difference between Schmitt's point that the sovereign gesture is based on the exception, and that this exception is legitimized by excluding chaos and anarchy—and then Agamben's point that this exclusion of chaos ultimately leads to the reduction of life to bare life, included as excluded. According to Agamben, the sovereign gesture is ultimately based on the production of bare life within the sphere of the law itself—that is, the normal situation.[18] And it is this monopoly on the production of bare life that the birth challenges. The transgression, in the form of the replicants' independent, "natural" reproduction or birth, is a threat that potentially changes the political coordinates of the present. The birth is truly a miracle, something nobody believed was possible. It basically constitutes a moment that potentially disrupts the permanent state of emergency, Wallace's—and before him,

Tyrell's—monopoly on life, a concrete life that breaks through the crust of power.

## Witnessing the Future

One could argue that the central event in the film is about witnessing a miracle: the physically impossible birth of a life beyond the monopoly of power, which, in a wider sense, abolishes or at least threatens the sovereign's monopoly on the enforcement of the death penalty. To enforce the death penalty on behalf of the sovereign—that is what K does, as Morton tells him when K comes to his house with the intention of arresting and probably killing him—because the latter has never witnessed a true miracle. It is a phrase echoing several times in K's head during the film; if one has seen a miracle—if one has concrete evidence that the impossible can happen—then it no longer makes sense to carry out the sovereign order of the death penalty.[19] Thus, to witness a miracle more specifically means having hope for the future—a different, better future where life becomes meaningful not just in and for itself, but also in relation to others, to the past, and to those still unborn, the generation that will inherit this world.

The film starts by witnessing this terrifying future. The first film begins with an eye that witnesses an explosive future (literally, images of explosions are reflected on the retina). The sequel also begins with an eye that, however, looks more natural and fragile. Nothing is reflected in the eye, as if there is no consciousness or self-reflection present. Its patterns coincide with the subsequent external images of endless, hypnotic circles of solar panels, and then Anthropocene fields—Wallace's artificial crops that saved humanity. It is, at the same time, a scenario suggesting the total production and exhaustion of Earth's potential.[20] Everything in this brave new world has been tainted by human interests. Nothing seems to escape this desperate desire for exploitation.

Whereas the first film opens with an eye witnessing the arrival of the future as a new, alluring, and outrageous adventure, the eye in the sequel is a blank and exhausted eye that has already witnessed the coming of the future and the fatal consequences it has had. It looks natural because the question of whether it is real or artificial is no longer really exciting or important.[21] While Vangelis's music in the first film is dreamy, grandiose, extravagant, expectant, and overwhelming, the music in the sequel is stifling, poisonous, and deadly, like the sound of monstrous turbines running amok. It is the sound of the death of nature. While the first film was cloaked in a permanent darkness, nothing is hidden in the sequel: the massive and devastating destruction of Earth appears in plain daylight.

Thus, the opening sequence places the film heavily within a temporality of *coming-after*, the time after the first film. Out of the artificiality of the first film's universe, its existential doubts about authenticity, something naturally was created: the birth of a child, but also, in a further symbolic sense, the rebirth of the natural. This is why the sequel constantly dwells on issues of fertility, reproduction, nature, ecosystems, and so forth. These issues move beyond narrow questions about selfhood and individual originality; they suggest that identity formation is ultimately related to something beyond the self. While the first film was really about the problem of the *lack* of originality, the sequel converts the first film into a kind of original, and hence "authentic," source. In the first film, Rachael was haunted by questions about her originality—the photos of her predecessors, whether they were genuine, and whether her feelings and memories were real or just copies of those of Tyrell's niece. In the sequel, Rachael has become a mother, just like the figure in her beloved family photo, except that this time the photo is not fake, precisely because the authenticity of this photo is confirmed and authenticated by the events of the first film. In a sense, the sequel is thus one long, dignified response to that devastating scene in the first film during which Rachael desperately attempts to convince Deckard that she is human, that she has a mother, and that her photos—her memories—are real.

## The Monstrous Hypothesis

It is in this context that we must understand the miraculous. *Blade Runner 2049* focuses intensely on the death of nature. The future we encounter in the film is one that has destroyed and erased almost everything from the old world, quite literally, through the event of the Blackout, which signifies a kind of rupture, as if the referential connection to the past has now been severed and hence denaturalized. It is a time *after* the world reached the point of absolute maximum production (in the 2020s, when the natural ecosystems collapsed, around the time the first film ends), the latter represented through Wallace's artificial farming, which averted worldwide famine. This is the normative situation: the private sector becoming more powerful than the state, and hence being in a position to challenge the latter's monopoly of power. After having resumed Tyrell's replicant production line (and presumably ignoring the state ban on the production of replicants, which was the reason why Tyrell's company eventually failed), Wallace retroactively attempts to rewrite the original. According to Wallace, Tyrell had discovered the technique of replicant reproduction, and he even indicates that Deckard and Rachael were always supposed to meet, fall in love, and have a child.[22] In the first film, replicants are given implants, treasured memories to which strong feelings are attached because this provides them with a psychological pad that makes them more resistant. Thus, when Wallace indicates that Deckard and Rachael were always supposed to develop a romantic relationship that might lead to reproduction—Tyrell's last trick, as he calls it—this is basically a natural evolution of an extreme biopolitical desire to create the perfect slave.

At the same time, this monstrous suggestion seems to be an almost violent intervention in our understanding of the first film, for was it not precisely the romance that ultimately opened a new vision of emancipation— the authentic love that made the other questions (who is human? on what basis?) irrelevant? Why is Wallace suggesting that the only "real" thing in the first film—love—was part of the biopolitical narrative? Clearly, this biotechnological development has not yet been put into production; Wallace is obviously obsessed with this opportunity, but at the same time, it is one that he is unable to control. This is ultimately why he is so obsessed with Deckard and the question of what actually happened in the first film.

K begins to suspect that his implant may be a real memory and that he might have been born, instead of artificially created, when he discovers the date inscribed in the tree at Morton's house. It arouses something in him, a scene from childhood when he was chased by other children who wanted to burn his wooden horse. On the wooden horse (and the tree), the date is engraved: 06.10.12—the child's birthday. Dates signify something specific and exact, but dates are also referred to because the timeline no longer occurs naturally, as if there is something broken and disrupted about natural time. In other words, there is a need for fixed points to anchor an absent or fragmented temporality in the plot. The box that K finds next to the tree, which contains Rachael's bones after she died in childbirth, has been buried for approximately thirty years. We also hear that Morton Saper has been a farmer there since 2020. It was around this time, as the opening crawl tells us, that Earth's ecosystem collapsed—and when the first film ends. The sequel takes place in the year 2049. Hence, Rachael and Deckard's child must be around thirty years old, about the same age as K.

The enormous Blackout that deleted all digital files lasted ten days, after which very little was left. This is the main reason why the timeline is so fragmented. As one of the archivists dryly points out, paper was the only thing that was preserved.[23] Ironically, it is this almost-clean slate that allows both Deckard and his child to remain hidden for all those years. The lack of information also allows K to begin dreaming that perhaps he was actually this child—a replicant family romance that causes anxiety (the fear of being original) but also generates a mad desire to be "real."[24]

When K starts to suspect that he may be the missing child, he promptly fails the police test, which is a kind of reverse Voight-Kampff machine in the sense that *failing* the test means that he is not replicant *enough*.[25] But in a further sense, failing the test also suggests that he has become more human. At this point, the same logic sets in: the ambiguity of who or what he is leads to the potential activation of the death penalty. Joshi gives him forty-eight years, after which he is "on his own," as she puts it—that is, after which he will be hunted down and executed by other blade runners.

## The Past as an Esper Machine

Memories play an ambiguous role in both films, typically representing an emancipatory desire (to be real), but also something that puts life in danger, something that potentially activates the death penalty. In the first film, Deckard uses the so-called Esper machine in his detective work, allowing him to scan depths and angles that would otherwise not have been possible in a normal photo. Whereas photos in the first film refer to memory (and hence something human)—which, however, can be manipulated (as with Rachael's false photos)—these play a much more fluid role in the sequel.[26] Here, people are generally far less obsessed with the photograph's referential, indexical status. This limit or law of referentiality seems to have been exceeded a long time ago. In fact, while Rachael in the first film is shocked to learn that her photos are false, K seems equally disturbed when he realizes that the photos of Rachael and her child are possibly genuine.

The sequel is a bit like one of these bottomless, inexhaustible photos in the first film; while the Esper machine in the earlier film allowed Deckard to trace replicants and their past, the visual metaphor of this technological device is extended in the sequel almost to the entire plot. In a sense, one could say that this is exactly how the sequel imagines the future of the future: as one of these unfathomable, endless photos containing an indefinite number of angles, traces, and stories. In the sequel, K moves around the landscape almost in the same way that Deckard did in connection with the photo of the snake woman in the first film to uncover the secret of the past, and thus the answer to the mystery of the present. Deckard is important in the sequel because he represents a transitional figure between the old world (the first film) and the new (the sequel)—in between which there is the Blackout, which has deleted virtually all connections. He is, furthermore, ambiguous, in the sense that he seems both natural and unnatural, perpetrator and innocent, assassin and victim at the same time. At one point, Deckard tells K that he once had his job, which indicates not only that Deckard might also be a replicant, but also the fact that, sooner or later, K himself will be hunted. It is through Deckard that the new world seeks answers about the old world. He represents the most tangible trace that connects the old world with the new one.[27]

## The Sovereign and *Homo Sacer*

Both K and Wallace attempt to recreate original circumstances. K is desperate to find out whether he was really born; Wallace is obsessed with the possibility of reproduction, how replicants can give birth. In the sequel, the character of Deckard first appears in a video clip from the first film,[28] which means that the erasure during the Blackout was not total. Wallace's archive seems to have survived, suggesting further that Wallace was possibly the one behind the Blackout and that it was part of his attempt to monopolize knowledge, and hence power.

Wallace first appears in a sequence in which he inspects a new replicant model, which is lowered down from a ceiling while immersed in transparent plastic packaging. It is a birth scene, albeit wholly artificial, one that vividly evokes the intimate relationship between the figure of the *homo sacer* and the sovereign. In the figure of Wallace, biopolitical sovereignty and traditional sovereignty coincide. Tenderly caressing the new replicant model, Wallace seems to be almost in love with his creature, but then he stabs it, for no other reason than to manifest his absolute sovereign power. As a father figure, he tells Deckard (who accuses him of being cruel because he has never had any children) that he has millions of children: the replicants. The wider project, as Wallace observes, is to create a slave army of millions of replicants to colonize the universe, or to "own the stars," as he poetically formulates it.

In the film, Wallace always appears in the same mysterious settings: subterranean spaces that are never quite bright or dark, illuminated by rays reflected through large water basins, creating a particularly intense atmosphere of something not only mythological and divine, but also organic and natural. It underlines his omni-paternal character, like a kind of doomsday prophet speaking on behalf of universal humanity, or simply a vessel for power itself. The film even indicates that Wallace himself might be a replicant. His eyes look misty, as if he is blind. At one point, Luv inserts a small electronic device into Wallace's neck, after which he is able to control small drones inspecting the new replicant model. While the Tyrell character represented a combination of shrewd business tycoon and scientist, Wallace is far more ambiguous and inscrutable—more apocalyptic, religious, psychopathic.

In the first film, Roy Batty returned to Tyrell like the lost son. In the sequel, K also makes a return like the lost son, albeit to Deckard, not Wallace. There is a genuine problem of paternity in the sequel: the question of the legitimate father. Wallace can recreate a perfect copy of Rachael, though not quite; Deckard can still tell the difference, even without the help of a machine, thus exposing the limitations of Wallace's biopolitical ambitions. Ironically, Wallace himself is an "illegitimate" or self-claimed heir, standing in the shadow of his "creator," Tyrell, whose identity (human or replicant) was never entirely clear either. There is no "natural" link between Tyrell's and Wallace's corporations *except* the same biopolitical ambition driving both characters. What Wallace manages to fulfill is the potential already formulated by Tyrell in the first film: the monstrous hypothesis, or the total and absolute inclusion of the excluded life—that is, the bare life.

## Conclusion

What is at stake here is ultimately an articulation of a biopolitical dynamic whose structure comes close to Agamben's figure of the *homo sacer*. Wallace has taken over the replicant project from Tyrell, refined it, and made it even more viciously biopolitical by discovering new ways of separating bios and zoé further—that is, the production of bare life. What happens in the film is that this bare life miraculously manages to transcend this distinction through the event of birth. It is the event of birth that represents the abolition of the biopolitical production of bare life, and thus ultimately heralds the birth of the political. As Hannah Arendt observes in *The Human Condition*, the

> miracle that saves the world, the realm of human affairs, from its normal, "natural" ruin is ultimately the fact of natality, in which the faculty of action is ontologically rooted. It is, in other words, the birth of new men and the new beginning, the action they are capable of at virtue of being born. (247)

Through the concept of natality, Arendt formulates an idea that a life being born enters the world with a promise that this world's future is full of opportunities for individual action—that is, a political existence.

In the sequel, a ghostly question emerges as we reach the outermost limit of biopolitics: now that bare life has been included in the most absolute sense, what has become of the sovereign's foundational gesture, to declare the state of exception in order to protect and ensure the survival of life at all costs? What Wallace, in reality, strives for at this absolute threshold of biotechnology is to rule over the very miracle of life, that which, ultimately, is the very reason for the political, or why we need the political in the first place. At this point, we find, on the one hand, the total coincidence of biopolitical sovereignty and traditional sovereignty, and on the other hand, bare life freeing itself through the autonomous miracle of birth.[29] It is this remainder of autonomy, the miracle, that escapes Wallace, and which he is so desperate to possess. As a doomsday prophet, Wallace proclaims his monstrous ambitions of colonizing the entire universe, the enormous worlds he wants to create, yet he is basically limited by the biological fact of birth, which raises the question of paternal legitimacy. Additionally, underneath this question of paternal legitimacy, we ultimately find the subversive question of sovereign legitimacy. In the first film, we see the culmination of the sovereign production of bare life, and, as a consequence a radical questioning of the border between humans and replicants.[30] Ultimately, the replicant constitutes the absolute boundary that divides life from its form (*homo sacer*) and also that which threatens to transform all life into bare life. Birth (and, more specifically, replicants giving birth), the theme of the sequel, is that which insists on the impossibility of separating zoé from bios: life and the form of life.[31]

*Blade Runner 2049* begins at a point in history where life cannot be further separated from its form, a biopolitical process already initiated in the first film. At the same time, the first film literally contained the possible seed of an act of transgression, even if, as Wallace suggests, Tyrell had planned this all along: the birth of Rachael and Deckard's child. The sequel rewrites this into an emancipatory project in which the birth again assumes the miraculous form that Arendt formulated through the concept of natality—or, in Agamben's vocabulary, where life is once again born into a state no longer radically separated from its form—and which subsequently becomes the potential beginning of a replicant revolution against the totalitarian regime of Niander Wallace.

The child, it turns out, is the Memory Maker, which ironically brings us back to that traumatic scene in the first film during which Deckard tells a desperate Rachael that all her childhood memories belong to someone else. In the sequel, Rachael's dignity is restored, one might say: the Memory Maker creating replicant implants is her own daughter, who, in a sense, retroactively authenticates Rachael's photo. It is in this way that the sequel imagines the possibility of life and its form of meaning brought together again, and hence, in a further sense, articulates a resistance narrative against those forces, represented by Wallace, who attempt to separate them by all means possible. The film ends with K lying on the stairs in the snow; meanwhile, the daughter conjures up images of snowflakes—a soothing, reconciliatory juxtaposition suggesting that the sharp distinction between implants and reality has now dissolved. As Deckard enters the building, he finally confirms the miracle of birth beyond the reach of sovereign power. Overall, *Blade Runner 2049* offers a glimpse of *the future of the future*, or a vision of what comes after *our* future—that is, the birth of a political subject no longer bound by the political coordinates of the present.

## Notes

1. In the sequel, blade runners still hunt outlawed replicants, and these blade runners are now clearly replicants themselves, in contrast to the first film, where it was unclear whether Deckard was a human or a replicant. The fact that—as the opening crawl explicitly mentions—they are *also* called "blade runners" indicates, perhaps indirectly, that the blade runners in the first film, including Deckard, were also replicants.
2. They are, in fact, direct competitors throughout much of the film. For example, Joshi, the police superintendent, does not reveal anything to Wallace about the discovery of the pregnant replicant; Luv, a replicant carrying out Niander Wallace's orders, subsequently kills one of the medical workers at the police station in order to obtain Rachael's bones, and later kills Joshi to obtain information about the child.
3. Scott's *Blade Runner* employed the detective genre (Deckard as a detective tracing escaped replicants in order to kill them), and Villeneuve's film likewise uses this genre—albeit in order to trace and reconstruct what actually happened in the first film. Thus, K meets and interrogates several characters from the first film, such as Detective Gaff and Deckard.
4. In reality, the only emancipatory possibilities in the first film were limited to escape, death at the hands of blade runners, "expiration," or suicide.
5. Quite literally, K starts to investigate the reality of his memories (which he believed hitherto were implants: that is, fake), and really does find a wooden horse—as he remembered it—in the furnace.
6. Citing Pompeius Festus's definition, Agamben writes: "The sacred man is the one whom the people have judged on account of a crime. It is not permitted to sacrifice this man, yet he who kills him will not be condemned for homicide; in the first tribunitian law, in fact, it is noted that 'if someone kills the one who is sacred according to the plebiscite, it will not be considered homicide'. This is why it is customary for a bad or impure man to be called sacred" (*Homo Sacer* 71). Additionally, one could understand "sacred man" to imply that this individual is no longer protected by humans, or human law; he is at the mercy of the gods (although the fact that he cannot be sacrificed suggests that the person is also excluded from this realm).

7. It is important to note that Agamben explicitly rejects the psychoanalytic notion of the ambiguous connection between the sacred and the filthy, unworthy. Historically, within ancient Roman law, punishment and sacrifice were closely connected; to be punished according to human law was, at the same time, to be cleansed, and hence prepared as a worthy gift for the gods (see Agamben, *Homo Sacer* 81). To be sentenced to death, one's life was thus reinvested with divine meaning—and this reinvestment is what the figure of the *homo sacer* is denied. What the *homo sacer* is denied is, ultimately, that his life may yet again become meaningful, formed (if only in the last moments of a person's life). It remains, in other words, bare life, even on the threshold of death.
8. See Agamben, *Homo Sacer* 83.
9. To Agamben, this means that "The paradox of sovereignty consists in the fact that the sovereign is, at the same time, outside and inside the juridical order. If the sovereign is truly the one to whom the juridical order grants the power of proclaiming a state of exception and, therefore, of suspending the order's own validity, then 'the sovereignty stands outside the juridical order and, nevertheless, belongs to it, since it is up to him to decide if the constitution is to be suspended *in toto*'" (*Homo Sacer* 15).
10. Here, Agamben follows Foucault in arguing that power is not simply an entity that excludes, but rather something that includes the excluded, or rather includes in the form of something being excluded. See Foucault, *Sexuality* 143.
11. See Agamben, *Homo Sacer* 84.
12. Thus, Agamben writes that "The fundamental categorial pair of Western politics is not that of friend/enemy but that of bare life/political existence, zoé/bios, exclusion/inclusion" (*Homo Sacer* 8).
13. Several times—for instance, at the police station, in the streets, and even in K's own apartment building—we see people hostile to the blade runners, or "skin jobs," as they are called condescendingly by humans as well as other replicants. This hostility was, more or less, entirely absent from the first film—thus possibly reflecting a change in attitude regarding the relation between humans and replicants.
14. In the sequel, K carries around a pocket device that turns out to be an updated version of the Voight-Kampff machine. In the first film, the subjects were solemnly asked a series of questions, while a huge device screened their eye movements—thus at least giving the impression of a normative, legal procedure of sorts; in the sequel, no questions are asked—the new pocket device simply scans the serial number inserted in the eyes of the suspected replicants. The difference suggests a further biopolitical intensification of the imperative to execute illegal life.
15. In the first film, replicants could apparently still escape; there were still spaces where refugees could hide. In the sequel, this off-the-grid space seems to have become either toxic (such as Deckard's place, a dystopian Las Vegas shrouded

in what looks like a sickly-red nuclear cloud), or a giant rubbish heap inhabited by tramps and dubious characters running child-slave orphanages.
16. K is portrayed as both sexual and asexual at the same time; when Joshi visits his apartment, she asks him—playfully—what happens if she drinks the rest of the bottle of liquor. In a further sense, Joshi here tests K to see if he is able to transgress the artificiality of his replicant persona—whether he has something akin to a "soul." This situation occurs while they are working on a case about love and reproduction, and about the impossible transgression of the synthetic and artificial. Later, Joi, K's hologram girlfriend, hires a prostitute to make love with K—which again underlines this attempt to transgress something physically impossible.
17. Interestingly, if Deckard really was a replicant, it means that Tyrell clearly lied to Roy (when the latter asked him about the possibility of living longer), and that he was willing to die for this lie. Rachael, on the other hand, dies while giving birth, which means that she could still have been a replicant with an in-built limited time span.
18. Agamben essentially reconfigures the friend/enemy distinction into the zoé/bios distinction as the most essential gesture of sovereign power. In the original *Blade Runner*, the friend/enemy distinction collapses, while the zoé/bios distinction is challenged and ultimately overcome in *Blade Runner 2049*.
19. K has clearly no reservations about killing the previous models; but Morton's sentence—"because you've never seen a miracle"—will haunt him throughout the rest of the film, much as Gaff's sentence ("too bad she won't live") haunts Deckard in the first film. In a sense, the slow-motioned flashbacks suggest glimpses of something new emerging: real, unique memories that K (like Deckard in the first film) will later authenticate and claim as his own. The use of real memories for replicant implants is illegal, as the so-called "Memory Maker" (who turns out to be Rachael and Deckard's child) tells K. This was clearly *not* illegal in the first film (that is, Rachael has the memories of Tyrell's niece).
20. The opening sequence shows images from the giant Noor Complex Solar Power Plant in Morocco.
21. When K later asks Deckard if his dog is real, the latter simply answers that he does not know: that is, it does not really matter. This contrasts with the first film, in which Deckard asks several times whether animals are real, and on each occasion is told that they are not.
22. At one point, Wallace asks Deckard: "Did it never occur to you that you were designed to fall for her . . . all to make that single special specimen . . . that is, if you were designed . . . love or mathematical precision?" He thus indicates, without being entirely clear or affirmative, that one of the secret plot maneuvers of the first film was to bring Deckard and Rachael together so that they could reproduce a child. Whether reproduction was an unexpected outcome, or whether it was intentionally planned all along, remains uncertain.

23. This is, however, not entirely true; when K seeks information about the child in a remote orphanage, he discovers that the pages of the book are missing. Likewise, not everything digital has been erased: Wallace still has video archival material about Deckard and Rachael's interview at Tyrell's corporation.
24. When K starts to believe that he is Rachael's child, Joi tells K that she always knew he was a "special boy:" that is, he was real. She even gives him the name "Joe," which—paradoxically—"completes" the allusion to the nightmarish situation of Kafka's "Joseph K."
25. That K must go through these tests every time he returns from a mission also indicates that the system does not trust the new blade runners.
26. In the sequel, the advertising billboards have become much more fluid, taking the form of holograms. On the one hand, the holograms are clearly commercial products, and thus an extension of the ubiquitous advertising columns in the first film, but on the other hand, they are personalized to such an extent that they appear to have some kind of unique personality. Thus, Joi is clearly a special character, while the film at the same time indicates that there is nothing special about her. Several characters—especially after Joi's console has been destroyed and she herself has been eliminated—have exactly the same figure, face, and voice.
27. When K finally manages to track down Deckard, his first line is to ask whether K has a piece of cheese. It is a reference, as K recognizes, to Robert Louis Stevenson's *Treasure Island*, which actually appears in a deleted scene from the first film. In this scene, Detective Holden (who was nearly killed by an escaped replicant) reads the book, while Deckard visits him in the hospital. The fact that this scene was not included in the first film, but is referred to nonetheless in the sequel, once again emphasizes the complicated relationship between the two works.
28. The video clip shown is Deckard's interrogation of Rachael to find out whether she is a replicant. Luv comments that it was difficult to tell what she was—thus acknowledging the fallibility of the Voight-Kampff machine.
29. While Agamben has a decidedly negative, biopolitical conception of birth, Hannah Arendt understands "natality" as an original, new beginning: "with each birth something uniquely new comes into the world" (*Human Condition* 9)—and which, in a further sense, embodies the very condition of possibility of action. While the negative, biopolitical dimension of birth is encapsulated in the production of K and the rest of the replicants, Rachael's ability to give birth seems to transcend this biopolitical horizon, hence gesturing towards the emancipatory possibilities inherent in Arendt's concept of "natality."
30. Hence the reason why Joshi and the doctors cannot see the difference between human being and replicant (that is, the boundary separating life from form), in the scene where they investigate Rachael's remains, is perhaps that this difference is so minimal that we need, ironically, a machine (or another replicant) to tell the difference (an irony already explored in the first film).
31. See Agamben, *Homo Sacer* 28; 104–11.

# Conclusion

The overall aim of this book has been to explore the political potential of sci-fi film from the late twentieth century to the beginning of the twenty-first century. Sci-fi is perhaps the aesthetic genre most insistently devoted to exploring the potential of the future, and more specifically, the collective future. It is the latter that links the sci-fi genre eminently to the specifically political. From a political perspective, the individual future is relatively insignificant. How we live *together* is a profoundly political question, a balancing act between collective security concerns and individual freedom—now and later, in the future. Political philosophy is essentially the history of how such a balance may be reached in any given present, and how such a present may be prolonged; the genre of sci-fi more specifically asks important questions about how and under what circumstances such a balance may be preserved in the future.

The future as defined here, via Schmitt, is that event which radically changes the political coordinates of the present. In this book, I have looked at sci-fi films that explore the political dimension of the imagination of the (Schmittian) future at a time when we, perhaps more intensely than ever before, have become aware of our own imaginative limits. This is the period that Fukuyama has called the end of history, a period precisely characterized by the difficulty of thinking *beyond* ourselves, the difficulty of imagining anything coming after ourselves that will fundamentally improve today's political coordinates. As Jameson has famously formulated it, "it is easier to imagine the end of the world than the end of capitalism" (*Archaeologies* 199)—which, in Jameson's view, is closely related to the surge in popular narratives of collective destruction (rather than utopian visions of the new Jerusalem). It is at this stage that we have begun to speculate intensely about, not a different present, but the *same* present in the future, what the future might bring *us*, and whether *we* might still be in possession of power and wealth in the time to come.

Each of the films discussed in this book attempts to imagine the impossible, the radically unpredictable future or, more specifically, the question of how to contain this impossible imagination within a political framework premised on the coordinates of the present. These are works that imagine the future realistically—that is, within a collective perspective, or, how we in the present may imagine the future for the entire political community. Within consolidated, stable, and individualized Western societies, the sci-fi film genre suggests that if the collective imagination of the present can no longer think beyond the notion of a post-political society, the sense of the political, albeit in deferred form, may be resuscitated precisely through a genre that intensely explores political images of our future, and hence, ultimately, rediscover the possibility of moving beyond the post-political malaise. In the post-political epoch, we tend to anticipate the future in the form of a state of exception, whose aim is to bring back the present. Sci-fi offers an important contribution to the understanding of this dynamic. It is a genre ultimately attempting to articulate the impossible, the prediction of the political implications of the event that remains radically unpredictable in the present: the future itself.

## Addendum

One of the things dominating the year 2020 and beyond was, of course, the spread of the pandemic, a truly worldwide event that shut down large parts of the global community. Amid all the death, misery, and fear it caused, the pandemic reintroduced the feeling of the future (the collective future) as radically unpredictable. In some sense, it was an experience of collective shock, partly because the notion of an unpredictable future had been almost completely absent before 2020, at least in many parts of the West. As a shock experience, the events of 2020 underlined the fact that, in those spaces where normality has established itself to an extreme degree, as in much of the West, it is difficult, if not impossible, to truly grasp the implications of the future proper—that is, as a phenomenon that seriously breaks with the life we live now.

It is possible that, in what may be called the post-COVID-19 era, we will be moving towards a more comprehensive understanding of the political implications of a radically unpredictable future. At the same time, there are no immediate indications that things will change drastically. State powers are responding to the future in the form of drastic emergency laws, as we have witnessed in large parts of the world. In the attempt to prevent the spread of COVID-19, vast arrays of authoritarian measures have been embraced that would have been entirely unacceptable in normal times: draconian lockdowns, police reinforcements, far-reaching surveillance technologies, invasive tracing apps, vast border closures, and visa suspensions, as well as numerous forms of segregation, camp-like quarantine arrangements, social distancing, and so on. This state of emergency is basically intended to prevent the future from arriving properly, and subsequently to ensure that we may return to the present at some point with everything as it was before. And yet, not quite; history shows us, time and again, that when states have once implemented a series of emergency laws, these will not be removed when the imminent threat is eliminated. They often remain intact, even when the normal state has returned. As I have discussed in this book, there is always the danger that the aftermath of a state of emergency becomes synonymous with its normalization. Thus, it is possible that, at some point, we may come to the realization that the future has already arrived. The sci-fi genre, as I have tried to demonstrate here, may help us to envision the political implications of this arrival.

# Works Cited

Agamben, Giorgio. *Homo Sacer: Sovereign Power and Bare Life*. Trans. Daniel Heller-Roazen. Palo Alto: Stanford University Press, 1998.
—. *State of Exception*. Trans. Kevin Attell. Chicago: University of Chicago Press, 2005.
*Alien*. Dir. Ridley Scott. Twentieth-Century Fox Productions, 1979. Film.
Alkon, Paul K. *Origins of Futuristic Fiction*. Athens: University of Georgia Press, 1987.
Ambrogio, Anthony. "Alien: In Space, No One Can Hear Your Primal Scream." In *Eros in the Mind's Eye*. Ed. Donald Palumbo. Westport, CT: Greenwood Press, 1986, pp. 169–79.
Andersson, Jenny. *The Future of the World: Futurology, Futurists, and the Struggle for the Post-Cold War Imagination*. Oxford: Oxford University Press, 2018.
Angenot, Marc. "The Absent Paradigm." *Science-Fiction Studies* 6 (1979): 9–19.
Arendt, Hannah. *The Human Condition*. Chicago: University of Chicago Press, 1958.
—. *The Origins of Totalitarianism*. New York: Harcourt Brace & Company, 1973.
Baker, Daniel. "Why We Need Dragons: The Progressive Potential of Fantasy." *Journal of the Fantastic in Art* 23:3 (2012): 437–59.
Balakrishnan, Gopal. *The Enemy: An Intellectual Portrait of Carl Schmitt*. London: Verso, 2000.
Balke, Friedrich. "Carl Schmitt and Modernity." In *The Oxford Handbook of Carl Schmitt*. Ed. Jens Meierhenrich and Oliver Simons. Oxford: Oxford University Press, 2016, pp. 629–59.
Barale, Michele Aina. "When Lambs and Aliens Meet: Girl-Faggots and Boy-Dykes Go to the Movies." In *Cross-purposes: Lesbians, Feminists, and the Limits of Alliance*. Ed. Dana Heller. Bloomington: Indiana University Press, 1997, pp. 95–106.
Barbour, Charles. "Sovereign Times: Acts of Creation." *Law, Culture and the Humanities* 6:2 (2010): 143–52.
Bell-Mettreau, Rebecca. "Woman: The Other Alien in Alien." In *Women Worldwalkers: New Dimensions of Science Fiction and Fantasy*. Ed. Jane B. Weedman. Lubbock: Texas Tech Press, 1985a. 9–24.
—. *Hollywood Androgyny*. New York: Columbia University Press, 1985b.

Bendersky, Joseph. *Carl Schmitt: Theorist for the Reich.* Princeton, NJ: Princeton University Press, 1983.

—. "Schmitt's Diaries." In *The Oxford Handbook of Carl Schmitt.* Ed. Jens Meierhenrich and Oliver Simons. Oxford: Oxford University Press, 2016, pp. 117–46.

Benjamin, Walter. "Critique of Violence." In *Walter Benjamin: Selected Writings.* Vol. 1. Ed. Michael W. Jennings. Cambridge, MA: Harvard University Press, 1996, pp. 236–52.

—. *The Origin of German Tragic Drama* [1928]. Trans. John Osborne. London: Verso, 2003.

—. "On the Concept of History." *Selected Writings 4 (1938–1940).* Ed. Howard Eiland and Michael W. Jennings. Cambridge, MA: Harvard University Press, 2006, pp. 389–400.

Benoist, Alain de. "On Politics." *Telos* 125 (2002): 9–36.

Ben-Yishai, Ayelet. *Common Precedents: The Presentness of the Past in Victorian Law and Fiction.* Oxford: Oxford University Press, 2013.

Berkmanas, Tomas. "Schmitt v. (?) Kelsen: The Total State of Exception Posited for the Total Regulation of Life." *Baltic Journal of Law & Politics* 3:2 (2010): 98–118.

Blackford, Russell. *Science Fiction and the Moral Imagination: Visions, Minds, Ethics.* Cham: Springer Nature, 2017.

*Blade Runner.* Dir. Ridley Scott. Warner Bros, 1982. Film.

*Blade Runner 2049.* Dir. Denis Villeneuve. Warner Bros, 2017. Film.

Bloch, Ernst. *The Principle of Hope* [1959]. Trans. Neville Plaice, Stephen Plaice, and Paul Knight. Cambridge, MA: MIT Press, 1995.

Bond, Cynthia D. "Law as Cinematic Apparatus: Image, Textuality, and Representational Anxiety in Spielberg's *Minority Report.*" *Cumberland Law Review* 37:1 (2006): 25–42.

Bould, Mark and Sherryl Vint. *The Routledge Concise History of Science Fiction.* London: Routledge, 2011.

Bredekamp, Horst. "From Walter Benjamin to Carl Schmitt, via Thomas Hobbes." *Critical Inquiry* 25:2 (1999): 247–66.

Brooks-Rose, Christine. *A Rhetoric of the Unreal.* Cambridge: Cambridge University Press, 1981.

Brown, Wendy. *In the Ruins of Neoliberalism: The Rise of Antidemocratic Politics in the West.* New York: Columbia University Press, 2019.

Bruno, Giuliana. "Ramble City: Postmodernism and 'Blade Runner'." *October* 41 (1987): 61–74.

Bussolini, Jeffrey. "Ongoing Founding Events in Carl Schmitt and Giorgio Agamben." *Telos* 157 (2011): 60–82.

Butler, Judith. *Precarious Life: The Powers of Mourning and Violence.* New York: Verso, 2004.

Canavan, Gerry. "The Suvin Effect." In Darko Suvin, *Metamorphoses of Science Fiction: On the Poetics and History of a Literary Genre.* Ed. Gerry Canavan. Bern: Peter Lang, 2016, pp. xi–xxxvi.

Carveth, Donald and Naomi Gold. "The Pre-Oedipalizing of Klein in (North) America: Ridley Scott's Alien Re-Analyzed." *PSYART: A Hyperlink Journal for the Psychological Study of the Arts*, 1999; http://www.psyartjournal.com/article/show/1_carveth-the_pre_oedipalizing_of_klein_in_north_a (last accessed October 2020).

Chu, Seo-Young. *Do Metaphors Dream of Literal Sleep? A Science-Fictional Theory of Representation*. Cambridge, MA: Harvard University Press, 2010.

Cobbs, John L. "Alien as an Abortion Parable." *Literature/Film Quarterly* 18:3 (1990): 198–201.

Cornea, Christine. *Science Fiction Cinema: Between Fantasy and Reality*. Edinburgh: Edinburgh University Press, 2007.

Creed, Barbara. *The Monstrous-feminine: Film, Feminism, Psychoanalysis*. New York: Routledge, 1993.

Cristi, Renato. *Carl Schmitt and Authoritarian Liberalism*. Cardiff: University of Wales Press, 1998.

Csicsery-Ronay Jr, Istvan. "Dis-Imagined Communities: Science Fiction and the Future of Nations." In *Edging into the Future: Science Fiction and Contemporary Cultural Transformation*. Ed. Veronica Hollinger and Joan Gorson. Philadelphia: University of Pennsylvania Press, 2002, pp. 217–37.

—. *The Seven Beauties of Science Fiction*. Middletown, CT: Wesleyan University Press, 2008.

Delany, Samuel R. *Starboard Wine*. New York: Dragon Press, 1984.

—. "About 5750 Words." In *The Jewel-Hinged Jaw: Notes on the Language of Science Fiction*. Revised edn. Middletown, CT: Wesleyan University Press, 2009, pp. 1–16.

Derrida, Jacques. *Of Grammatology*. Trans. Gayatri Chakravorty Spivak. Baltimore: Johns Hopkins University Press, 1974.

—. *The Other Heading: Reflections on Today's Europe*. Trans. Pascale Anne Brault and Michael Naas. Bloomington: Indiana University Press, 1992.

—. *The Politics of Friendship*. Trans. George Collins. London: Verso, 2005.

Descartes, René. *Discourse on Method*. New York: Bobbs-Merrill, 1960.

Desser, David. "The New Eve: The Influence of *Paradise Lost* and *Frankenstein* on *Blade Runner*." In *Retrofitting Blade Runner: Issues in Ridley Scott's Blade Runner and Philip K. Dick's Do Androids Dream of Electric Sheep?* Ed. Judith B. Kerman. Wisconsin: University of Wisconsin Press, 1997, pp. 53–65.

Dick, Philip K. *Do Androids Dream of Electric Sheep?* New York: Doubleday, 1968.

—. *Minority Report* [1956]. London: Gateway, 2014.

Dillman, Joanne Clarke. "*Minority Report*: Narrative, Images, and Dead Women." *Women's Studies* 36 (2007): 229–49.

Doherty, Thomas. "Gender and the Aliens Trilogy." In *The Dread of Difference: Gender and the Horror Film*. Ed. Barry Keith Grant. Austin: University of Texas Press, 1996, pp. 181–99.

Duncan, Ian. *Scott's Shadow: The Novel in Romantic Edinburgh*. Princeton, NJ: Princeton University Press, 2007.

*Elysium*. Dir. Neill Blomkamp. Sony Pictures, 2013. Film.
Ermarth, Elizabeth Deeds. *Realism and Consensus in the English Novel*. 2nd edn. Edinburgh: Edinburgh University Press, 1998.
Fisher, Mark. *Capitalist Realism: Is There No Alternative?* London: Zero, 2009.
Foucault, Michel. *The History of Sexuality, vol. 1*. Trans. Robert Hurley. New York: Pantheon, 1978.
—. "About the Concept of the 'Dangerous Individual' in Nineteenth-century Legal Psychiatry." In *Power*. Ed. James D. Faubion. New York: New Press, 2000, pp. 176–200.
—. *"Society Must be Defended". Lectures at the Collège de France 1975–1976*. Trans. David Macey. Ed. Mauro Bertani and Alessandro Fontana. New York: Picador, 2003.
Franklin, H. Bruce. "Visions of the Future in Science Fiction Films from 1970 to 1982." In *Alien Zone: Cultural Theory and Contemporary Science Fiction Cinema*. Ed. Annette Kuhn. London: Verso, 1990, pp. 19–31.
Freedman, Carl. *Critical Theory and Science Fiction*. Middletown, CT: Wesleyan University Press, 2000.
Fukuyama, Francis. *The End of History and the Last Man* [1992]. New York: Perennial, 2002.
Gallagher, Catherine. *Nobody's Story: The Vanishing Acts of Women Writers in the Marketplace 1670–1820*. Berkeley: University of California Press, 1994.
Gallardo-C., Ximena and C. Jason Smith. *Alien Woman: The Making of Lt. Ellen Ripley*. New York: Continuum, 2004.
Geduld, Harry. "Return to Méliès: Reflections on the Science Fiction Film." In *Focus on the Science Fiction Film*. Ed. William Johnson. Englewood Cliffs, NJ: Prentice-Hall, 1972, pp. 142–7.
Glass, Fred. "Totally Recalling Arnold: Sex and Violence in the New Bad Future." *Film Quarterly* 44:1 (1990): 2–13.
Goode, Tabitha. "Abstract Representational Space: Uncanny Aliens and Others (Pandora, or Prometheus's Return)." *Camera Obscura* 40–1 (1997): 245–74.
Greenberg, Harvey R. "Reimagining the Gargoyle: Psychoanalytic Notes on Alien." *Camera Obscura* 15 (1986): 86–109.
—. "Fembo: Aliens' Intentions." *Journal of Popular Film and Television* 15:4 (1988): 165–71.
Gregory, Derek. "Drone Geographies." *Radical Philosophy* 183 (2014): 7–19.
Greiner, Rae. *Sympathetic Realism in Nineteenth-Century British Fiction*. Baltimore: Johns Hopkins University Press, 2012.
Gross, Raphael. "The 'True Enemy': Antisemitism in Carl Schmitt's Life and Work." *The Oxford Handbook of Carl Schmitt*. Ed. Jens Meierhenrich and Oliver Simons. Oxford: Oxford University Press, 2016, pp. 96–116.
Harrison, Lawrence E. and Samuel P. Huntington. *Culture Matters: How Values Shape Human Progress*. New York: Basic Books, 2000.
Harvey, David. *The Condition of Postmodernity*. Cambridge: Blackwell, 1990.

Heil, Susanne. "Gefährliche Beziehungen": *Walter Benjamin und Carl Schmitt.* Stuttgart: J. B. Metzler, 1996.

Hell, Julia. "*Katechon*: Carl Schmitt's Imperial Theology and the Ruins of the Future." *The Germanic Review* (2009): 283–326.

Herman, Chad. "'Some Horrible Dream about (S)mothering': Sexuality, Gender, and Family in the Alien Trilogy." *Post-Script: Essays in Film and the Humanities* 16:3 (1997): 36–50.

Hobbes, Thomas. *Leviathan* [1651]. Cambridge: Cambridge University Press, 1991.

—. *Behemoth or The Long Parliament* [1681]. Oxford: Clarendon Press, 2010.

Hoffman, A. Robin. "How to See the Horror: The Hostile Fetus in *Rosemary's Baby* and *Alien*." *Lit: Literature Interpretation Theory* 22:3 (2011): 239–61.

Huemer, Michael. "Free Will and Determinism in the World of *Minority Report*." In *Science Fiction and Philosophy: From Time Travel to Superintelligence*. 2nd edn. Ed. Susan Schneider. Malden, MA: Blackwell, 2016, pp. 104–13.

Huiskamp, Gerard. "*Minority Report* on the Bush Doctrine." *New Political Science* 26:3 (2004): 389–415.

Huntington, Samuel P. *Who Are We?* New York: Simon and Schuster, 2005.

Jameson, Fredric. "Postmodernism and Consumer Society." In *The Cultural Turn: Selected Writings on the Postmodern 1983–1998.* London: Verso, 1998, pp. 1–20.

—. *Archaeologies of the Future: The Desire Called Utopia and Other Science Fictions.* London: Verso, 2005.

Jeffords, Susan. "'The Battle of the Big Mamas': Feminism and the Alienation of Women." *The Journal of American Culture* 10:3 (1987): 73–84.

Jennings, Ros. "Desire and Design: Ripley Undressed." *Immortal, Invisible: Lesbians and the Moving Image.* Ed. Tamsin Wilton. New York: Routledge, 1995, pp. 193–206.

Johnston, Keith M. *Science Fiction Film: A Critical Introduction.* Oxford: Berg, 2011.

Kagan, Robert. *The Return of History and the End of Dreams.* New York: Vintage, 2008.

—. *The Jungle Grows Back: America and Our Imperiled World.* New York: Penguin Random House, 2018.

Kalyvas, Andreas. "Carl Schmitt and the Three Moments of Democracy." *Cardozo Law Review* 21 (1999–2000): 1525–65.

Kavanaugh, J. H. "Son of a Bitch: Feminism, Humanism and Science in *Alien*." *October* 13 (1980): 90–100.

Kowalski, Dean A. "*Minority Report*, Molinism, and the Viability of Precrime." In *Steven Spielberg and Philosophy: We're Gonna Need a Bigger Book.* Ed. Dean A. Kowalski. Kentucky: University of Kentucky Press, 2008, pp. 227–47.

Landon, Brooks. *The Aesthetics of Ambivalence: Rethinking Science Fiction Film in the Age of Electronic (Re)production.* London: Greenwood Press, 1992.

Lazzarato, Maurizio. "From Biopower to Biopolitics." *Pli: The Warwick Journal of Philosophy* 13 (2002): 112–25.

Le Guin, Ursula. "Do-It-Yourself Cosmology." *The Language of the Night: Essays on Fantasy and Science Fiction*. Ed. Susan Wood. New York: G. P. Putnam's Sons, 1979.

Linder, Christian. "Carl Schmitt in Plettenberg." In *The Oxford Handbook of Carl Schmitt*. Ed. Jens Meierhenrich and Oliver Simons. Oxford: Oxford University Press, 2016, pp. 147–68.

Littmann, Greg. "What's Wrong with Building Replicants? Artificial Intelligence in *Blade Runner, Alien*, and *Prometheus*." In *The Culture and Philosophy of Ridley Scott*. Ed. Adam Barkman, Ashley Barkman, and Nancy Kang. Lanham, MD: Lexington, 2015, pp. 133–44.

Locke, John. *Second Treatise of Government* [1690]. Ed. C. B. Macpherson. Cambridge: Hackett, 1980.

Lucchese, Filippo del. *The Political Philosophy of Niccolò Machiavelli*. Edinburgh: Edinburgh University Press, 2015.

Luckhurst, Roger. *Science Fiction*. Cambridge: Polity, 2005.

McCormick, John. "Teaching in Vain: Carl Schmitt, Thomas Hobbes, and the Theory of the Sovereign State." In *The Oxford Handbook of Carl Schmitt*. Ed. Jens Meierhenrich and Oliver Simons. Oxford: Oxford University Press, 2016, pp. 269–90.

MacLeod, Ken. "Politics and Science Fiction." In *The Cambridge Companion to Science Fiction*. Ed. Edward James and Farah Mendlesohn. Cambridge: Cambridge University Press, 2003, pp. 230–40.

Mearsheimer, John J. *The Tragedy of Great Power Politics*. New York: W. W. Norton, 2014.

Meierhenrich, Jens. "Fearing the Disorder of Things: The Development of Carl Schmitt's Institution Theory, 1919–1942." In *The Oxford Handbook of Carl Schmitt*. Ed. Jens Meierhenrich and Oliver Simons. Oxford: Oxford University Press, 2016, pp. 171–216.

Melzer, Patricia. *Alien Constructions: Science Fiction and Feminist Thought*. Austin: University of Texas Press, 2006.

Menand, Louis. "Francis Fukuyama Postpones the End of History." *New Yorker*, August 27, 2018; https://www.newyorker.com/magazine/2018/09/03/francis-fukuyama-postpones-the-end-of-history (last accessed October 2020).

Merry, Robert W. *Sands of Empire: Missionary Zeal, American Foreign Policy, and the Hazards of Global Ambition*. New York: Simon and Schuster, 2005.

Meuter, Günter. *Der Katechon: Zu Carl Schmitts fundamentalischer Kritik der Zeit*. Berlin: Duncker & Humblot, 1994.

*Minority Report*. Dir. Steven Spielberg. 20th-Century Fox and DreamWorks Pictures, 2002. Film.

Mouffe, Chantal. *On the Political*. London: Routledge, 2005.

Mulhall, Stephen. *On Film*. London: Routledge, 2008.

Nietzsche, Friedrich. "Zarathustra's Prologue." In *Thus Spoke Zarathustra* [1883–5]. Cambridge: Cambridge University Press, 2006, pp. 254–63.

*Oblivion*. Dir. Joseph Kosinski. Universal Pictures, 2013. Film.

Paik, Peter. *From Utopia to Apocalypse: Science Fiction and the Politics of Catastrophe.* Minneapolis: University of Minnesota Press, 2010.

Penley, Constance, ed. *Close Encounters: Film, Feminism, and Science Fiction.* Minneapolis: University of Minnesota Press, 1991.

—. "Time Travel, Primal Scene and the Critical Dystopia." *Liquid Metal: The Science Fiction Reader.* Ed. Sean Redmond. New York: Wallflower Press, 2004, pp. 126–35.

Petrey, Sandy. *Realism and Revolution: Balzac, Stendhal, Zola, and the Performances of History.* Ithaca, NY: Cornell University Press, 1988.

Polak, Fred. *The Image of the Future.* Trans. Elise Boulding. Amsterdam: Elsevier Scientific, 1973.

Pope, Richard. "Affects of the Gaze: Post-Oedipal Desire and the Traversal of Fantasy in *Blade Runner*." *Camera Obscura* 73:25 (2010): 69–95.

Redmond, Sean. "Film Since 1980." In *The Routledge Concise History of Science Fiction.* Ed. Mark Bould and Sherryl Vint. London: Routledge, 2011, pp. 134–43.

Renault, Gregory. "Science Fiction as Cognitive Estrangement: Darko Suvin and the Marxist Critique of Mass Culture." *Discourse* 2 (1980): 113–41.

Rieder, John. "On Defining SF, or Not." *Science Fiction Studies* 37 (2010): 191–209.

Roberts, Adam. *Science Fiction.* 2nd edn. London: Routledge, 2006.

Rousseau, Jean-Jacques. *Discourse on Political Economy* and *The Social Contract* [1762]. Trans. Christopher Betts. Oxford: Oxford University Press, 1994.

Rowlands, Mark. *The Philosopher at the End of the Universe: Philosophy Explained Through Science Fiction.* London: Ebury, 2005.

Runciman, David. *How Democracy Ends.* New York: Basic Books, 2018.

Rushing, Janice Hocker. "Evolution of 'The New Frontier' in *Alien* and *Aliens*: Patriarchal Co-optation of the Feminine Archetype." *The Quarterly Journal of Speech* 75:1 (1989): 1–24.

Russ, Joanna. "Towards an Aesthetic of Science Fiction." *Science-Fiction Studies* 2:2 (1975): 112–19.

Ryan, Mike. "New 'Alien' and 'Chappie' Director Neill Blomkamp On 'Elysium': 'I F*cked It Up'." *Uproxx*, February 26, 2015; https://uproxx.com/movies/neill-blomkamp-elysium-alien/ (last accessed October 2020).

Sammon, Paul. *Future Noir: The Making of Blade Runner.* New York: Harper, 1996.

Sava, Nadia. "The State of Exception: Between Decision and Norm." *International Journal on Humanistic Ideology* 7:2/3 (2017): 15–29.

Schmitt, Carl. *Dictatorship: From the Origin of the Modern Concept of Sovereignty to Proletarian Class Struggle* [1921]. Trans. Michael Hoelzl and Graham Ward. Cambridge: Polity Press, 2014.

—. *Political Theology: Four Chapters on the Concept of Sovereignty* [1922]. Trans. George Schwab. Cambridge, MA: MIT Press, 1985.

—. *The Concept of the Political* [1932]. Trans. George Schwab. Chicago: University of Chicago Press, 1996.

—. *Legality and Legitimacy* [1932]. Trans. Jeffrey Seitzer. Durham, NC: Duke University Press, 2004.

—. *The Leviathan in the State Theory of Thomas Hobbes: Meaning and Failure of a Political Symbol* [1938]. Trans. George Schwab and Erna Hilfstein. Westport, CT: Greenwood Press, 1996.

—. *Ex captivitate salus: Erfahrungen der Zeit 1945/47* [1950]. Berlin: Duncker & Humbolt, 2002.

—. *Nomos of the Earth in the International Law of the Jus Publicum Europaeum* [1950]. Trans. G. L. Ulmen. New York: Telos, 2003.

Schwab, Georg. *The Challenge of the Exception: An Introduction to the Political Ideas of Carl Schmitt between 1921 and 1936*. 2nd edn. New York: Greenwood Press, 1970.

Seed, David. *Science Fiction: A Very Short Introduction*. Oxford: Oxford University Press, 2011.

—, ed. *Future Wars: The Anticipation and the Fears*. Liverpool: Liverpool University Press, 2012.

Shaw, Harry E. *Narrating Reality: Austen, Scott, Eliot*. Ithaca, NY: Cornell University Press, 1999.

Shippey, Tom. *Fictional Space*. London: Humanities Press, 1991.

Silverman, Kaja. "Back to the Future." *Camera Obscura* 9 (1991): 108–32.

Sobchack, Vivian. *Screening Space: The American Science Fiction Film*. New York: Ungar, 1988.

—. "American Science Fiction Film: An Overview." In *A Companion to Science Fiction*. Ed. David Seed. Oxford: Blackwell, 2005, pp. 261–74.

Specter, Matthew. "What's 'Left' in Schmitt?" In *The Oxford Handbook of Carl Schmitt*. Ed. Jens Meierhenrich and Oliver Simons. Oxford: Oxford University Press, 2016, pp. 426–54.

Stern, J. P. [Joseph Peter]. *On Realism*. London: Routledge, 1973.

Strauss, Leo. *The Political Philosophy of Thomas Hobbes: Its Basis and Genesis*. Chicago: University of Chicago Press, 1952.

Suvin, Darko. *Metamorphoses of Science Fiction*. New Haven, CT: Yale University Press, 1979.

Taleb, Nassim Nicholas. *The Black Swan: The Impact of the Highly Improbable*. 2nd edn. New York: Random House, 2010.

Tanaka, Hiroshi. "Carl Schmitt and Fascism: Schmitt, Germany and Japan." *Hitotsubashi Journal of Social Studies* 22 (1990): 1–6.

Taubin, Amy. "The 'Alien' Trilogy: From Feminism to AIDS." *Women and Film: A Sight and Sound Reader*. Ed. Pam Cook and Philip Dodd. Philadelphia: Temple University Press, 1993, pp. 93–100.

Telotte, J. P. *Science Fiction Film*. Cambridge: Cambridge University Press, 2001.

Toffler, Alvin. *Future Shock*. New York: Random House, 1970.
Tönnies, Ferdinand. *Thomas Hobbes: Leben und Lehre*. Stuttgart: Bad Cannstatt, 1971.
Torry, Robert. "Awakening to the Other: Feminism and the Ego-Ideal in Alien." *Women's Studies: An Interdisciplinary Journal* 23:4 (1994): 343–63.
Turing, Alan. "Computing Machinery and Intelligence." In *The Essential Turing: Seminal Writings in Computing, Logic, Philosophy, Artificial Intelligence, and Artificial Life: Plus The Secrets of Enigma*. Ed. Jack Copeland. Oxford: Oxford University Press, 2004, pp. 441–64.
Vardoulakis, Dimitris. "Autoimmunities: Derrida, Democracy and Political Theology." *Research in Phenomenology* 48 (2018): 29–56.
Vaughn, Thomas. "Voices of Sexual Distortion: Rape, Birth, and Self-Annihilation Metaphors in the Alien Trilogy." *The Quarterly Journal of Speech* 81:4 (1995): 423–35.
Virilio, Paul. *Speed and Politics* [1977]. Trans. M. Polizzotti. New York: Semiotext(e), 1986.
—. *L'Insécurité du territoire*. 2nd edn. Paris: Galilée, 1993.
—. *Bunker Archaeology* [1967]. Trans. George Collins. New York: Princeton Architectural Press, 1994.
Wegner, Phillip E. *Imaginary Communities: Utopia, the Nation, and the Spatial Histories of Modernity*. Berkeley: University of California Press, 2002.
Weigel, Sigrid. "The Martyr and the Sovereign: Scenes from a Contemporary Tragic Drama, Read through Walter Benjamin and Carl Schmitt." *CR: The New Centennial Review* 4:3 (2004): 109–23.
Weinstock, Jeffrey A. "Freaks in Space: 'Extraterrestrialism' and 'Deep-Space Multiculturalism'." *Freakery: Cultural Spectacles of the Extraordinary Body*. Ed. Rosemarie Garland Thomson. New York: New York University Press, 1996, pp. 327–37.
Wells, H. G. *The Discovery of the Future with The Common-sense of World Peace and The Human Adventure* [1902]. Ed. P. Parrinder. London: PNL Press, 1989.
Westfahl, Gary, Kin Yuen Wong, and Amy Kit-sze Chan, eds. *Science Fiction and the Prediction of the Future: Essays on Foresight and Fallacy*. Jefferson, NC: McFarland, 2011.
Wolin, Richard. "Carl Schmitt: The Conservative Revolutionary Habitus and the Aesthetics of Horror." *Political Theory* 20:3 (1992): 424–47.
Wood, Robert E. "Cross Talk: The Implications of Generic Hybridization in the Alien Films." *Studies in the Humanities* 15:1 (1988): 1–12.
Wright, David. "Alternative futures: AmI scenarios and *Minority Report*." *Futures* 40 (2008): 473–88.
Žižek, Slavoj. *In Defense of Lost Causes*. London: Verso, 2008.
—. *The Year of Dreaming Dangerously*. London: Verso, 2012.

# Index

Agamben, Giorgio
  and biopolitics, 82
  and exception, 14, 80, 109, 110
  and *homo sacer*, 45, 49n24,
    50n31, 81–2, 122n12, 127,
    129–30, 131, 138
  on the sovereign gesture, 133
*Alien*
  ambiguity, 37, 39–41
  conflict, 19, 20, 36–9
  feminist perspectives, 32–3
  literalness, 33–4, 44
  politics, 41–2, 45
  power, 42–4, 46
  psychoanalytic perspectives, 32
  structure, 39
Alkon, Paul K., 24n15
Andersson, Jenny, 1–2
Angenot, Marc, 8
Arendt, Hannah, 139

Barbour, Charles, 30n62
Bell-Mettreau, Rebecca, 32
Ben-Yishai, Ayelet, 9
Benjamin, Walter
  and exception, 30n67, 118, 120
  and the sovereign, 106, 109–10

  and violence, 62
biopolitics
  Agamben and, 82
  in *Blade Runner*, 95–6, 99–100,
    129, 132–3, 139
  in *Blade Runner 2049*, 127, 132,
    133, 139–40
  definition of, 50n37
  in *Elysium*, 73, 75, 76, 83
  Foucault on, 83
biopower, 21, 94–5, 99, 101
Blackford, Russell, 24n20
*Blade Runner*
  biopolitics, 95–6, 99–100, 129,
    132–3, 139
  and difference, 98–9
  fear of the future, 134–5
  the Human, 91–4, 100–1, 135–6
  memories, 137, 140
  music, 134
  the sovereign, 21, 91–3, 97, 99,
    126–7, 134, 138
*Blade Runner 2049*
  biopolitics, 127, 132, 133,
    139–40
  fear of the future, 135–7
  the Human, 137

*Blade Runner 2049* (*contd.*)
   memories, 137–8
   music, 134
   opening crawl, 127–8
   plot, 22, 126
   the sovereign, 140
   temporality, 136
Bloch, Ernst, 25n25
Bond, Cynthia D., 71n34
Bredekamp, Horst, 122n10
Brooks-Rose, Christine, 8
Bruno, Giuliana, 103n20
Butler, Judith, 13

Canavan, Gerry, 24n18
Chu, Seo-Young, 10
Cobbs, John L., 32
Cold War, 1–2
Cornea, Christine, 24n20, 25n22
COVID-19 pandemic, 3, 146–7
Csicsery-Ronay Jr, Istvan, 5,
   25n25, 25n27, 26n36, 31n68

Delany, Samuel R., 23n14, 122n11
Derrida, Jacques, 24n19, 28n49,
   51n47
Descartes, René, 103n22
dictatorship, 15, 27n42, 109
Dillman, Joanne Clarke, 68n3,
   70n29

*Elysium*
   characterization, 82–3
   exception, 21, 73, 80–1, 84, 85
   human rights, 76, 81, 86
   plot, 20–1, 72–3, 86–7
   political dimension, 72, 73, 75,
      77, 82, 84–5, 86, 87

   the sovereign, 76–9
   technology, 73, 74–7, 78, 79,
      83, 86
exception
   *Elysium*, 21, 73, 80–1, 84, 85
   *Oblivion*, 21–2, 105–8, 110–12,
      113, 114, 115, 116–17,
      118–19, 120–1
   Schmitt and, 13–16, 19–20, 37,
      57–9, 118
   science fiction and, 16–19
   sovereign and, 11, 19–20
   and temporality, 108–10

fantasy
   *Elysium*, 73, 74, 87
   *Minority Report*, 56
   *Oblivion*, 117
   and science fiction compared, 8,
      25n27, 26n28, 26n29, 26n31,
      26n35, 30n66
Foucault, Michel
   *History of Sexuality*, 21, 50n36,
      91, 94–5, 96, 97–8, 101
   on power, 83, 142n10
   on race war, 112
Franklin, H. Bruce, 6
Freedman, Carl, 26n29
Fukuyama, Francis: *The End of
   History*, 1, 3, 4, 28n50, 55,
      68n7, 72, 145
future, the,
   concepts of, 4–5, 8
   and exception, 14, 15
   fear of, 1–3, 134–7
   and liberalism, 11
   political dimension of, 145, 146–7
   prediction of, 54

Geduld, Harry, 122n13
Glass, Fred, 6

history: science fiction and, 5, 6;
    see also Fukuyama, Francis
Hobbes, Thomas: *Leviathan*,
    15–16, 30n64, 35–6, 38–9,
    49n25, 68n6, 76, 80, 84,
    88n2, 123n21; *see also under*
    Schmitt, Carl
Hoffman, A. Robin, 32

Jameson, Fredric, 4, 6, 145
Jeffords, Susan, 32
Johnston, Keith M., 5

Kagan, Robert, 1, 23n13
Kalyvas, Andreas, 28n45
Kavanaugh, J. H., 32
Kelsen, Hans, 28n51, 68n11
Kowalski, Dean A., 70n30

Le Guin, Ursula, 26n35
liberal democracy, 1, 16, 23n10;
    *see also* rights
liberalism
    and depoliticization, 2–3, 12–13
    and the future, 11
    Schmitt and, 37, 56, 57
Locke, John, 49n26

McCormick, John, 48n9
Machiavelli, Niccolò, 27n42
*Mad Max* franchise, 1
Marx, Karl, 56
Meierhenrich, Jens, 121n1
*Minority Report*
    exception, 63, 64, 65–7
    fantasy, 56
    plot, 53–5, 60–4, 65
    political dimension, 20, 54, 56,
        60
    power, 53–4
    prediction of the future, 54–5,
        58, 60–1, 62, 64, 67
    technological premise, 59, 64,
        65, 67
Mouffe, Chantal, 23n9
Mulhall, Stephen, 47n2

Nietzsche, Friedrich, 42
novum: Suvin's concept of, 7–8,
    9–10, 17, 54

*Oblivion*
    exception, 21–2, 105–8, 110–12,
        113, 114, 115, 116–17,
        118–19, 120–1
    fantasy, 11
    the Human, 111, 113–14,
        115–18
    plot, 105–6, 111–12, 114–15

Paik, Peter, 6, 26n32, 26n36
Polak, Fred, 23n5

race war: Foucault's notion of,
    112
realism, 6–7, 8, 9
Renault, Gregory, 25n27
Rieder, John, 25n22
rights
    to die, 94, 100–1
    human rights, 49n26, 76, 81, 86
    to life, 91–3, 94, 95, 101
Roberts, Adam, 25n22

Rousseau, Jean-Jacques, 48n12, 48n13
Rushing, Janice Hocker, 32

Sava, Nadia, 15, 28n48
Schmitt, Carl, 2
  concept of the future, 4–5
  concept of the political, 10–13, 34, 35, 36, 37, 44, 46, 51n43, 55–6, 89n16, 94, 102n16, 108, 123n14, 124n25
  concept of the state of exception, 13–16, 19–20, 37, 57–9, 118
  and Hobbes's *Leviathan*, 15–16, 30n64, 36, 38–9, 41, 49n25, 50n38, 68n6, 122n10
  and liberalism, 37, 56, 57
  and the sovereign, 11, 13–16, 20, 22, 37–8, 55, 57–9, 64, 85, 94, 106, 108–9, 110, 127, 130–1, 133
Schwab, Georg, 29n55, 30n63
science fiction
  and history, 5,6
  meaning of, 3–4
Seed, David, 25n22
sex: Foucault on, 97–8
Shippey, Tom, 8
Sobchack, Vivian, 6
sovereign, the
  Agamben and, 45, 80–1, 133
  Benjamin and, 110
  *Blade Runner*, 21, 91–3, 97, 99, 126–7, 134–5, 138
  *Blade Runner 2049*, 140
  and the death penalty, 95–7
  *Elysium*, 76–9

  Foucault and, 21, 94, 96
  future, 18–20
  Hobbes and, 84–5
  *Minority Report*, 59–60, 65
  Schmitt and, 11, 13–16, 20, 22, 36, 37–8, 41, 55, 57–9, 64, 85, 94, 106, 108–9, 110, 127, 130–1, 133
  and violence, 63
Stern, J. P., 9
Strong, Tracy B, 28n51, 29n56, 29n61
Suvin, Darko, 23n14
  concept of the novum, 7–8, 9–10, 17, 54

Taleb, Nassim Nicholas, 29n59
technology
  breakdown of, 18
  *Elysium*, 20–1, 73, 74–7, 78, 79, 83, 86
  future, 6, 7
  *Minority Report*, 20, 53–5, 64, 67
  and progress, 55–6
  Schmitt on, 12
Telotte, J. P., 25n27
*Terminator 2: Judgment Day*, 31n68
time travel, 30n68
Toffler, Alvin, 2
Torry, Robert, 32
Turing, Alan, 102n4

utopia, 4

Vardoulakis, Dimitris, 86
Vaughn, Thomas, 33

violence
    and death, 96
    founding, 62–3
    and law, 93–4, 99–100, 109
    protection from, 77

Wells, H. G., 68n4
Wyeth, Andrew, 123n19

Žižek, Slavoj, 24n19, 28n50

EU representative:
Easy Access System Europe
Mustamäe tee 50, 10621 Tallinn, Estonia
Gpsr.requests@easproject.com

www.ingramcontent.com/pod-product-compliance
Lightning Source LLC
Chambersburg PA
CBHW071848230426
43671CB00012B/2109